W9-BIS-480

BY NICK DE SEMLYEN

The Last Action Heroes
Wild and Crazy Guys

THE LAST ACTION HEROES

THE LAST ACTION HEROES

THE TRIUMPHS, FLOPS, AND FEUDS OF HOLLYWOOD'S KINGS OF CARNAGE

...

NICK DE SEMLYEN

CROWN
NEW YORK

Published in the United States by Crown,
an imprint of Random House, a division of
Penguin Random House LLC, New York.

CROWN and the Crown colophon are registered trademarks of
Penguin Random House LLC.

LIBRARY OF CONGRESS CATALOGING-IN-PUBLICATION DATA
Names: De Semlyen, Nick, author.
Title: The last action heroes / Nick de Semlyen.
Description: New York: Crown, [2023] |
Includes bibliographical references and index.
Identifiers: LCCN 2022057087 (print) | LCCN 2022057088 (ebook) |
ISBN 9780593238806 (hardcover; acid-free paper) |
ISBN 9780593238813 (ebook)
Subjects: LCSH: Action and adventure films—History and criticism. |
Actors—United States—Biography. | Heroes in motion pictures.
Classification: LCC PN1995.9.A3 D4 2023 (print) |
LCC PN1995.9.A3 (ebook) |
DDC 791.4302/8092511 [B]—dc23/eng/20230208
LC record available at https://lccn.loc.gov/2022057087
LC ebook record available at https://lccn.loc.gov/2022057088

Printed in the United States of America on acid-free paper

crownpublishing.com

2 4 6 8 9 7 5 3 1

First Edition

Book design by Edwin A. Vazquez
Title-page art: © Serhii Holdin, stock.adobe.com (texture),
© dmitr1ch, stock.adobe.com (texture)

For MC

If you wage war, do it energetically and with severity.

—Napoleon Bonaparte

I'm gonna hit you with so many rights, you're gonna beg for a left.

—Chuck Norris

CONTENTS

...

THE LAST ACTION HEROES

PROLOGUE

...

THEY CAME FROM THE SKY. And with their arrival went any chance of peace.

It had been shaping up to be a Cannes Film Festival like any other. As the sun rose on a sleepy Saturday—May 12, 1990—across the coastal French city there were flickers of activity. The world's most prestigious celebration of motion pictures was commencing for the forty-third time.

On the Promenade de la Croisette, caked in chalk-white makeup, an Andy Warhol impersonator was enjoying his fifteen minutes of fame. Cineastes who had been lucky enough to attend the opening gala, a screening of *Dreams,* the latest by Japanese auteur Akira Kurosawa, debated its themes and discussed the surprising cameo by Martin Scorsese as Vincent van Gogh. Others looked forward to the gems of thought-provoking cinema to come, such as Sergei Solovyov's Russian comedy *Black Rose Is an Emblem of Sorrow, Red Rose Is an Emblem of Love.*

It was a mecca for those who liked their films dense in subtext and their *cafés allongés* scalding hot. Notes would be taken. Applause would be meted out. The human condition would be considered.

Then, with a roar, the jet touched down.

It was a chartered luxury 747 out of Los Angeles, a hulking

tube of metal polished to a high gleam. It had traveled a little over six thousand miles to its destination. And it was stuffed with an astonishing array of American power players—stars, directors, executives—few of them renowned for making art-house fare.

"The Hollywood of 1990 is on the frickin' plane," recalls James Cameron, who had been the last to board in California, having scrambled to finish typing up his first draft of *Terminator 2: Judgment Day*. "When I got to the airport, they all gave me a snarky clap for being late."

"It was an amazing flight, a magic trip," says Renny Harlin, the director who had just blown up two airplanes and half an airport for the yet-to-be-released *Die Hard 2*, but who hadn't been banned from high-altitude travel. "There was no shortage of caviar and champagne and that kind of thing."

More potent refreshments were apparently available, too. "We stopped in Maine to refuel, and after we'd been flying for another twenty minutes somebody gets on the speaker and says, 'We are now outside of American airspace,'" remembers Steven de Souza, writer of the original *Die Hard* and *Commando*. "And all of a sudden the drugs come out. People are doing cocaine on the drop-down trays. Then I get tapped on the shoulder and it's Michael Douglas passing me a joint."

If Douglas was literally riding high, he was also doing it figuratively, with *Wall Street* and *Fatal Attraction* recent hits in his rearview mirror. But the biggest dogs on board were two movie stars whom few would have expected to share oxygen for over ten hours. Arnold Schwarzenegger and Sylvester Stallone, after more than a decade of bitter warfare, had finally been convinced to appear in public together. The event: a huge party to celebrate Carolco Pictures, the bankroller of many of the bombastic action movies that had ruled the box office for the past decade.

At the airport in Cannes, the disembarking VIPs were each handed an envelope containing 2,000 French francs, spending money for the weekend. Then they were led to a convoy of waiting black Mercedes-Benzes and drivers, at their disposal for the next three days. The vehicles, blue and red lights flashing on their tops, roared down the coast to the decadent Hôtel du Cap-Eden-Roc. There, a $1 million soiree—the most expensive ever thrown in the history of Cannes—awaited. One of the world's hottest bands, the Gipsy Kings, flown in on a separate jet from Spain, performed songs at high volume. And 240 guests joined those from the plane to mill around a massive terrace overlooking the sea, including Mick Jagger (who ended up dancing on top of a table next to girlfriend Jerry Hall), Jean-Claude Van Damme, Dolph Lundgren, Sharon Stone, and Clint Eastwood, who happened to be staying in the hotel and thought he'd check out what all the noise was about.

As the sun went down and fresh seafood was served, the party's grandest flex was deployed. Rockets blasted up into the Cannes sky, spelling out the names of Carolco's upcoming projects and the people attached to them. "This firework display said 'TERMINATOR 2' in gigantic letters out over the Croisette," remembers a still-impressed Cameron.

It was a day nobody who attended will ever forget, a showcase of pure excess. Not to mention a cacophony that probably sent Cannes's more sober visitors—who until that moment had been mulling over the ins and outs of Russian comedy—running back to their lodgings. "It's the best party ever done," brags Carolco cofounder Mario Kassar, who put it together. "Everybody was at that party and probably nobody could have done it again."

There was just one moment of panic along the way. The evening's coup de grâce had been devised by Kassar: a moment of showmanship to rival even magical fireworks, and which demanded equally careful handling. Schwarzenegger and Stallone, the two titans of action cinema, whose work had brought in millions upon millions of dollars and who were now living, breathing icons, would make a dramatic entrance midway through the event. They had never been convinced to star in a movie together, but tonight they would share a terrace. It would be Carolco's greatest PR stunt yet, a détente to rival any feat of international diplomacy. Except neither Stallone nor Schwarzenegger would concede on a key point: which of them would enter the party first. That old rivalry, pacified for a while, had suddenly flared back up.

"They were waiting outside, and everyone was asking the question 'Who's coming in first, who's coming in second?'" Kassar remembers. A chill swept through the gaggle of Carolco party-planners. After so much expense, could a clash of egos make it all fall apart? Anybody aware of the history between the two stars knew it was a distinct possibility. So Kassar moved fast.

"I took some photos with them—one on the left, the other on the right," he says, "and they held my hands up in the air. Then I said, 'Okay, let's go in now!' And I came in with both of them. So that resolved that problem."

Inside the party now, Schwarzenegger, wearing a green-and-yellow Hawaiian shirt, appraised the dance floor like a Terminator scanning a biker bar. Stallone, in a button-up shirt, blazer, and designer sunglasses, did the same. And then, to the amazement of all, the pair turned to each other, locked hands, and started to dance, waltzing in circles around the terrace.

The famous faces in the crowd looked on, delighted. They were present for a monumental moment, a long-awaited truce, two colossal egos finally aligning in perfect harmony.

Then, abruptly, Stallone grimaced and stopped.

"Goddammit," he told Schwarzenegger. "You're leading. I hate that."

AMERICA IN THE 1970S was crying out for a hero. In the last year of the previous decade, the nation had conquered the moon. But now things had gone awry. Abroad, a cataclysmic defeat in Vietnam had dented national pride. At home, the president was being indicted and swarmed by protesters, some wielding signs in which the x in "Nixon" was replaced by a swastika. The economy, which had boomed in the wake of World War II, was wilting, the stock market plummeting 40 percent in an eighteen-month period and joblessness rampant. Everywhere was a newfound sense of despair, felt so keenly and widely that in 1979 President Jimmy Carter addressed it in a speech. "It is a crisis that strikes at the very heart and soul and spirit of our national will," he declared with a stony face. "We can see this crisis in the growing doubt about the meaning of our own lives, and in the loss of a unity of purpose for our nation."

Heroes were in short supply, not least on the big screen. Clint Eastwood's "Dirty" Harry Callahan thrilled the masses, but returns were diminishing (third sequel *Sudden Impact* would feature a farting bulldog named Meathead). Gene Hackman's violent, wild-eyed Popeye Doyle in *The French Connection,* another lawman, was intentionally tough to root for. Hong Kong martial arts icon Bruce Lee emerged as a brief, blazing light but died tragically on the cusp of mainstream American success, just a month before *Enter the Dragon*'s Hollywood premiere. As for the blaxploitation wave, the Richard Roundtree–starring *Shaft* had made $13 million from a $500,000 budget and inspired dozens of films throughout the 1970s, featuring charismatic actors from Pam Grier to Jim Brown. But while the subgenre had a huge impact, even inspiring the James Bond film *Live and Let Die,* by the late 1970s it was fading away.

As any fan of action cinema knows, though, it's when things are bleakest, when all hope is lost, when the villains are smirking and innocent civilians are on their knees, that fresh footsteps are heard, hailing the arrival of a savior. Or, in this case, eight of them.

First came the titans. The one they called "the Italian Stallion": Stallone, a onetime brawler with a sensitive soul and a flair for mayhem. And then the one they called "the Austrian Oak": Schwarzenegger, a former bodybuilder with a boyish smile and a gonzo torso. In their wake arrived lither but no less deadly specimens: Swedish black belt Dolph Lundgren, Chinese dynamo Jackie Chan; Belgian killing machine Jean-Claude Van Damme; glowering, ponytailed Steven Seagal, whose origins nobody could ever quite pin down. Two all-American dudes would join the fray, too: karate master Chuck Norris and the smirking, noncommittal Bruce Willis.

Each of these stars had a distinct way of plying their deadly art. But between them they gave America, and beyond, a renewed sense of purpose—one that Jimmy Carter probably didn't have in mind.

Razing entire armies, toppling legions of hit men, brutalizing terrorists, they restored a sense of clarity that had been lost somewhere along the way. Whether their adversaries were Soviet soldiers or street-level drug dealers, their philosophy was simple, one even a child watching secretly from behind a couch could understand: never give up, never stop shooting, never lose. "Running from your fear is more painful than facing it," sermonized Chuck Norris in *The Hitman*. His *Missing in Action* series rewrote the Vietnam War to give it a happy ending.

There were many other movie stars kicking ass at this time, from Sigourney Weaver in *Aliens* to Harrison Ford in the *Indiana Jones* franchise to the somewhat scrawnier Ralph Macchio in *The Karate Kid*. Others such as Fred Williamson, Linda Hamilton, Cynthia Rothrock, and, later, Wesley Snipes had the talent, the physique, or both, but were offered fewer opportunities by Hollywood of the 1980s and '90s. The charismatic Carl Weathers came tantalizingly close to channeling his *Rocky* and *Predator* cachet into proper action stardom, headlining the raucous *Action Jackson,* but when a sequel failed to materialize he moved into TV. This particuar octet, though, had a purity to their big-screen exploits, rarely distracted by the siren calls of drama and comedy, and unrivaled in their cultural dominance. They obsessively sculpted their bodies, chugged protein shakes, and marched back into battle again and again and again. In return for their sacrifices, they were given the keys to Hollywood, with hordes of screaming fans so devoted they would even spend $8.95 on a strudel based on Schwarzenegger's mother's recipe. These stars acquired floods of cash, groupies, state-of-the-art private jets, access to all areas. Even the new president wanted to be in on the action. In 1985, ahead of a visit by invitation to the White House, Stallone was asked to bring a signed poster of *Rambo: First Blood Part II*. It now resides in the Reagan Presidential Library and Museum.

Today, these action movies have a complicated legacy. Many look primitive, a relic of an ancient world (often with a strong undercurrent of xenophobia, depicting those from foreign cultures, be they Arabs or Africans or Russians, as villainous monsters intent on destroying America). And inspiring as these movies were—sometimes even influencing freedom fighters around the globe, such as those in Nicolae Ceaușescu's Romania, to battle for democracy—there was a shadow side to both the myriad action movies and the men who made them. Claims of sexual assault and harassment followed several of them throughout their careers. The heightened sense of masculinity they portrayed on-screen had the potential to warp and corrupt. And not just for the men wielding the weapons, but sometimes for those who worshipped them. If life was cheap on-screen, it could be cheap off-screen, too.

What's undeniable, though, is that they still pack one hell of a punch. Seen as a whole, they are the product of a unique time in history—a surely-never-to-be-repeated golden age when multiplexes echoed to the sound of artillery fire, when quips came as fast as a southpaw punch, when Cro-Magnon warriors stood steady as a skyscraper. Before every movie hero had superpowers and digital effects boosted every brawl, they were the canvas on which viewers could project their hopes and fantasies. Whatever the battlefield, whether it be a jungle or a mountaintop, a thirty-five-story building or an ice rink, Earth or Mars or a humble boxing ring, they got fists pumping, and they still do today.

And it all started with eight hungry men, looking for a fight.

CHAPTER 1

...

THE STALLION

LION URINE IS AN ACRID LIQUID. It stings the eyes. It burns the throat. It smells foul. So when Sylvester Stallone got drenched in the stuff, it pretty much ruined his day.

It was 1970, and the twenty-four-year-old was at his new job in New York. Each morning he took the subway from his $71-a-month apartment on 56th Street and Lexington, a rented abode so filthy that Stallone joked to friends he was subletting to cockroaches. After a short stroll through the urban jungle, he'd enter an actual one: the five-and-a-half-acre Central Park Zoo. He walked past souvenir carts hawking balloons and animal crackers, past the legendary sea lion pool, past the bear pit, until he reached the red-brick building that housed the big cats. From inside, he was eyeballed by the leonine residents he was charged with looking after, including King Kado, who had been mysteriously found as a cub inside a parked car years earlier, and Bobby, who liked to devour twenty pounds of horsemeat a day.

At first it hadn't seemed a bad gig. But now Stallone wasn't grinning. For one thing, he was being paid just $1.12 an hour. For another, he was shoveling shit, literally—clearing up the lions' leavings with a broom and a hose. And when his trousers got splashed, leaving them so foul-smelling that on the subway ride home people fled from his car, he decided this wasn't the life he wanted to be stuck in.

"Not too many people ever have the thrill of seeing lions taking giant leaks," he said a few years on. "Let me tell you, they're accurate up to 15 feet, and after a month of getting whizzed on, I quit."

It was a low point. But Stallone had recently had plenty of those. Shortly before his stint at the zoo, his determination to become a performer, whatever it took, led him to transform into a creature himself, for a production of the sole play written by Pablo Picasso, *Desire Caught by the Tail*. Written by the painter in a feverish three days in 1941, the bawdy, rarely performed burlesque had drawn controversy in the late 1960s when put on in France, after rumors that the actors were urinating for real onstage. And the version starring Stallone, as a capering Minotaur-like creature, would elevate some eyebrows itself.

Stallone liked to think of himself as an enlightened artist in the making. At the University of Miami, he had pored over highbrow literature, from Albee to Zola. An immersion in the world of experimental theater sounded like the exact kind of thing he should be doing. Forget that it was taking place not on Broadway, or even off-Broadway, but on what Stallone termed "off-off-Broadway"— Pelham Parkway in the Bronx. This could prove to be the first step of a monumental career. The only trouble was, when he got his copy of the script, he barely understood a word.

"It's the only play that Picasso ever wrote, and for a reason, because it was horrible," Stallone was to explain. The plot was nonexistent. The characters were named things like Onion, Fat Anguish, and the Bow-Wows. There was to be simultaneous laughing and farting. One of the more lucid stage directions read, "The dancing shadows of five monkeys eating carrots appear." And when Stallone was presented with his costume, he began to get a *really* bad feeling. To become his half-man/half-bull character, he would don red horns, a scarlet fright wig on his groin, and a huge fake penis, which caused him particular problems. "It was a giant red appendage that you had to wrap around and stick in your G-string, because it was bothering you," he recalled. "You really couldn't walk."

One night, as he hobbled around the ramshackle stage, the penis escaped its cloth prison and bounced up and down like a spring, provoking a wave of unintentional laughter. On a subsequent evening, Stallone ended up in the hospital after one of the other actors blasted a fire extinguisher in his face, freezing shut his lips and eyes. The incident saw the play close after a grand total of three weeks and Stallone's face turn an unnatural shade of brown for the next four months.

This absurd odyssey into absurdist drama would have seen less committed folk scurry home for an ordinary life. But no bull-monster's genitals, or even lion's genitals, could discourage Sylvester Stallone. Whenever doubts clouded his mind, he took a deep breath and drove them back out.

After all, his literary hero Edgar Allan Poe had provided words for just such occasions. "They who dream by day are cognizant of many things," Poe had written, "which escape those who dream only by night."

FROM THE BEGINNING, Stallone's biggest problem was his face. It wasn't a bad face; in fact, it was a highly expressive one, with soulful eyes and sensuous lips. But on July 6, 1946—the rainy, wind-lashed New York day on which he was born—something had gone wrong. The doctor on duty clamped forceps onto his head as he emerged from the womb and pulled, too hard, severing a facial nerve above his jaw.

The injury affected the way Stallone spoke. "Reminiscent of the guttural echoings of a mafioso pallbearer," he once joked of his gravelly, slightly slurred voice. And it affected the way he looked, making the left side of his face droop a little. At school, kids taunted him with the nicknames "Slant Mouth," "Sylvia," and "Mr. Potato Head." "I *was* like Mr. Potato Head, with all the parts in the wrong place," he told a reporter in 1990. To another, he said, "I was like a poster boy for a nightmare. In a contest between me and a bulldog, you'd say the bulldog's better."

With a nurturing home life, the bullying might have had less impact. But his home life—in Hell's Kitchen and then, from the age of five, Montgomery Hills in Maryland—was anything but. His father, Frank, was a tough fireplug of a man who dreamed of being a singer, but in fact was flailing unsuccessfully to get a hair salon off the ground. His mother, Jacqueline, hawked cigarettes at nightclubs. Money was scarce, emotional support even scarcer. He would remember only two occasions on which his mother kissed him, while he compared his father to Stanley Kowalski, the emotionally pent-up brute at the center of *A Streetcar Named Desire*, even claiming that he witnessed Frank eating a raw sparrow, punching out a horse, and stitching up a wound without anesthetic—admittedly, not all on the same occasion. Savage beatings for Sylvester and his brother Frank Jr. were frequent, accompanied by two repeated questions: "Why can't you be smarter? Why can't you be stronger?"

Rage began to build inside him. Stallone looked like a low-rent gangster, and soon started to act like one, too. He'd prowl the neighborhood and use a brick to smash flies he saw crawling across cars. One day he jumped off a roof holding an umbrella, breaking his collarbone and prompting his father to say to his mother, "This boy will never become President. You've given birth to an idiot." By the time he was twelve, he'd broken ten other bones, too. He got kicked out of school after school; at one of them, the teachers unanimously voted him "Student Most Likely to End Up in the Electric Chair."

The first big change was a divorce; his parents called it quits in 1957. Then came Philadelphia, with Jacqueline starting a new life there with the city's pizza king, Tony Filiti. And then came the movie that changed everything. When Stallone, age thirteen, sat down in a movie theater to watch *Hercules Unchained*, starring former Mr. Universe Steve Reeves, it wasn't the performance that jolted him. After all, he'd fallen asleep watching *On the Waterfront* not long before. Instead, it was the *power:* Reeves's sinews straining, veins popping, muscles so vast that they threatened to burst the screen.

"It was like seeing the Messiah," Stallone would recall. "I said, 'This is what I want to be.'"

Could strength be the way to break out of it all: the bullying, the beatings, the bitterness? The teenage misfit grabbed on to the concept. Every piece of furniture in the house became impromptu gym equipment; every time somebody pointed a camera at him, he flexed like he was Steve Reeves, minus the manly beard and toga. His mother, who had swapped nightlife for fitness herself, opening a gym for women called Barbella's, smiled indulgently, even when he strapped cinder blocks to the ends of a broomstick and started hoisting it in the air.

That brutal question from his father, "Why can't you be stronger?," had become irrelevant. So Stallone tackled the other one: "Why can't you be smarter?" He purchased a dictionary, and instead of using it to bash his glutes, he read it, learning one new word a day. As his vocabulary expanded, so did his imagination. At school he wrote a four-hundred-word essay about what it would be like to eat a car. It got an F-minus.

He was still a shitkicker and a delinquent, firing arrows out of classroom windows and slugging any kid who made fun of him, but a sensitive inner artist began to take form. And when his mother read about a college in the Swiss Alps that was desperate for new scholars and would take even this straight-D student, he ended up in Europe, at an altitude of 4,500 feet, in an environment that would nurture that growth. "The lack of oxygen kept me dizzy at first," recounted Stallone. "Everybody was wearing berets and goatees and talking French, and I didn't know *what* to do." So he tried some new things. He read Walt Whitman poems into a tape recorder and played them back, altering his voice. He began painting and writing verse himself. Belatedly, he was getting book smart, although his street smarts remained: he taught his fellow students how to fake asthma attacks for $20 a pop.

Until Switzerland, acting had been of little interest. When Stallone let himself consider his future, he daydreamed about being a shepherd or a blacksmith, something solitary and masculine. Though he'd had a taste of performing at the age of eight, playing the lower half of Smokey the Bear in a Cub Scout play, doing it as an adult seemed soft. Even so, he allowed himself to be talked into auditioning for a college production of *Death of a Salesman,* improvising the sentence "I tell you, darling, I can't offer you anything but a handful of stars and a slice of immortality." The drama teacher said, "Not bad for a guy who looks like a Neanderthal." Stallone landed the role of Biff, and one night, through an unintended calamity, he had his second moment of revelation.

"I was onstage, and I wasn't feeling nervous at all—I felt in control of the situation," he was to remember. Then a scene went wrong: Stallone threw a radio, as planned, but this time it slammed through a backdrop, causing a large segment of the set to collapse. "Everyone started laughing. But the drama that was happening onstage was so in control of the audience that it didn't knock them out of concentration. I knew then, 'This is what I was made to do.'"

After all, how many professions reward you for trashing a room?

IN 1969 STALLONE arrived in New York, broke but hell-bent on becoming a star. He set up base in a flea-ridden apartment for six days, then spent the next eleven sleeping on a bench in a bus station, tuning out the sounds of junkies shooting up. His paltry possessions were stashed each night in a twenty-five-cent locker. In the daytime he roamed the city's streets, looking for a break. But one was not forthcoming. His first audition—for the film *Fortune and Men's Eyes*—was a bust; Zooey Hall, future star of *I Dismember Mama,* would end up playing the role, a character named Rocky, instead.

Instead, Stallone's first appearance was in a soft-core porn film, *Party at Kitty and Stud's,* which took two days to shoot, involved a nude game of Ring Around the Rosy, and saw him perform his first-ever action sequence, leaping over a fence in a snowy Central Park. It paid $200 and got him out of the bus station, but attempts to get an agent were met with the same response: "There is no call for your particular type." In real life, he often made people uneasy—one shopkeeper pulled a gun on him, assuming he was a stick-up man—but when he tried to get cast as a mugger in Woody Allen's *Bananas,* Allen dismissed him as insufficiently intimidating. That is, until Stallone and his friend Johnny, another aspiring actor, rubbed soot on their faces, ran Vaseline through their hair, and returned, scaring Allen into giving them parts.

Stallone's dream of somebody recognizing his poetic heart was not working out. He scored a substantial role in the 1973 counter-culture drama *No Place to Hide,* then was cast in the next year's *The Lords of Flatbush,* about the adventures of four leather-clad dudes in Brooklyn, but his heart wasn't fully in either. And on *Flat-bush,* he clashed with co-star Richard Gere over the unlikely sub-ject of condiments. "He would strut around in his oversized motorcycle jacket like he was the baddest knight at the Round Table," Stallone recalled of Gere, before describing a fracas in the back of a Toyota after Gere climbed in holding a chicken-and-mustard sandwich. "A small, greasy river of mustard lands on my thigh. I elbowed him in the side of the head." Gere exited the proj-ect.

One person who did see promise in the unknown Stallone was B-movie producer Roger Corman. The aspiring actor ended up being cast in two 1975 Corman projects. In *Capone,* a film Stallone would later describe as "the inbred cousin of *The Godfather,*" he played a gangster who betrays the titular mob boss; in *Death Race 2000* he was "Machine Gun" Joe Viterbo, who has a giant switch-blade strapped to the fender of his car. "He projected for *Death Race* the particular kind of pseudo-macho thing I was after," re-members Corman.

With another mugger gig booked the same year—this time op-posite Jack Lemmon in *The Prisoner of Second Avenue,* though in that film he turns out not to be a criminal after all—Stallone was at least racking up credits. But he was depressed. That rush he'd experienced in Switzerland performing *Death of a Salesman* had long faded. So he turned to something that offered him a sense of control: writing.

When he'd first arrived in New York, he'd had with him a copy of the *Easy Rider* screenplay. It wasn't because he liked Dennis Hopper, Peter Fonda, and Terry Southern's turns of phrase. In fact, when he'd watched the biker film that summer, he'd felt he could do better. And he got scribbling, aiming to prove it.

Stallone's early efforts weren't much more coherent than his school essay about the edible car—he would later refer to an epic screenplay he penned, with the title *Cry Full and Whisper Empty in the Same Breath*, as "180 pages of garbage"—but they gave him a sense of accomplishment. And while he failed to sell a single script, he seized opportunities to contribute dialogue to projects he was involved in. For *Death Race 2000* he pitched the line "You know, Myra, some people might think you're cute. But me, I think you're one very large baked potato." When the director, Paul Bartel, pushed back on the alteration, Roger Corman intervened to allow it. Recalls Corman: "I said, 'Sly's rewrite is really better than what's in the script. Stay with him and let him go.'"

Between parts, Stallone took any job he could get: theater usher, bouncer, fish-head cutter. But always he was writing, often under fake names such as Q. Moonblood or J. J. Deadlock. One notion he had was about a rock star with an illness that can only be cured by bananas. It ended with the singer dying onstage mid-gig; Stallone titled it *Sad Blues*. Another, *Till Young Men Exit,* was about unemployed actors so frustrated that they first kidnap a producer, then put him in a blender—no need to read between the lines there. All were rejected. He sprayed black paint onto all the windows of his apartment and carried on writing, ideas spilling out of his head. One day, in a marathon fourteen-hour session, he wrote six half-hour TV pilots. Not one was bought.

He could have given up there. Most people would have. Stallone, though, was a fighter, and so he started writing again. This one was what he called a "vile, putrid, festering little street drama," zooming in on "a good guy surrounded by rotten people." It was about another fighter. A guy named Rocky Balboa.

IRWIN WINKLER, the Hollywood producer who was one half of Chartoff-Winkler Productions, was a busy man. And he had little time for the hulking brute who had just stepped into his office. "It was one of those awkward meetings where you keep glancing at your watch and wondering how long it will be before you can ask him to leave," Winkler recalls. "We were very reluctant to meet him because we didn't have a movie we were casting. He didn't have a big list of credits. There was nothing much to talk about."

The conversation lurched on, with the wannabe actor failing to make much of an impression: his biggest film to date, *The Lords of Flatbush,* was one neither Winkler nor his partner, Bob Chartoff, had gotten around to seeing. Finally the meeting ground to a halt, and their guest headed dolefully for the door. Then, stopping and turning, Stallone blurted out, "Oh, by the way, I'm a writer."

Winkler was skeptical—most writers looked like Woody Allen, rather than someone who asks Woody Allen to hand over his wallet—but he was also intrigued. The first screenplay Stallone sent over, about some scheming opportunists in 1940s Hell's Kitchen, was rejected. But the second, about a down-on-his-luck boxer, showed some promise. "We were at the time trying to get the rights to a John Garfield boxing picture that Paramount owned, but Paramount was giving us a hard time," Winkler says. "So this solved that problem."

Where that Paramount film, 1947's *Body and Soul,* was about the corrupting power of money—a small-time slugger winds up becoming a puppet for mobsters—*Rocky* had a nobler figure at its core. Shortly before he met Winkler and Chartoff in 1975, Stallone had witnessed the legendary fight between world heavyweight champion Muhammad Ali and Chuck Wepner, aka "the Bayonne Bleeder," in Ohio. The cocksure Ali won, and it was his name that the crowds chanted, but Stallone was mesmerized by the underdog

Wepner, who had trained out in the wilderness of the Catskill Mountains and managed to go the distance, lasting fifteen rounds. The Bayonne Bleeder bled plenty, but as Stallone said shortly after, "He can hold his head up high forever no matter what happens." Wepner's dogged determination was channeled into the character of Rocky Balboa, aka the Italian Stallion, in Stallone's latest script.

So, too, was the actor's own pain. By now he was living in Los Angeles with his wife, Sasha, but his financial situation had not improved; in fact, he was terrified. With $106 in the bank, he joked darkly that they were so broke that their bull mastiff, Butkus, had to eat his own fleas. On the page, at least, he was able to craft the arc for Rocky that life was refusing to give him. The Philadelphia pugilist would be given a shot against all the odds, training for a fight against preening world champion Apollo Creed, and managing to make it fifteen rounds, just like Wepner.

When Winkler and Chartoff showed interest, Stallone frantically fleshed out the ideas he'd scribbled down, staying up for three and a half days straight, Sasha typing up his wild scrawls. "We'd watch the sun go up and the sun go down and we'd eat standing up and she would struggle and slap herself in the face at the typewriter to keep herself awake," he recalled two years later. The story slowly got lighter, the supporting characters less vile, Rocky himself more virtuous, though hardly smart, and the relationship between him and girlfriend Adrian unabashedly romantic. The producers read it and were charmed. They also figured they could make it for peanuts.

United Artists, the studio Chartoff-Winkler had a deal with, was less enthusiastic. "They turned it down flat," says Winkler. "They said, 'Nobody's going to see a fight movie. He's an ugly duckling. She's an ugly duckling. They got this crazy brother Paulie. Why would a champion give him an opportunity? Women don't go see fight movies.' They give us a whole list, like a studio can do when they don't want to make something."

There was another problem. Stallone insisted that he be not only the writer but also the star. After all, who could understand this Philly palooka better than him? But United Artists wanted a

heartthrob, Burt Reynolds or Ryan O'Neal, not a droopy-eyed unknown who'd just turned up in Hollywood in a rusty Oldsmobile.
The studio kept offering Stallone more and more money to walk
away from the role, eventually a cool million, but he refused every
time. Then the producers managed to work out a solution: if they
made the movie for the minuscule sum of $1 million, drawing on a
special clause they had in their contract with UA, and paid for any
overages themselves, they couldn't be stopped. "At that point,"
Winkler admits, "we were making the movie out of spite."

Thrilled, despite receiving just $23,000 to star, Stallone started
getting in shape. He began waking at four A.M., spending days in
the gym, punching bags until his knuckles bled and his thumbs
bent back, clumsy but determined to look like a convincing fighter
in the ring. And on December 3, 1975, he, Sasha, and their dog—
which at his lowest point Stallone had been forced to sell but had
managed to buy back—boarded a train from LA to Philadelphia to
begin the shoot.

The journey quickly turned into an ordeal. "Sly was stuck in a
small compartment with Butkus, who had a flatulence problem,"
explains Winkler. Stallone puts it more colorfully: "These blasts of
gas would come thundering across the room and nearly drive me
and Sasha into convulsions. I almost considered whittling a cork
and blocking up the foul passage." As he went over his screenplay
again and again, the toilet in the tiny room repeatedly flushed of
its own accord, and stewards' whistles blew incessantly. At one
point, when water flew out of the basin onto the crimson carpet on
which he was rolling, Butkus turned beet red; the Stallones spent
the next eleven hours rinsing him clean.

The shoot itself was so fast-paced and cheaply funded—with a
van functioning as the production office and Stallone changing in
the wardrobe vehicle—that few involved thought the project had
much of a chance. Garrett Brown, the camera operator whose test
for his new Steadicam rig had inspired the look of one of the movie's biggest scenes, in which Rocky triumphantly jogs up the
seventy-two stone steps of the Philadelphia Museum of Art, found
it a far cry from the two slick studio pictures he was also working

on, *Bound for Glory* and *Marathon Man*. "My first meeting with Stallone was unforgettable," Brown says. "He occupied the middle of our lone motor home in his gray sweats. Catering had the dinette forward and the odoriferous bathroom was aft. I asked him if the latter was functional and he muttered, 'Don't sling any iron in there and you'll be all right.'"

So puny was the budget that the entire cast and crew stayed in a motel. For lunch they'd head to the nearest Italian restaurant and guzzle cheap pasta. And there was no time for lavish set builds or multiple takes. "There's one shot where he walks across the parking lot and you see the big fucking 5K light in the background," says editor Richard Halsey. "Everybody said to me, 'You can't use that.' I said, 'It's dramatic! Who gives a shit? Nobody's going to be paying attention to that.'" Winkler, who was working on Martin Scorsese's $14 million *New York, New York* simultaneously, says, "It was really kind of guerrilla warfare. We had to cheat a lot of stuff to make it look, frankly, reasonable."

Yet the cheapjack vibe fit both the material and the location. Rocky's humble, whatever-it-takes approach to life bled into the production, with Stallone happily jogging miles and miles and miles over the first few days of shooting, whatever it took to get the right footage for the training montages. "We ran all over town," Brown remembers. "In the train yards and on the rubble-strewn fields and the elegant paths among the Delaware and Schuylkill Rivers. Everywhere we shot was evocative and new." And when they returned to LA to shoot interiors, people on the crew began to look at each other and say, "Have we actually got something here?"

For editor Scott Conrad, drafted in by Halsey to help grapple the eighty-four thousand feet of fight footage into shape, the realization came when he sat down to do a rough cut of the scene in which trainer Mickey, played by Burgess Meredith, comes to Balboa's apartment to ask to be his manager. "I needed your help about ten years ago, right?" Rocky tells Mickey, all his pent-up frustration shaking loose. "You never helped me. You didn't care." Says Conrad: "When I looked at all the dailies, the guy won me over then. He went toe-to-toe with Burgess Meredith. I get goose bumps now thinking about it."

Stallone filled the film with personal touches: the photos tacked to Rocky's mirror are of his own family; his father, Frank, rings the bell during the big fight; even Butkus makes an appearance as Rocky's pet, as well as two turtles, Cuff and Link, which Stallone had found in a pet store himself. The line between character and actor was blurred. And although John Avildsen was officially directing the movie, Stallone frequently had his own notes to offer. "He was all over John, all over the other actors, and I'm being complimentary," says Winkler. "He was really, really committed to helping out in every aspect of the film."

This didn't always go down well with Avildsen, a veteran of nine previous films. Not least when *Rocky* got into postproduction. Sometimes when Stallone swung by the cutting rooms at MGM Studios, there was levity. "Sly would pull up in this new car with black-and-white cowhide upholstery," says Halsey. "Of course, everybody made fun of him—it was so pretentious. He was a good bloke, you know?" Stallone even brought Butkus by. "We all liked the dog, but he was really pissed off that Butkus was so gentle," Halsey recalls. "Somehow the dog lost his voice, so he sent him to training school."

Sometimes, however, things felt more adversarial. "I provided them with a presence they wouldn't fool around with," Stallone would recall. "They wouldn't just say, 'Hey, let's cut out this close-up of Sly'—not when I'm sitting two feet away. By being there, I got them to respect my screenplay and my performance." En route one day, the star had worked himself up into such a rage imagining a scenario in which Avildsen insisted on deleting a scene with Rocky and Adrian—"I was a raving lunatic"—that he bellowed at the director as soon as he entered the room. At the close of another day, as Avildsen and the two editors prepared to end a long session in MGM's Screening Room 9, Stallone made a surprise appearance, to the dismay of the director. "Avildsen did his best to keep him out of the editing room," says Conrad. "Stallone had been calling for days and days, trying to get in to see John. John kept putting him off and putting him off. Avildsen was down on the Moviola when he got a call from the front gate that Stallone was on his way in to see him. He picked up his stuff, packed his bag as fast as he could, and he's careening out the door, when in comes Rocky."

Avildsen attempted to squeeze past his leading man in the narrow doorway. Stallone, undeterred, blocked him, saying, "John, I want to talk to you about the film."

"I gotta go," mumbled Avildsen. "I've got a meeting."

There was a little more back-and-forth. Then, abruptly, Stallone grabbed the director, picked him up off the ground, and set him back inside the screening room.

"Like I said," he repeated, *"I want to talk to you about the film."*

UNITED ARTISTS continued to see *Rocky* as a no-hoper, even after it had been cut together and Bill Conti's triumphant music was layered on top. Studio chairman Arthur Krim fell asleep in a preview screening, while UA's president, Eric Pleskow, sent the producers a letter saying they were considering sending it direct to TV. It was decided not to submit it to the Cannes Film Festival.

The buzziest movies in 1976 were gloomy, cynical pictures—*Taxi Driver, Carrie, Network*—in which the lead character either died or was left splattered in blood. *Rocky,* while gritty and raw in places—and even though the good guy didn't exactly win—had a different message. You could punch your way out of a jam, all on your own, if you never, ever gave up.

There was, from some quarters, distaste for this sunny philosophy. *New York Times* critic Vincent Canby called *Rocky* "a sentimental little slum movie." But far more were delighted by it. At a screening for Academy of Motion Pictures Arts and Sciences members, the film was met with a standing ovation. And when it came out, it grossed $117 million in the United States, more money than was made by *Taxi Driver, Carrie,* and *Network* put together, KOing Hollywood and becoming the number-one hit of the year.

There was, it was clear, a sudden, revived appetite for pictures with a message of hope. "We'd all gone through Vietnam, and the youth rebellion, and Nixon, and the plumbers and Watergate," says Winkler. "And all of a sudden this film comes along and says, 'If you believe in yourself, there's a wonderful opportunity for you.' It told a story people wanted to hear at the time."

This was it: the start of a new wave of action movies featuring a lone man pitted against the world, buckling but refusing to break. And Stallone made for a new kind of hero: not wiry and intense, like De Niro, Pacino, or Redford, but bulky and a little gauche. Or maybe an old kind of hero, back from the dead; the *Philadelphia Bulletin* ran a story about Rocky headlined "The Hollywood Movie Hero Has Returned." When Stallone was nominated for the Best Actor Academy Award, as well as Best Original Screenplay, to some it seemed unbelievable. Would this guy even fit into a tux? He did, and the experience that had started with an eighty-four-hour writing marathon and a farting dog ended in a visit to LA's Dorothy Chandler Pavilion, in a rented jacket (the bow tie fell off en route), where Stallone shadow-boxed with Muhammad Ali on the stage.

He didn't end up winning either Oscar, despite *Rocky* netting the night's big prize. "I'll tell you, the fact he didn't get anything really killed him," says Conrad, who along with Halsey picked up the award for Best Film Editing. "We sat behind him one row and over to the right, and you could almost see him wince every time he got passed over." Even so, Stallone was riding a huge high, having written his way out of rags and into riches with his rags-to-riches tale. "The movie has made Sylvester Stallone the hottest new star of 1976," declared the *Hollywood Reporter*. "As Frank Capra might put it, 'It *can* happen here.'"

He was now mixing with the cream of the movie industry, as well as some fellow rising stars, including an Austrian even bigger than he was. At the Golden Globes, Stallone had glared in disbelief at the person who picked up Best New Talent. The man, who had been seated at the same table as him, looked pleased with himself, and he had an eyebrow-raising name: Arnold Schwarzenegger.

"He's gloating and gloating and gloating," Stallone was to re-call. "And then finally it's time for *Rocky*. And we're not getting this category, and then I lose Best Actor. I go, 'Jesus, this is a night-mare.'" As the evening wound on and his temper frayed, Stallone couldn't stop looking over at this Schwarzenegger guy. Finally, dis-appointment gave way to triumph as *Rocky* was announced as Best Motion Picture. But instead of focusing on the stage, Stallone found himself aiming his emotions in a different direction—specifically, across the table, at the night's Best New Talent. "I manage to grab this giant bowl of flowers," he said, "and heave it in his direction."

As the pot crashed down and high-end petals spilled onto the immaculate carpet of the Beverly Hilton Hotel, attending celebri-ties, from Robert Wagner to Farrah Fawcett, gasped. Stallone and Schwarzenegger locked eyes. Though nobody there knew it yet, not even the two of them, a new period of Hollywood history had begun. A war, launched by roses.

And shrapnel was going to fly.

CHAPTER 2

...

THE TANK

LIKE STALLONE, Arnold Schwarzenegger had some close encounters with lions in his formative years. Not that he actually got inside a cage. Instead, he'd stand outside the metal bars, intently watching them stretch and snarl, so that he could replicate their movements later in the gym.

"You always have to stretch like the big cats," he told people, never failing to mention that his star sign was Leo. "When I read what a lion is supposed to be and I check what I am, it's exactly the same thing."

This confidence, so robust that Schwarzenegger felt a rapport with a 420-pound African predator, was there from the start. Born in the Austrian farm village of Thal in 1947, as a boy he managed to charm the occupying American soldiers, so each morning an armored transport equipped with 40 mm cannons would stop outside his family's cottage and take him to school. Nobody who knew the young Arnold was too surprised that he'd managed to finagle a military escort. After all, this kid was not your average resident of Thal. "I didn't get certain things I needed as a child," he wrote in 1977, "and that, I think, made me hungry for achievement, for winning in other ways, for being the best."

His home was, in some ways, a hushed haven from the world. His mother, Aurelia, played the zither and sang lullabies to Arnold and his older brother, Meinhard. Cats scampered around. And the yellow cottage looked out onto a forest in which nestled the ruins of an ancient castle. It was like something from a fairy tale. But it came complete with an ogre: Arnold's father, Gustav, an ill-tempered man who had been a member of the Nazi Party and was left racked with anger and guilt when Hitler's regime toppled. Gustav would frequently aim these emotions in the direction of his two children. "My hair was pulled. I was hit with belts," Schwarzenegger remembered five decades on. "Many of the children I've seen were broken by their parents, which was the German-Austrian mentality."

This child, however, was not going to break.

Instead, he got tough. Schwarzenegger saw himself as a piece of iron and every challenge that came his way as a hammer, forging him into steel. A smack on the face? A chance to prove he could brush off pain. No toilet in the house? He'd use a pot, like the hero in an ancient myth. When one of the family cats, a black-furred firecracker named Mooki, raked claws across his face, Arnold just laughed.

Weight training, when he discovered it at the age of fifteen, was just the next natural step in the fortification process. His new body would be a suit of armor, one he would never take off.

It began with a photograph in a newspaper Schwarzenegger picked up at school. In it, Mr. Austria, Kurt Marnul, was bench-pressing more than four hundred pounds—raw power. The teenage schoolkid was hooked. His first workout was a disaster; he overdid it and, legs wobbling like jelly, rode his bicycle into a ditch on his way home. But in no time he was bulking up, part of a new community, learning unfamiliar words like "intercostals," "deltoid," "lower latissimus." He plastered his bedroom walls with posters of scantily clad musclemen, causing his parents to panic, fearing he was gay. His mother summoned a local priest to talk to him, while his father resorted to a more brutal tactic: his fist. "He said my weight training was garbage," Schwarzenegger recalled. "That I should do something useful and go out and chop wood."

But wood held less appeal than iron. Finally he had started to feel alive. He met Marnul himself, who agreed to train him, and began taking part in contests, finding he could lift more easily when egged on by the cheers of a crowd. Women began to be drawn to him; he returned their interest, and then some, but didn't pursue a relationship or allow his hedonistic adventures to interfere with his training.

One Sunday morning, after another long, wild night out, Schwarzenegger arrived at the gym to find the door locked and the lights out. No problem—he scaled the roof and broke in through a skylight. Then he worked out alone, shivering in the cold. This way, at least, there was no wait for the weights.

FUELED BY ENDLESS MEAT—he called the bull's testicles he enjoyed "Arnold's Protein Burger"—Schwarzenegger grew and grew. When fellow lifters pointed out that he had feeble calves, he spent a year punishing them until they bulged like boulders. Those perfected, he battered his deltoids into submission. He wrote down a mantra—"Arnold, you are a winner"—and repeated it aloud to himself a dozen times a day. There was no doubt that the professional bodybuilding circuit was the right track for him to be on. After all, where else could you get anointed with a title as grandiose as Mr. Universe?

There was only one small detour along the way: a compulsory year of service in the Austrian army. But even there he was able to bolster his macho image, being selected for a tank unit. Each day the eighteen-year-old clambered into an M47 Patton, a fifty-ton metal monster named after the American general, and rolled into action. Schwarzenegger looked the part but proved to be a poor soldier, on one occasion leaving the vehicle without its brakes on (it rolled into a river) and on another smashing through a garage door and bursting a water pipe. He became familiar with the concept of solitary confinement but didn't mind it, using the time to do push-ups. When he wasn't in the M47 he was training anyway, for at least four hours a day, his body expanding so fast he had to be issued a larger uniform.

Post-army, he continued creating goals, then demolishing them. He began visualizing himself as King Kong when he stood onstage, except instead of craving Fay Wray in his clutches he thought only of trophies. "Whatever I thought might hold me back, I avoided," he said. "I crossed girls off my list—except as tools for my sexual needs. I eliminated my parents too." He visited London and even South Africa, where the platform he was on collapsed under the combined weight of brawn and metal.

It was America, though, that held the most allure. As a child in sleepy Thal, Schwarzenegger had imagined the United States as being the most glamorous place in the world, and one where any dream could come true. After all, it was where his beloved Johnny Weissmuller Tarzan films had been manufactured. And when he had sat down to write out what he called "the Master Plan," Step 1 had read, "I will come to America, which is the country for me. Once there, I will become the greatest bodybuilder in history." After that, he would learn English, get a business degree, invest in real estate, start making movies, and make a million dollars by the age of thirty.

And so, after winning Mr. Universe—at the age of twenty, he was the youngest person ever to do so—in 1968 he arrived on the shores of California for the very first time.

He was, at first, disappointed. Where were the famous American skyscrapers? And what was up with Hollywood, which he now saw was just a dumpy-looking place in the middle of Los Angeles? "I was looking for giant signs and neon lights," he recalled. "But this was nothing."

Schwarzenegger was underwhelmed, too, by the legendary Gold's Gym, two blocks from LA's Venice Beach; to him the gym looked small and shabby. Still, he dove in, making friends there, bodybuilders with nicknames like "Snail" and "Fat Arm Charlie." Schwarzenegger himself acquired a new, ironic moniker: "Chubby." America didn't turn him soft; in fact, he became even more competitive, sometimes doing squats until he passed out, regaining consciousness five minutes later and carrying on. "A lot of other athletes are afraid of this," he said. "So they don't pass out. They don't go on." And soon he was a mainstay in fitness magazines, the focus of ghostwritten articles such as "Bombing the Forearms with the Double Split!" and "How I Terrorized My Thighs into Massive Growth!"

The Master Plan was under way. While over on the East Coast of America Stallone was poring over poetry, Schwarzenegger was rumbling forward, unstoppable, with no time for diversions. "I never saw him read a book for pleasure, or take a vacation that did not involve a business or promotional connection," recalled George Butler, who would direct him in the bodybuilding documentary *Pumping Iron*. And one item on Schwarzenegger's list was about to be ticked off, even faster than he'd imagined.

The Austrian with the unpronounceable name was about to make a movie.

ONE MUGGY MORNING in the summer of 1969, Arthur Allan Seidelman walked into a coffee shop on Columbus Avenue and 72nd Street in Manhattan. Having just been hired for his first film as director, he had been asked by its producers to meet their freshly cast leading man. This person, he had been told, was an accomplished European thespian who had performed in numerous Shakespeare plays. So it was something of a surprise for Seidelman when he came face-to-face with a person who not only could barely speak English but also in stature more closely resembled the Globe Theatre than a typical Hamlet.

"The thing that stands out in my mind is how huge he was," remembers Seidelman. "I mean, I spent the meeting talking to his right arm."

A few other things about Arnold Schwarzenegger caught the director's attention that day. One was the size of his appetite. "He had a massive breakfast," Seidelman says. "It was, as I recall, four eggs, two baked potatoes, and two waitresses." Another was his charm; Schwarzenegger was refreshingly unpretentious, shoveling food into his mouth and flashing an easy grin. And then there was his honesty. Instead of bullshitting about art, he was remarkably up-front about his ambitions. "I asked him why he had decided to come to America," the director recalls. "And very candidly, he said, 'To make money.'"

Schwarzenegger did in fact have a personal connection to the project. As a teenager he had loved a 1961 film called *Hercules in the Haunted World,* pitting Reg Park, one of his bodybuilder heroes, against an army of zombies. That had been part of a string of Italian Hercules movies that had proven a mini-craze throughout the 1960s, romps with titles such as *Hercules, Prisoner of Evil* and *Hercules in the Vale of Woe.* The cycle was now winding down, and a small production company called RAF Industries had decided to jump in with a spoof for Italian television, originally titled *Hercules Goes Bananas* before ending up as *Hercules in New York.* Schwarzenegger would take a role previously occupied not only by Park but also by Stallone's hero Steve Reeves.

Moving to New York from October to mid-December 1969, he threw himself into acting with the same intensity with which he had sculpted his body, regardless of how ridiculous the sequence might be. And *Hercules in New York* was not short on those. Following the illegitimate son of Zeus as he is flung down to earth by his father, the tale depicts a sprawl of Greek mythology on a budget far from Titan-sized. "We shot it all in and around Central Park," says Seidelman. "If you listen carefully at the Gates of Hell, you can hear the traffic going by on Central Park West." As for the sequence in which Hercules grapples with a marauding bear, an aspiring actor was convinced to don an animal costume, which turned out to be not entirely convincing. "I decided that there's no way I'm going to be able to convince anybody above the age of two and a half that this is a real bear," admits the director. "So I asked the guy just to have fun with it. That was the modus operandi of the bear."

Schwarzenegger, despite the nonexistent production values and lousy lines, remained eager to please. Again and again, he would ask, "Was that good? How can I make it better?" Exuding a goofy, breezy charm in front of the camera, he was happy just to be there.

One day he and Seidelman took advantage of a break and

headed up to the top of the Empire State Building. "Even though I was a native New Yorker, I had never been up there," says Seidelman. "And Arnold had never been up there, either. I remember standing looking out over the city, next to him, and being very moved by his response to being there." Like King Kong, his bodybuilding role model, Schwarzenegger had clambered to the roof of Manhattan's most famous building, though he would make it down again in less dramatic fashion.

Hercules in New York, to no one's surprise, made little impact, and was derided by those who did see it. For Schwarzenegger, there were other reasons not to point at it with pride—not only was his name changed to "Arnold Strong" in the credits, but his voice was dubbed over, too. Still, as his star began to rise, he refused to disown his ignominious beginnings.

"He's a much too honest guy to sweep it under the carpet," says Seidelman, who has made over fifty movies with the likes of Elizabeth Taylor and Ellen Burstyn but still gets asked most about his $30,000 muscleman-versus-grizzly flick. "I sent him a note recently about my ill health, and he sent me back a very sweet one that said, 'Are you ready to do a sequel?' I learned to be proud of the film by following Arnold's example."

IN THE DECADE AHEAD, Schwarzenegger would appear in only four other films; *Hercules in New York* had not, it was accurate to say, gotten Hollywood's attention. But any frustrations he might have felt were channeled into his workout regime, which wasn't getting any milder. In 1970 he won not only the Mr. Olympia contest but Mr. Universe and Pro Mr. World, too, a hat trick never before achieved. In his 1977 book, *Arnold: The Education of a Bodybuilder*—billed as "a super-man's program for super-fitness"—he laid down his rules for getting a body like his, which he referred to as "a work of art."

> "If you concentrate hard enough, you will be able to send blood to a particular muscle just by thinking about it."

"After you are no longer able to do full reps, do partial reps until the calf literally refuses to move."

"Guys who do not row never win a contest."

"Keep your mind hungry."

Hunger—a never-ending appetite for new experiences, new victories—was what drove Schwarzenegger's every move. In the same book, he openly proclaimed it as his philosophy: "For me, life is continuously being hungry. The meaning of life is not simply to exist, to survive, but to move ahead, to go up, to achieve, to conquer." Like the tank he had driven back in his army days, he rolled forward, looking for situations to size up and subdue. While he had finally gotten into a long-term relationship, with a California waitress named Barbara Outland—a change from the casual flings that had usually started with Schwarzenegger strolling up to a woman and asking if she wanted to have sex—it fell apart in 1975 when it became clear he wasn't going to be content with settling down and having a normal life.

As it happened, the breakup came about because of a movie, aptly titled *Stay Hungry*. Schwarzenegger couldn't say no to the project; for one thing, the writer was his pal Charles Gaines, who had tailored the role of weightlifter Joe Santo to him. For another, the director was Bob Rafelson, indie darling and maker of the likes of *Five Easy Pieces* and *The King of Marvin Gardens*. The meandering tale of a slacker (Jeff Bridges) who gets embroiled in the affairs of the denizens of a gym, it didn't have much more of a budget than *Hercules in New York*, but it was a far more serious production. This was something he couldn't bumble through.

Rafelson had at first reacted badly to the suggestion that this untrained novice take on the role. But eventually he agreed, calling his friend Jack Nicholson and asking the star to recommend an acting coach. The answer was Eric Morris. And nine weeks of intense one-on-one lessons were arranged, to happen at Morris's LA studio.

"I'm talking to Bob on the telephone and I say, 'Well, okay, how am I going to recognize him?'" Morris recalls now. "There was dead silence. Ten seconds go by. And then he says, 'Eric, you can't miss him.' "

Morris, whose style of teaching pushed the pioneering approach of Stanislavski even further, spent six weeks probing Schwarzenegger, urging him to divulge memories, to tell him what made him happy, what upset him, what he thought of his parents. The bodybuilder, who had spent years trying not to betray any emotion, was at first bewildered, then resistant, then, eventually, cooperative.

"I was collecting the jelly beans," says Morris. "Specifics about his life that I knew I could translate specifically to every scene in the film. I milked him dry." Only in the final three weeks did the *Stay Hungry* screenplay come out; at that point, the dots were connected. "I would say, 'Arnold, remember you told me that story about how you climbed through the skylight at the gym? That's the way you have to feel in this scene.' "

It worked. Besides the crash course in acting, Schwarzenegger had slimmed down from 240 pounds to 209 at Rafelson's request and even taken fiddle lessons (Santo turns out to have a surprising flair for bluegrass). And when he arrived in Birmingham, Alabama, for the shoot, he impressed everyone there. In one scene, Santo is mocked by some yahoos for his fiddle-playing—"Let's hear it for the Muscle Beach Symphony Orchestra!"—and whatever painful memory Schwarzenegger drew on for the moment pays off; it's the actor at his most unguarded and affecting.

Far from the embarrassment of *Hercules in New York*, the free-form *Stay Hungry* earned warm reviews. And while the *New York Times* write-up did describe Schwarzenegger as appearing "to be trapped inside a huge, grotesquely muscled body that has no relation to the conventional head on top of it," it was also a good bit of PR for the bodybuilding community, presenting them as likeable, three-dimensional people rather than oversized freaks. It was certainly good PR for Schwarzenegger, who went on to win the Golden Globe award that riled up Stallone so much. Encouraged, he went back to Morris to develop his acting techniques even further, joining the tutor's class for over a year.

There, it seemed, he was game for anything. "I had him ranting, screaming, doing antisocial experiments," says Morris. "Abandonments, where you lie on the floor and have a fit. He did Vesuvius, one of my exercises where a guy gets up onstage and does a large expurgatory dump"—a wild bellow, venting repressed emotions, "a way to prime the pumps and get out all of your internal shit that you're gunnysacking and pushing down, so you're ready to act."

There were two moments that convinced Morris that Schwarzenegger had the makings of a great actor. One was an electrifying performance of a scene from Tennessee Williams's *Sweet Bird of Youth,* a young female student playing the ruined, drug-addled Alexandra Del Lago, he her boy toy Chance Wayne. The other was a role-playing exercise where Schwarzenegger flashed back to being a young boy in Thal, Austria, opening presents on Christmas morning. "The way he did that brought tears to everybody's eyes," Morris recalls. "And I think he teared up, too."

But even as Schwarzenegger's psychological armor was being stripped away, he was being tugged in another direction, too. The bodybuilding documentary *Pumping Iron,* which came out the year after *Stay Hungry,* saw him at his most macho and outrageous, playing tricks on his competitors and saying things like, "Milk is for babies. When you grow up, you have to drink beer." A huge success, *Pumping Iron* thrust him into the limelight and gave him his first taste of real stardom.

"Arnold has a gift that cannot be acquired no matter how hard an athlete trains, no matter how many pep talks replete with references to Michelangelo's sculpture he absorbs," wrote an awed Richard Schickel in *Time.* "It is, of course, the gift of charisma."

One night in Eric Morris's class, after the film's release, Schwarzenegger had a dark look on his face. Morris asked him to stand up and share what he was feeling.

"I saw an agent just now," the Austrian explained. "He doesn't like my body. He doesn't like my name. And he doesn't like my accent. But *fuck him*—I'm going to be a superstar."

Later that evening, as the class dined at a Mexican restaurant, Schwarzenegger leaned over to Morris and told him, "I love what you do. But that's not the direction I want to go. I want to be an action-adventure actor."

Class was dismissed.

WHILE SHOOTING *STAY HUNGRY,* Schwarzenegger had gone with Bob Rafelson and Sally Field on a trip to an Alabama movie theater to watch the summer's smash hit, *Jaws*. And it's possible that the man who once identified with King Kong may have also seen kinship with the ravenous great white shark. A killer, yes, but also a perfect physical specimen, larger and more efficient than any of its kind, hell-bent on achieving its objectives.

Because as the 1970s ended and the 1980s began, the Austrian was closing in on Hollywood with his mouth wide open.

There were near misses, such as when he was deemed too short to play the Incredible Hulk in a TV series (his pal Lou Ferrigno, one inch taller at 6'4", bagged the part) and too bulky to play Flash Gordon. His audition for the latter saw him come into the orbit of Italian mega-producer Dino De Laurentiis, a character every bit as colorful as Schwarzenegger. Hackles instantly rose on both sides.

"Why does a little man like you need such a big desk?" the actor asked as he entered De Laurentiis's office.

The producer erupted. "You have an accent! I cannot use you! Flash-a Gordon has no accent!"

"What do you mean, I have an accent? I can barely understand *you*," Schwarzenegger retorted. The meeting, he would claim, lasted a total of one minute and fourteen seconds.

Even so, it was another De Laurentiis project that would provide the big break he was waiting for. It originated with Edward Pressman, another producer, who saw a rough cut of *Pumping Iron* and immediately began calculating which movie to drop Schwarzenegger into. "It was not an intellectual process that I went through," recalls Pressman. "It was just an immediate response to this amazing human marvel. I was friendly with a guy named Ed Sumner, who had a comic book store on the Upper East Side of Manhattan. And he started showing me Conan comics, especially the covers by Frank Frazetta. Which, you know, looked like Arnold. It was such an easy connection."

It did seem like a no-brainer; as drawn by Frazetta, Robert E. Howard's fantasy hero Conan the Barbarian was even more hulking than the Hulk, a primitive force of nature who drives a chariot drawn by polar bears and wields weapons bigger than most people. Pressman approached Schwarzenegger one day in 1977 at a Sunset Boulevard restaurant, hooking him with a quick pitch.

Conan the Barbarian took six years to get off the ground, beset by rights issues and a torturous quest to find a director. Ridley Scott expressed interest, prompting Pressman to fly to London to meet him, but had changed his mind by the time the producer touched down. Adrian Lyne came and went. Ralph Bakshi, who had directed an animated version of *The Lord of the Rings,* took a meeting with Schwarzenegger at LA eatery Musso & Frank, which quickly went sour. "It turned into a nightmare," says Pressman. "The whole thing fell apart right at the table. Ralph is pretty headstrong and didn't like being told what to do. I guess as an animator, he was used to having total control over everything."

And then there was Oliver Stone. At that point better-known as a writer than as a director, he had typed out a sprawling *Conan* screenplay, with a possible view of him and Bakshi directing together. His 140-page script was berserk in its ambition, marinating in the baroque craziness of the Hyborean Age and featuring mutant armies, legions of whirring insects, and references to Dante's *Inferno.* Whether it was filmable will never be known, because Dino De Laurentiis entered the scene, offering to finance the project. "We were into Dino-world," remembers Stone unhappily. "And Dino does things his way, which means cutting every fucking thing you can in the script."

Another thing De Laurentiis wanted to cut: the man who had mocked his desk. "Part of our contract said the actor had to be Arnold," Pressman explains. "And Dino fought that. He said, 'He can't speak English. People will laugh at us. This will never work.'" Attempts to melt the ice by getting the two together backfired when De Laurentiis accused Schwarzenegger of being a Nazi. And so other, svelter actors were investigated. One was Christopher Lambert. Another was David Carradine. But Pressman stuck doggedly to his original choice, and finally De Laurentiis caved, although he refused to allow Schwarzenegger to record the film's narration. The movie began to shoot in Spain in early 1981, with maverick director John Milius behind the camera.

"Conan is a barbarian," says Milius now, of *Conan the Barbarian,* "and I related to that instantly. I love Genghis Khan, I love the Vikings, I love the Apaches, and all primitive warrior cultures. I was the only guy in Hollywood who could have wrote and directed *Conan* the way I did, because I'm some sort of unreconstructed barbarian myself."

It would prove an eventful shoot. Almost as soon as filming began, there was an attempted coup in the country, with tanks rolling through the streets. The sets slithered with snakes; the film's villain, Thulsa Doom, runs a serpent cult, and so Milius had hired an eccentric herpetologist named Dr. Tiva, who had an entourage of beautiful female assistants, to bring in truckloads of reptiles. The swimming pool of the hotel that housed cast and crew had water snakes writhing in it, to prevent them from getting dehydrated, while Milius liked to unwind by wrapping a boa constrictor around his neck. "I'm interested in pagan mythology," he said with a smile in a moment of downtime, "and they've allowed me to make a pagan movie."

Again, Schwarzenegger was up for anything. His daily training routine was fearsome: horseback riding while clad in heavy armor, a thirty-minute run, an hour of weights, sword practice with an instructor named Yamazaki. On his first morning of filming, he cut himself on a blade and had to be stitched up by a medic. Another day, while being chased by wolves, he was caught by one and dragged along the ground by his clothes. During the shooting of a scene where Conan discovers a secret burial chamber, he fell from a height.

"Look, I'm bleeding real blood," he told Milius.

"Leave it, it looks great," the director replied.

Schwarzenegger, well used to putting his body through hell, had told Milius early on, "You must treat me like a trained dog." He forensically studied the Marlon Brando film *One-Eyed Jacks* for a scene in which Conan wields his mighty Atlantean sword, didn't complain when an orgy scene was shot in an ice-cold truck factory, and didn't flinch when an arrow, fired by Milius himself, whizzed past his head and into a giant animatronic snake. "I put Arnold through his own Wheel of Pain," says Milius with a laugh. "Whatever I threw at him, he was game. I even got him to resculpt his physique so his musculature would reflect a more ancient warrior's type body than that of a modern bodybuilder."

Later on in the shoot, Schwarzenegger found himself shackled to the actual Wheel of Pain, a giant wooden instrument of torment, with powerful wind machines blasting cold air into his face. He requested hot tea with some schnapps in it, then mulled over a Friedrich Nietzsche quote he had memorized: "Whatever doesn't kill you, makes you stronger."

ON A CHRISTMAS TRIP to Nairobi at the end of 1981, Edward Pressman was leafing through a newspaper when he spotted an ad for an early screening of *Conan the Barbarian*. The producer was surprised—few major American films open first in Kenya, and nobody had notified him of the plan. Then again, he was out of the loop with *Conan,* being preoccupied of late with getting Universal's *The Pirates of Penzance* off the ground. He and his wife bought tickets and watched the swords-and-sorcery drama unfold. And what they saw filled Pressman with dread.

"It was a kind of shapeless form of *Conan,*" he remembers. "There were sequences that would just go black for ten seconds and you'd sit there and something else would pop up. It wasn't even a first cut. I was just distraught: 'What happened?' It turned out that Dino had a tax deal and it had to open in one major city in the world before the end of the year. So he picked this city that no one would know about, Nairobi, and showed the film as a tax maneuver."

In fact, things weren't nearly as dire as they seemed. When the movie test-screened in Las Vegas in early 1982, it was a triumph; the packed audience, many of them bikers in black leather and chains, cheered when a drunken Conan punched a camel and screamed at the dark-magic conniving of James Earl Jones's Thulsa Doom. Recalls Milius: "The test-screening process is very overrated, and usually misused by Harvard MBA types to fuck a good movie up. With *Conan* it worked in my favor, though." After the movie finished, Robert Rehme, the head of Universal, proclaimed with a grin, "We're moving the date up." The film was released in May, then one of the earliest-ever releases for a big summer movie; it ended up grossing over $70 million from a $20 million budget.

Not everyone was pleased. *Time* called the film "a sort of psychopathic *Star Wars,* stupid and stupefying." And when Oliver Stone saw the finished product, he was appalled. "I mean, even the cactus looked ridiculous," he says. "People with costumes that are badly done. Phony stuff. At the end it feels like a cult of hippies, especially with John's casting—his surfing buddies or whatever."

But the numbers spoke: it was a victory, not least for its star. While Schwarzenegger's on-screen hero was hardly more textured than his two-dimensional comic-book counterpart, the performance fit the movie perfectly. He was suddenly bankable, not as Mr. Universe but as himself: nobody would ever tell him his name was too silly for a movie poster again. "My goal is to be equal to Clint Eastwood or Robert Redford or any of those guys," he told a reporter at the time. "I'm very well on my way."

At one point in *Conan the Barbarian,* a mysterious wizard known as Mako shares some advice with the hero: "Success can test one's mettle as surely as the strongest adversary." Schwarzenegger was about to find out for himself if that was true.

CHAPTER 3

...

TOOLING UP

AFTER ROCKY, Sylvester Stallone should have felt like a super-hero. For one thing, he found himself in the running to play one. In early 1977 he met *Superman* director Richard Donner to discuss the possibility of playing the Last Son of Krypton. Stallone was excited—at age eight he had dyed a shirt blue, crayoned on an *S*, then pulled back his outerwear in class to reveal it—but Donner decided he wanted an unknown. The star shrugged; he had plenty of other offers coming in.

Stallone's lifestyle had been upgraded in sync with his career. He used his *Rocky* earnings to buy a lavish house with private beach in Malibu. Inside, dotted everywhere, were mementos of his miraculous breakthrough: metal figurines of boxers; the gloves he had worn for Balboa's bouts hanging up; fan letters from the likes of Elvis Presley, Frank Capra, and Kirk Douglas strewn about.

"I've been down, and I've been up," Stallone remarked. "And up is better."

But it actually felt more like he'd moved sideways, to a different kind of trouble. Instead of success eliminating the problems in his life, they were multiplying. There was attempted blackmail, when the producers of his film debut, the tawdry *Party at Kitty and Stud's,* tried to coerce him into giving them $100,000 by threatening to widely release the film. And there was a fistfight on an LA street, with a driver who Stallone claimed drove into the back of his car. "In true Rocky fashion, I hit him with a wide, arcing left," he explained. Rather than making him money, this time a punch cost him $15,000.

Another loss was his marriage to Sasha. Having been together since they met as ushers in a New York movie theater, they separated soon after *Rocky*'s release. Even that movie, which had brought him so much fortune (both from his $2.5 million payday and from future career opportunities) and which he had atypically watched again and again when it came out—he claimed to have sat through it forty times—was not free of misery. While it had earned $225 million worldwide, Stallone would claim he had been given no ownership stake in the franchise, something that would rankle him for decades to come.

And despite the many effusive reviews, he felt sore about the notices that hadn't gone his way. One piece of writing, in particular, had dug in like a splinter: Vincent Canby's slam for the *New York Times*. "People like Canby and real loose screws of that nature . . . eventually they're going to meet their Waterloo," Stallone thundered in 1977. "I'd like to have Canby come up to me and call me a fourth-rate actor. I defy him."

There were more bad reviews to come. Plenty more, in fact. His two follow-ups to *Rocky*, both arriving in 1978, had far from the same reception as his boxing drama. Even if the first one was titled *F.I.S.T.*

That project had looked like the perfect next move. Diametrically opposed to *Rocky*, it was a serious drama about a labor union called the Federation of Inter-State Truckers. The director, Norman Jewison, was the veteran of respected Oscar contenders *In the Heat of the Night* and *Fiddler on the Roof*. And Stallone's role was that of a Cleveland warehouse worker, Johnny Kovak, who ends the film by delivering an emotional monologue at a Senate hearing, then getting shot by Mafia goons. But while Stallone inveigled his way into the writing process, getting paid an extra $150,000 on top of his $350,000 acting fee for punching up Joe Eszterhas's script, this time he was not permitted access to the editing room. This, he was to claim, damaged the movie. "The director never used my most fiery takes, so I came off lukewarm," he griped.

For his next film, *Paradise Alley,* he was determined not to be cut out of the loop again. In fact, he'd be running the show. The script was Stallone's, a resuscitation of the story Winkler and Chartoff had rejected a few years earlier; he would direct for the first time; and he would even sing the incongruous theme song, "Too Close to Paradise," a collaboration with *Rocky* composer Bill Conti. A tale of hustlers in postwar New York, with a subplot about a dancing monkey, a glib turn from Stallone as earring-wearing hero Cosmo Carboni, and characters including Franky the Thumper, Rat, and Burp, it was not subtle stuff, but it was at least personal, set in Hell's Kitchen (where Stallone was born) in 1946 (the year he was born). Once again, though, he was outmaneuvered in postproduction, with Universal removing dozens of scenes and, in Stallone's mind, ruining the film.

It wasn't the one-two punch for which he had hoped. *F.I.S.T.* actually found a supporter in Stallone's nemesis Vincent Canby, but otherwise came out to yawns; *Time* summed it up as "nearly two and a half hours of unmitigated boredom." The denunciations mostly suggested that Stallone had strayed too far from what he did best. On the other hand, *Paradise Alley* was decried for being too close to *Rocky.* Canby, back in antagonistic form, called it "*Rocky* warmed over and then thrown out." Pauline Kael tutted, "Stallone tries to work our emotions in exactly the same ways, and there's no surprise to the shamelessness this time."

Sitting in Malibu, the newly minted A-lister felt dazed by the barrage. "I received the worst reviews since Hitler," he said. "They would actually ignite, they were so hot."

IN LATER YEARS, Stallone would refer to Rocky Balboa as his "best friend." But as the 1970s ended, his feelings toward the character were less genial.

When Stallone was invited to a White House state dinner, President Jimmy Carter extended an arm with a grin and said, "Pleasure to meet you, Rocky." On a trip to the Senate chamber, Ted Kennedy did the same, then asked him to scrawl an autograph, as Balboa, for his kids. It would happen in less refined locations, too, with well-wishers yelling the name at him across the street. They all meant well, but the more he heard it, the more Stallone's blood boiled. Something *Rocky* editor Scott Conrad was to learn the hard way in late 1978. "I was doing a picture over at Warner Hollywood Studios, and saw him across the way," Conrad recalls. "When we were maybe ten feet away, I go, 'Yo, Rock!' We used to kid around about that. And he turned around slowly, and looked at me, and walked away."

Rather than it being just an indicator that everyone loved the character he'd created, Stallone believed that he and Balboa, the slurring stumblebum, were being perceived as one and the same. Whenever he tried to assert himself in production meetings, he was met with thinly veiled derision. "They say, 'Who is he? He's right off the streets. He shouldn't be earning that kind of money. He should feel lucky and keep his mouth shut and sit in a corner,'" he told Barbara Walters in 1979. He sensed the attitude even from his friends and gradually cut himself off from people in his life, one by one.

The notion of returning to Balboa, then, initially had little appeal. But finding himself sleeping on a bed in an office at Universal Studios post–*Paradise Alley*, with his family gone, his loyal manager Jane Oliver dead from cancer, his confidants sparse, and a thick folder full of withering reviews, Stallone finally came to the conclusion that another round couldn't hurt.

Rocky II would be brawnier in every way than the scruffy original. The budget was, at $7 million, seven times larger; no more stinky motor home or cheap spaghetti lunches. And this time Stallone himself would be in control, properly. "We felt he was so involved in every part of the making of *Rocky* that when we decided to make *Rocky II* I asked him to direct it," says Irwin Winkler. "He hesitated and then agreed." The studio, United Artists, was less happy about this news, given the box office of *Paradise Alley*, but finally relented.

They were soon glad they did. The 1979 sequel undeniably

played it safe—Stallone ditched a notion of finishing the film with a fight in the Colosseum in Rome, complete with a cameo from the pope, instead keeping the action in Philadelphia, and the final reel saw Rocky win, properly this time. But it was a huge crowd-pleaser, giving the characters and milieu a glossy sheen while retaining the charm. "A great movie," exclaimed Muhammad Ali, who had written Stallone a poem after seeing the original. "It has all the ingredients: love, violence, emotion." There were no Oscar nominations this time, but it made $200 million worldwide, not much less than its predecessor had. "It was a resuscitator," Stallone said a couple of years later. "It came at a time when I needed it most."

It wasn't enough, however, to allow him to shake off his funk. After a brief reunion with Sasha, the relationship blew up once again. In New York to shoot *Nighthawks*, a grimy cop thriller that both begins and ends with Stallone wearing a woman's wig, he agreed to a stunt in which he would be dangled 250 feet above the East River on a cable, a scenario so dangerous that he took a knife up with him, claiming it was so he could kill himself quickly on the way down should it go wrong, rather than have his body explode on impact with the water. Perhaps due to the stress of this type of working day, he partied hard at the city's clubs at night. When he visited an acupuncturist, they told him he had the body of a seventy-five-year-old.

His brain didn't feel much sprightlier. The same year, he found himself in Hungary, playing a goalkeeper in a project called *Escape to Victory*, about POWs who plot to escape during a soccer match against their Nazi captors. His castmates were an eclectic bunch: Michael Caine, Max von Sydow, Pelé, numerous members of Ipswich Town Football Club. But rather than quaffing pints with them, Stallone would retire to his hotel room alone, plunging back into that old depression.

"I felt that it was over. I was finished. This was it," he said in 1982. "This film would probably be my last. The fame game had gotten to me. I had lost. I had hit basically emotional rock bottom."

At the time, *Escape to Victory* felt like neither an escape nor a victory. But it was during that production that Stallone found an item that would salve his soul. It was a small green book with a big title: *The Keys to Reality*. Written by a man named Alan Osman, whose wife had been introduced to Stallone by his secretary Linda, it was full of mystical sentences, which the star studied as he sat in the hotel. One became his daily mantra: "I accept the responsibility to be in divine love at all times."

Slowly he felt his heart begin to lighten. And he turned once more to the sure-fire resuscitator: Rocky Balboa. The new screenplay Stallone tapped out came easily, even more so than the two times before. Because just as he had hewn *Rocky* out of all his New York anguish, into *Rocky III* went his mixed feelings about his LA fame. Balboa was now a huge deal, immortalized as both a bronze statue and a pinball machine. But in the process, he has started to alienate those who love him: distanced from his wife, Adrian, and spurning the advice of his trainer, Mickey, to keep things simple, opting to train in a glitzy gym instead. The once-humble hero has gone showbiz. Enter hungry new fighter Clubber Lang—as purely ambitious as Stallone had once been—who thrashes and humiliates him.

In a scene on a beach with Adrian, Rocky lays it all bare. "I don't believe in myself no more—don't you understand?" he tells his wife. "I'm *afraid*, all right? You wanna hear me say it? You wanna break me down? All right, I'm afraid. For the first time in my life, I'm afraid."

Once again, Stallone had poured his raw emotions into a script. And once again it worked. *Rocky III* was another huge hit, opening in nine hundred theaters around the United States and ultimately grossing $270 million. The film's theme tune, "Eye of the Tiger," which had been commissioned by Stallone after Queen denied him permission to use "Another One Bites the Dust," became a 1982 chart-topper for the band Survivor. And though critics were starting to get sniffy about the series—Pauline Kael called it "shrewd and empty and inept"—Stallone himself had fallen back in love with the character. Not even the fact that the two-thousand-pound bronze statue of Balboa he had donated to the Philadelphia Museum of Art was moved following complaints from grumbling citizens (one particularly furious letter to a newspaper demanded it be dumped in the Schuylkill River) could ruin the moment.

"I am quite aware that I'm locked into this image forever," Stallone finally admitted. "I could live ten lifetimes—I'll always be Rocky. But maybe that's the way it's supposed to be. Maybe that's what I was born to do."

Around his neck, he had begun wearing a gold chain. Affixed to it, bearing a single diamond, was a tiny boxing glove.

ARNOLD SCHWARZENEGGER was having a rather different experience acclimating to the Hollywood life. "He was a movie star," says Edward Pressman of his *Conan the Barbarian* leading man, "before he was a movie star."

Schwarzenegger liked to envision himself on a scale of 1 to 10, with 1 being a normal person, a schmuck, and 10 being a superhuman, where he strove to be. "Now I'm an 8, so I have two more steps to go," he announced as he wrapped on *Conan;* not bad, but room for improvement. While he waited for the inevitable boost up to the final level, he refined his lifestyle, sculpting himself into what he thought an 8 should look like.

On his thick right wrist gleamed a gold Rolex Oyster Perpetual, which he had procured after walking into the brand's store on Fifth Avenue and charming them into giving it to him for free. He began smoking a briar pipe behind the huge oak desk in his office in Venice, California, where a portrait of three stern, mustachioed Austrian strongmen glared at him. Photos of himself were strewn around the high-ceilinged room, plus an enormous *Conan* poster. Among the fine art hanging on the walls of his home, meanwhile, was a Marc Chagall painting of a topless mermaid, a man's hand clutching her right breast.

That last item was an indication that this barbarian was not entirely civilized. And 1983 saw Schwarzenegger indulge his old libidinous tendencies. Flying to Brazil for the filming of a TV movie called *Carnival in Rio,* he strolled the city, savoring the beauty he saw with a permanent grin on his face. "I can absolutely understand why Brazil is totally devoted to my favorite body part," he rhapsodizes at one point, over footage of him clutching a female dancer from behind. "The ass." At another point, under the pretext of giving another, startled-looking Brazilian woman an English lesson, he pushes a small carrot in and out of her mouth.

It was sleazy stuff. But back home, at least, he was trying to go respectable. He was now a member of LA's toniest dinner club, where he showed up clad in custom-fitted clothes. He skied, played tennis, went horseback riding and target shooting. He was also now dating a Kennedy—Maria Shriver, who stood by his side when he became an American citizen in September 1983. A girlfriend who connected him to one of the most beloved US presidents of all time was final affirmation that the nobody from a tiny Austrian village was now a somebody, in the country he loved most.

"I would pay anything for my father to be alive again for just one hour," Schwarzenegger said that year about the man who had beaten him and whose funeral he had declined to attend in 1972. "To see what I'm doing today."

More movies, more money, more power awaited. First he got busy on a Conan sequel. *Barbarian* had been conceived as the first in a franchise, and to stoke fans' excitement yet higher there was a new Conan attraction at Universal Studios, a live show set in a cave where a Schwarzenegger surrogate capered around, dodging fireballs, lasers, and a seventeen-foot-high mechanical dragon. The canny star, seeing an opportunity, convinced Universal to hand over more money. "We had made a deal for three pictures with Arnold," says Pressman. "Everyone thought I was crazy because it was $250,000 for the first film, $500,000 for the second film, and $750,000 for the third film, and they thought these were wildly excessive numbers. But after the film, he renegotiated his deal. It was too low."

Schwarzenegger netted a cool million for *Conan the Destroyer*, the most he'd ever gotten, though he griped to Maria that Stallone was making triple that amount. But while his wages went up, the original *Conan*'s mad-eyed intensity would be dialed down. The sixty-seven-year-old veteran director Richard Fleischer replaced the wild John Milius, and the studio ruled that the sequel had to get a PG rating. "We've taken just about all of the blood out," admitted Fleischer. Despite the big personalities on set—including musician Grace Jones, whom the stuntmen feared, given that she did not seem to understand the concept of fake blows, and basketball star Wilt Chamberlain, a seven-foot titan who claimed to have slept with twenty thousand women—the barbarian had become tamed.

On the plus side, Schwarzenegger already had another film in the can, with a director he had vibed with a great deal more than Fleischer. And this one wasn't going to be PG-rated.

AT TWO A.M. one night in March 1984, Schwarzenegger sat in a trailer on a crumbling corner in downtown LA. Wearing a red-striped sweatshirt and picking at his belated dinner, he told a visiting journalist, "I am ambitious; maybe the most ambitious person I know. But I am also careful. Very careful."

This was true: he weighed and reweighed every career decision he made. But the project he was in the middle of filming was raising eyebrows all around town. Because after making his name as a bare-chested hero who inspired kids worldwide to swing sticks at each other, Schwarzenegger was now in a leather jacket, shooting a cheap, schlocky-sounding thriller with a nobody filmmaker. Worse, he was playing the villain. And a particularly inarticulate villain at that.

When *The Terminator* was first brought to him, the role offered was that of Kyle Reese, the hero who goes back in time to save waitress Sarah Connor from certain death. Reese got the girl, the dialogue, and the heroic death, but Schwarzenegger wasn't particularly enticed. Still, urged to take a good look at the script by girlfriend Maria, who had been hooked by it when it arrived at their home, he agreed to meet its writer-director for lunch.

Neither man was eager to be at the chic Santa Monica eatery Schatzi that day. James Cameron hadn't wanted Schwarzenegger in the running in the first place, and his palms were perspiring at the thought of having to say no to Conan the Barbarian. Before leaving his office, he had told co-writer William Wisher, "If it doesn't go well, you can have the chair and stereo." But at the German deli, a regular Schwarzenegger haunt, the conversation went surprisingly well. Out came the Austrian's trademark giant cigars, Cameron managing to sample one without choking. And then Schwarzenegger began enthusing about Cameron's vision, in particular the villain, an unstoppable robot killer dispatched by a malevolent AI network called Skynet: how he should walk, how he should reload his weaponry. "*Man,* that bone structure," Cameron thought as he looked across the tablecloth. "If he put his mind to it, he could be a really scary motherfucker." By the time dessert came, the director realized his metal assassin had arrived with it.

"You've got to play the Terminator," Cameron announced.

Cinema history was in motion, but that wasn't immediately evident to all. "Nobody in town wanted to do that movie. It was turned down everywhere," says Mike Medavoy, whose company, Orion Pictures, financed the movie. "I'd be lying if I said I was gung-ho and ready to go." Michael Biehn, the actor who ultimately signed on as Reese, was just as unimpressed. "Anybody who tells you they read that script and went, 'Oh my God, this thing's going to be the greatest thing in the world' is lying," he insists. "I read it and thought, 'Well, this could be really, really bad.'" Cameron had, after all, been fired from his directorial debut, something called *Piranha II: The Spawning*. And the filmography of Biehn's on-screen nemesis was no more glittering. "De Niro, Pacino, Dustin Hoffman, Jack Lemmon—these are the people I wanted to work with. At the time nobody thought Arnold was going to become an actor beyond *Conan*."

For most of the $6.5 million shoot, Schwarzenegger lurked alone, working up the intensity he needed for the role. Remembering lines wasn't a problem—he speaks just fifty-eight words in the film—but for the first time in his career he would transform himself, suppressing his natural charisma, learning how to load firearms without looking, to fire without blinking, to speak without emotion. His co-stars began to look on in awe. "You know, I trained in New York, so I was a little bit of a theater snob," remembers Linda Hamilton, who was cast as Sarah Connor. "At the start I was like, 'Uh, Arnold? I don't know.' Most days we didn't see each other, because our characters were barely sharing a space. But I was curious. So I went to set when they were underground with him in a parking garage, to watch him do his best cyborg. And I thought, 'This could work. This could work really well.' There was just something very kinetic in the way he played it." And as the shoot rumbled on from February to May, plagued by a heat wave and an infestation of fruit flies, the Austrian star regularly impressed his Canadian director.

Despite his thin resume, Cameron was a cinema obsessive—stumbling out of a movie theater after his first viewing of *2001: A Space Odyssey,* he had been so overwhelmed by what he'd seen that he'd vomited. With *The Terminator* he was finally getting images out of his head and onto the screen. "I had a toy tank that could be remote-controlled, about two feet long," Cameron recalls of his childhood. "And I used to build kind of humanoid robotic torsos and put them on top of that and drive them around. That was a precursor to the treaded Hunter Killers."

Much of this movie was already in his imagination; after all, the Terminator had been born in a bad dream. "My nightmares are quite rich and fertile ground," Cameron says with a laugh. "Bad elevator nightmares, bad tidal wave nightmares, bad cyborg nightmares—I got them all." But in Schwarzenegger's granite jaw and stiff gait he was inspired to see something new, huge, mythic. John Wayne with a leather jacket and a grim scowl, not protecting a desert town but haunting it.

While Cameron could be a screamer and a swearer on set—at one point, he barked at Biehn, "That's exactly what I *don't* want"—he and Schwarzenegger rarely argued. And not just because the latter was packing an AMT Hardballer Longslide with laser-lock sight. They were simpatico. And their preferred method of unwinding was, of course, to shoot more guns. "I have a photo of Arnold, John Milius, me, Jim Cameron, and Franco Columbu, Arnold's pal who played the Terminator in the dream sequence, all holding automatic weapons," says Biehn. "The five of us went out tearing up the countryside with these assault rifles."

Despite Schwarzenegger's relaxed demeanor, the film, coming after the disappointment of *Conan the Destroyer,* could have been a huge setback. He didn't necessarily help himself: perhaps buoyed by a preview screening put on for LAPD officers where the real-life cops applauded the T-800 wrecking a police station, he blithely gave away the ending of the movie in an interview. And some of the early reviews for *The Terminator* were machine-cold. Gene Siskel called it "Erector Set toy-making"; the *Philadelphia Inquirer*'s Desmond Ryan wrote, "Protected by the impenetrable thickness of his accent, Schwarzenegger cannot be stopped by bullets. . . . It is the kind of nonsense that cries out for the summary termination of his career in movies."

But others were hotter. "Arnold Schwarzenegger was born to play the Terminator," hyped the *Hollywood Reporter.* "There's something downright satisfying about seeing this big, lovable lug play a remorseless heavy. *Terminator II,* where are you?"

At $33 million, the film only came in at number twenty-one in the chart of the year's top-grossers, beaten by the likes of *Revenge of the Nerds, Breakin',* and *Bachelor Party.* But those who experienced it had the sensation they were seeing something significant. A pulsing sci-fi film as lean and hungry as its creator, it was powered by a mighty piece of anti-casting: a goofy warrior transformed into a mirthless machine. By the time it hit home video, the movie had mustered up word of mouth enough to make it the second-most-rented video of 1985.

At the start of the previous year, Conan, not the Terminator, had seemed the safest bet. But only one of those characters would be back, and it wasn't the one in the furry boots.

LEGEND PERSISTS that Sylvester Stallone turned down the role of the Terminator. "Not true," says Mike Medavoy. By the time that movie came along, in fact, Stallone already had another iconic action role under his belt—a character every bit as formidable, and monosyllabic, as anything Skynet could whip up. And the part had arrived just in the nick of time.

Though the star had come to terms with Rocky Balboa, pretty much everything else he tried had failed. "Stallone's career was stalled," remembers *First Blood* director Ted Kotcheff. "The perceived wisdom in Hollywood was that Stallone only sold tickets as Rocky, and they were hesitant about casting him in anything else. But that kind of thinking didn't cut it with me."

First Blood came together through a series of strange connections. Mario Kassar and Andrew Vajna of Carolco Pictures managed to obtain the rights for the source material, a 1972 novel by David Morrell about a Vietnam veteran driven back to violence, from Warner Bros., which had been trying to wrestle it into shape as a Steve McQueen vehicle. Carolco was at the time a little-known company that had previously distributed movies, rather than make them; the first one they had picked up, titled *Chatterbox,* was about a young woman who discovers she has a talking vagina. The Lebanese-Italian Kassar and Hungarian Vajna were now moving into making films themselves, but they only knew one director: Kotcheff. "I used to cook pasta for him," Kassar explains.

As for Stallone, it took a while for anyone to think of him. "I think they were going to lab animals before they got to me," the star later joked. "They went through every actor in the system: 'De Niro . . . Nick Nolte . . . Zippy the monkey . . . '" But Kassar shared a lawyer with the star, and Kotcheff was eager when the casting idea was proposed. "I screened all the films he starred in," the director remembers. "He always gave interesting performances, and I thought that with the *First Blood* material and my direction, he could give a performance as good as De Niro and Pacino. I sent the script to Stallone's agent on a Thursday night. And for the first and only time in my long life of working as a film director, I received a yes the very next day."

However, Stallone had two conditions. Hands-on as ever, he wanted to work with Kotcheff on the script. And he wanted a big payday from Carolco: $3.5 million instead of his standard $2 million. "We had to pay the price," Kassar says with a shrug. "What you call the membership dues."

The material that had grabbed Stallone's attention was a long way from the dry monologues of *F.I.S.T.* Even more of a loner than Balboa, taciturn Vietnam veteran John Rambo goes to the small town of Hope, Washington, to visit an old comrade. There, mistreated by the town's police force, he snaps and goes on the run, hunted through the woods by cops, Dobermans, and ultimately the National Guard. So stealthy and resourceful is he that his pursuers might as well be chasing a ghost.

"You don't seem to want to accept the fact that you're dealing with an expert in guerrilla warfare," growls Trautman, Rambo's former commanding officer, to the sheriff who has sparked off the whole mess. "With a man who's the best, with guns, with knives, with his bare hands. A man who's been trained to ignore pain, ignore weather, to live off the land, to eat things that would make a billy goat puke."

The spare tale jibed with Stallone's feeling about the war and how America had let down those who fought in it. Like *Rocky*, it featured another hero pulling off unbelievable feats through sheer force of will. Still, he got increasingly jittery as the shoot loomed closer, convinced the subject matter was too heavy. "He changed his mind at one point," says Kassar. "He didn't want to do it anymore. Andy and I left his manager's office and we looked at each other." Then, in the elevator down to the parking garage, Kassar had a brainwave, and the two producers hurried back up to Stallone's manager, Herb Nanas. "I said, 'Herb, you know, we don't want him to act. But nobody knows the character better. Can he at least polish it so it's easier to cast somebody else?' He said, 'Well, for $50K he'll do it for one week.' Obviously, the whole thing was done in such a way that when he starts writing his character, he falls back in love with him."

Stallone not only was coaxed back into the role but also made two key contributions to the script. First, he insisted that the M60-wielding Rambo shouldn't kill anyone. Second, he declared that Rambo should not commit suicide at the end. "Remember *Rocky*," he pointed out. "Never kill your heroes."

This topic was to trigger countless arguments throughout the shoot and beyond. Kirk Douglas, who had been cast as Trautman, stormed off the film early on, furious at the change to the book's tragic ending, and his role was recast with Richard Crenna. "I got a very early call saying, 'Mr. Douglas is on his way to the airport,'" says Kassar. "He had had a big argument with Stallone in his trailer, because one wanted to kill the other guy and the other one didn't want to die." Kotcheff and Carolco got into it also when the director insisted on shooting the scene both ways. "I don't take orders from producers, so I told them to piss off and continued shooting," Kotcheff says with a chuckle. Only when it came to the first test screening, with the suicide intact, was the argument settled: the audience voted overwhelmingly for Rambo to live.

It had been a brutal production, with action staged atop cliffs in freezing temperatures. Stallone not only injured his back during a scene where he's assaulted with police billy clubs but broke three ribs jumping two hundred feet from one of those cliffs onto a tree. His mood was not enhanced by his *First Blood* diet: twelve eggs a day and a lot of fish, to make him look gaunt on-screen. And his feeling that the movie had bad juju, that it was somehow cursed, persisted into postproduction; shown a rough cut, he and his manager both reacted badly. "I think we both retched together in the alley," Stallone claimed later. "We tried to buy it back and burn the negative."

He failed in that attempt, and *First Blood* became a hit, the kind the actor had been chasing since 1976. At a screening of fifty-two minutes of the film, on Wilshire Boulevard in Hollywood, nine hundred industry people applauded wildly. "By the time we all walked from the theater to Orlando Orsini, the Italian restaurant where we were holding a little disco afterwards, the whole world was sold," says Kassar. Remembers Kotcheff: "The distributors went totally crazy for my film. Three competing Japanese distributors pushed Andy against the wall in the lobby, waving fat checks in his face."

It was an unlikely crowd-pleaser: a bleak character study of a broken man who barely speaks. But it struck a nerve, making $47 million domestic in 1982, more than any other movie that fall, proving even more profitable overseas, and getting strong notices, too. The likes of *The Deer Hunter* and *Coming Home* had provided harrowing depictions of Vietnam veterans; this movie fused a similar message—respect our vets—with bombastic action thrills. Memories of the conflict, which had ended seven years earlier, were not fading: only that year, a new memorial was installed in Washington, DC, bearing the names of fifty-eight thousand fallen American soldiers. But gradually the national sense of despair over the calamitous war was morphing into righteous anger. At the memorial's dedication, new president Ronald Reagan declared, "We're beginning to understand how much we were led astray at that time. We are just beginning to appreciate that [our troops] were fighting for a just cause." In John Rambo, audiences could see that just cause personified.

"It's a perfect reluctant hero," says Mike Medavoy. "It's the Alan Ladd character in *Shane*. A guy that comes to town, doesn't want to fight with anybody, and then finally finds himself having to do it. *First Blood* was one of the first films we distributed at the new Orion, and the stock went crazy."

Carolco suddenly had a future; Kassar bought a license plate for his Rolls-Royce that spelled out "RAMBO." As for Stallone, he now had two roles that had jolted pop culture. "I'd sort of conditioned myself to accept the fact that I wasn't too popular outside of *Rocky*," he said. "All of a sudden *First Blood* took off and I couldn't believe it. I never thought the public would like it at all. I thought it would be the most expensive home movie ever made."

While in Vancouver shooting the movie one rainy day, Stallone had, on a whim, asked a taxi driver where he could buy a fur coat. The driver took him to a family-run store downtown called Pappas Furs, where the star surveyed a sea of wild mink, lynx, and beaver. The owner's brother-in-law happened to be in the store and saw an opportunity, asking Stallone if he'd consider posing in fur. He agreed.

The resulting campaign, with the actor swathed in luxury garments, exploded the popularity of the business, which had previously sold just thirty coats a year. And for Stallone, it marked the beginning of a new, more extravagant phase. Rambo had set him free.

CHAPTER 4

...

THE COWBOY AND THE CANNONBALL

CHUCK NORRIS STOOD in a spot where thousands of men had been brutally killed. There, sweat trickling down his brow, he faced the deadliest man on earth.

It was a baking-hot morning in 1972, and Norris was at the Colosseum in Rome. His opponent was Bruce Lee who, in the previous films *The Big Boss* and *Fist of Fury,* had torn through enemies like a hurricane through a shed. Norris, who had barely stepped in front of a camera before, was feeling at a disadvantage in more than one respect. After arriving on a flight from America to shoot *Way of the Dragon*, his exit from the plane recorded by the thrifty Lee for use in the film, he had been told by a producer that he needed to bulk up for the battle royal.

"I'd never been in a movie, and I'm intimidated," Norris recalls. "So I started eating pasta. Then I stopped working out for almost a month. I went from 167 pounds to 185, and that's why you don't see me doing any jump-kicks in that movie. I didn't think I could get off the ground."

Even with a spaghetti handicap, Norris had been selected by Lee as the most formidable adversary possible. When the martial arts master had called him, out of the blue, Norris had replied, "So, Bruce, you want to beat the world champion, huh?" Lee had responded, quick as his fists, "No, I want to *kill* the world champion." But underpinning that was a deep respect. When Norris pointed out that everyone who faced Lee on-screen got annihilated, Lee promised this battle would be different.

And so it proved, the legendary nine-minute finale of *Way of the Dragon* swinging back and forth, its moves plotted out together by the two actors and shot partly in the Colosseum, a location that had been procured only via a deal between Lee and the Sicilian mob, and largely on a soundstage at Golden Harvest Studios in Hong Kong. Throughout, Norris's Colt is portrayed as a worthy opponent, vanquished only by a combination of explosive punches, kicks, elbow strikes, and, in one unforgettable moment, the ripping out of chest hair. When Colt finally hits the ground for good, witnessed by the fight's sole observer—a kitten—Lee's Tang Lung places Colt's *gi* and black belt on his corpse as a symbol of honor.

Even so, Norris calls Colt the only real villain he's ever played on-screen. "Bruce made me out to be a gladiator, not a bad guy," he says. "But that's the closest I came."

AS A CHILD IN OKLAHOMA, Chuck Norris dreamed not of becoming a two-fisted, two-footed killing machine but of being a cowboy. He watched endless John Wayne and Gene Autry movies with a nickel bag of popcorn on his lap. Then he'd patrol the streets of the prairie town of Wilson like a tiny sheriff, stopping only to covet the toy pistol in the window of a local store.

Alas, his parents couldn't afford it. In fact, they couldn't afford much. His father, Ray, was a drunk, prone to frequent fits of rage, who fainted during Norris's birth and was rarely around for other big events in his son's life. His mother, Wilma, while kinder, was constantly broke.

Norris could have gone sour and rebelled. "I went through a very difficult time," he says. "Having no male role model, I grew up with a lot of physical and psychological insecurities." But something inside him, maybe the thought of what his imaginary dad John Wayne would do, kept him on the straight and narrow. In the epic backyard battles he coordinated, using clothespins instead of toy soldiers, the righteous always came out on top. And even in the face of relentless bullying at school—born Carlos Ray Norris, he was part Cherokee—he resisted the urge to turn to violence.

"Chuck Norris came up harassed," says Robert Wall, a lifelong friend of the star, and himself an on-screen adversary of Bruce Lee in *Enter the Dragon*. "Mother and father got divorced. Father killed in a car accident, drunk. But through all that, he remained respectful, kind, a triple-A-plus human being. He can kick your ass, but he doesn't."

Those legendary abilities can be traced back to one night in South Korea in 1958. There, stationed at Osan Air Base as a military cop, Norris was taking a walk when he heard strange yelling. Following the noise, he came across a group of Koreans in white robes practicing *tang soo do,* a form of karate. Norris was intrigued. And so he threw himself into it, studying for five hours a day, six days a week. Soon he was supplementing that with four hours of judo every Sunday. Returning to America and his wife, Dianne, his high school sweetheart, he started his own martial arts school.

A decade on, Chuck Norris was a big deal. A multi-award-winning karate champion, he was friends with Bruce Lee, having stayed up all night talking to him in a hotel corridor on their first encounter. And other tough guys were starting to seek him out. In 1967, Arnold Schwarzenegger started visiting his school. "He would ask me, 'What are your future plans?'" recalls Norris. "And I would say, 'I want to teach for the rest of my life. Martial arts are my life's endeavor.' Schwarzenegger said, 'Not me. I'm going to become a real-estate mogul and then a movie star.' I was thinking to myself, 'Movie star? You can barely speak English.' But Arnold is a very focused individual."

Norris was noncommittal, yet Hollywood had its eye on him. In 1969, Lee, who was working as stunt coordinator on the Dean Martin comedy *The Wrecking Crew,* talked him into taking a tiny role. Three years later, he was being destroyed by Lee in front of a kitten in Rome. And in 1977 he and Wall, now business partners, financed his first proper star vehicle, the dire *Breaker! Breaker!,* which was shot in eleven days and cast Norris as a trucker with lethal feet. "The reason he became so successful as an actor is because he went through the humiliating, embarrassing *Breaker! Breaker!*," says Wall. "He had a lot of learning to do. In films as in martial arts, he had to go from white belt to green belt to brown belt to black belt."

Norris's next lead role would teach him some new moves. Partly written by the karate champion himself, *Good Guys Wear Black* followed former members of a black-ops unit, the Black Tigers, being hunted by CIA assassins in the wake of a double cross in the Vietnamese jungle. Norris's character, Major John T. Booker, is a lecturer in political science, but also a tough hombre, albeit one with dubious seduction skills; when he invites a beautiful woman to his house for dinner ("I don't eat lunch"), it's at five-thirty in the afternoon and she has to do the cooking, finding only frozen halibut in the fridge. Still, she jumps into Booker's bed with little hesitation, shortly before boarding an airplane that explodes.

Norris saw *Good Guys Wear Black* as potentially as successful a star vehicle as *Dirty Harry,* boasting a spectacularly overblown moment in which Booker drop-kicks a moving car. Few others saw it the same way, studio after studio turning it down. It was in his final meeting, with the last producer on his list, that he desperately argued, "There are four million karate people in America. They all know who I am. And if only half of them go to the movie, that's a $6 million gross on a $1 million budget." The producer greenlit the project.

After an arduous publicity tour by Norris, who did over two thousand interviews and developed laryngitis from all the talking, the film ended up making $18.3 million, reaping a huge profit. Its success amazed everyone, including his business partner. "Carlos couldn't talk to three people when I met him, he was so shy," says Wall. "When he first told me he was going to act, I came home to my wife and said, 'He'll never make it. Oh my God, what a bad decision.' Which shows what a genius I am."

An unlikely star had been launched at the age of thirty-eight, his arrival coinciding with a craze in America for all things martial arts. While Eastern fighting styles had drawn adherents for decades (Teddy Roosevelt even installed a special judo gym in the White House), in the 1970s karate and kung fu crossed over into the mainstream. On the big screen, besides Bruce Lee's work, pictures such as *Billy Jack* and Bond film *The Man with the Golden Gun* featured whirling kicks. On television, series such as *The F.B.I.*, *Mannix,* and *Mission: Impossible* showcased karate techniques; *Kung Fu* delivered exactly what its title promised. The cult movie *Five Fingers of Death,* produced by Warner Bros., brought the house down at its Times Square premiere in 1973, then got spoofed by Marvel in an issue of *Howard the Duck* ("Master of Quack Fu!"). And a host of magazines dedicated to roundhouse kicks and colored belts sprang up, from *Action Karate* to *Professional Karate* to *Self-Defense World.*

Chuck Norris, who would appear on the cover of *American Karate* magazine doing a flying kick over the head of the Statue of Liberty, was the right man in the right place to spearhead the movement. Now he just had to adjust his acting style, since *Good Guys Wear Black,* which had him deliver the lines, "Check your history, Morgan! Most of our expedient wars ended in failure!," proved too talky for most. "I wrote it with too much dialogue and critics crucified me on it," he admits. "I took Steve McQueen to see it and he said, 'Let me give you some advice. Give your co-stars all the BS dialogue and only speak when there's something important to say.'"

Norris took the advice to heart. From now on, he would let his legs do the talking.

IN A PARALLEL DIMENSION, Norris might have played the Terminator. He had the impenetrable-fortress physique, after all, and a face that on-screen rarely betrayed emotion. "I probably would have done it," he says of the role, "but it really fit Arnold's persona more than mine."

Norris's persona was something that preoccupied him greatly. His cowboy heroes had had a staunch set of morals, and he sought to follow their example. On the mat, in countless tournaments, he had demonstrated unflinching strength in the face of great odds; now he aimed to do the same on the screen, inspiring people to hold out against the corrupting forces in their lives.

There were wobbles in his own, like the time he cheated on his first wife in the early years of their marriage, fathering an illegitimate child. Or when he succumbed to ego after he had a taste of stardom. "I started forgetting what my real values were," he says. "I was angry all the time, thinking, 'I've got it all. Why aren't I happy?' There was a hole in my heart." But he never truly went off the rails. And, though appearances may suggest otherwise, he chose his roles with exceptional care. "I turned down a lot of things that I didn't feel fit the character I was trying to portray. I wanted to adopt a certain image: a guy who fights against injustice."

The movies that followed *Good Guys Wear Black* were outlandish, violent fantasies, in which injustice took many forms. In *Silent Rage,* it's a genetically enhanced killer, a schlocky Frankenstein's monster who inspired the tagline "Science created him. Now Chuck Norris must destroy him." In *Forced Vengeance,* it's a Hong Kong crime syndicate. In *An Eye for an Eye,* it's Christopher Lee, cutting heroin deals with the Triad. In *The Octagon,* it's ninjas ("They've been outlawed for three hundred years!"). The formula was there from the start: bad guys kill somebody close to the stoic hero, who finally snaps and embarks on a dialogue-light rampage of revenge. Again and again, the frequently bare-chested Norris proved there was no situation he could not kick his way out of, with the odd jab punch for good measure.

To quote another of his taglines: "Chuck Norris doesn't need a weapon . . . he *is* a weapon!"

The critics were confounded. This kind of thing had an air of respectability when it was Bruce Lee dispensing the pain, but what to make of this mayhem machine from the Midwest? "He has fluffy blond hair, performs his stunts in chinos and a down vest, and looks less like a killer than a good-natured golf pro," sniffed the *New York Times*. The *Washington Post* jibed, "Clearly *The Octagon* is no real threat to *War and Peace*."

Norris, though, was unperturbed by sniping from the East Coast intelligentsia. "My acting was atrocious, to say the least," he happily admits. His films were catching a national mood, with their painting of perils from abroad seeking to corrupt innocent Americans. And he was a relatable role model to kids across the country, who could never grow up to become Bruce Lee but could imagine themselves becoming Chuck Norris. They could even pay $19.95 for a pair of Chuck Norris Action Jeans ("The special jeans I wear during movie stunt fights are now available to you").

He didn't womanize. When he went to a bar he'd sip a Chuck Norris Kicker—a beverage he'd devised in Hong Kong in 1972, consisting of iced tea with a shot of Grand Marnier—and stop, every time, after his third glass. And despite having real karate powers, he never got into real fights, no matter how hard he was provoked.

This was put to the test in 1978 on the set of *A Force of One*. The film, about a San Diego karate teacher recruited by cops to help them take on a drug gang, climaxes with a fight in a sports arena. While they were shooting the sequence, a large gang of bikers started throwing bottles into the ring, ruining take after take. Eventually Norris had had enough.

"Carlos goes over there in a break," recalls Robert Wall, "and sits on a step below the head of these Hell's Angels types. The subdog position. And he talks to them: 'Guys, we're doing a film. I would appreciate it if you would stop bothering people.' Then he says, 'You want to be in the movie?' 'Yeah!' So we filmed them. We edited them out, but we filmed them."

This patient approach extended to his career, too. Churning out film after film, Norris waited for the one that would really connect. And in 1983, along it came. *Lone Wolf McQuade* had been turned down by Clint Eastwood when it was offered to him as a potential *Dirty Harry* sequel, but Norris saw in it the Western he'd wanted to make since he was a kid. Texas Ranger J. J. McQuade is bearded, righteous, and, yes, a lone wolf, who also happens to own a literal wolf. A man who reads a magazine called *Combat Handguns* and can single-handedly take down a gang of horse thieves, he was

Norris's slickest fantasy figure yet, and this time even the critics were impressed. "What Norris was really looking for," said Roger Ebert, "was the right character. That's what he's found in *Lone Wolf McQuade*." The hard-to-please Vincent Canby conceded that "Mr. Norris is good." The movie made almost triple its $5 million budget.

It was a major win. But for Norris the memory he'd take away from the whole experience was that of a five-year-old boy, terminally ill with leukemia, whose dying wish had been to receive a photograph of his hero. Norris did one better and flew to his bedside to meet the child, who had watched *Lone Wolf McQuade* on videocassette thirty times. Shortly after, Norris received word that the boy had died in the middle of yet another viewing of the film.

It made him resolve to think even harder about what he was putting out into the world. He'd fought bikers, ninjas, and surgically enhanced abominations. But his next on-screen conflict would be closer to his heart, turning an old family tragedy into something cathartic.

Chuck Norris was going to war.

A YEAR BEFORE crushing Norris in the Colosseum, Bruce Lee shared a scene with another future star. It was winter 1971, and the seventeen-year-old Jackie Chan had talked his way onto the set of *Fist of Fury* at Golden Harvest Studios in Hong Kong, to study the workings of the Dragon up close. Hired as a bit player, to be tossed about however Lee deemed most cinematic, Chan that day found himself dangling from a wire, preparing to be dropped onto the ground. Except a crew member got overexcited, releasing him too early. Chan crashed down before he was braced and ready.

Lee sped over to the youngster and helped him to his feet. Chan, brushing off the pain, was just ecstatic that his hero had noticed him.

Two years later, history repeated itself. This time, on *Enter the Dragon,* Lee accidentally smacked Chan in the face with a stick. "Are you okay?" Lee asked. Again Chan beamed with joy.

Despite the agonizing red welt on his face, he was just where he wanted to be. Chan had come into the world looking for action—he was born weighing an incredible twelve pounds, inspiring his parents to nickname him "Cannonball"—and had begun *hung ga* martial arts training at the age of four, practicing Iron Wire Fists and Tiger Cranes with his father, Charles. Once he enrolled in the China Drama Academy (CDA), eighteen-hour days of almost non-stop physical activity, beginning at five A.M., became the norm. He never learned to read, write, or do arithmetic, but Chan perfected flying kicks, stick-fighting, and acrobatic flips. His ten years at the CDA, from the age of seven to seventeen, were hard: so austere were the teachers that when he developed a fever one day, they only increased his training program. If children became too exhausted to keep fighting on the mat, they'd be told to sit down and keep slapping each other instead.

It was a brutal upbringing—a Dickens novel crossed with a Shaolin myth. Chan would later describe it as his "decade of darkness." But he emerged on the other side as honed and resilient as a diamond bullet. As for how he would put all that training to use, well, there was only one choice. "My master wanted me to do opera," he recalls. "But nobody wanted to see opera. My teachers didn't know this—they were old-fashioned. They didn't want me to become an action star."

If there was any doubt in Chan's mind, seeing Lee up close dispelled it immediately. Even better, the two became friendly, after Lee spotted Chan on the street in 1972 and asked if he wanted to go bowling. The pair headed by taxi to the nearest alley, and when people there began shouting "Bruce Lee! Bruce Lee!," Chan immediately began shielding his new friend, telling the horde to stop taking photos.

Lee's sudden death in July 1973 left the world shocked and opened up a vacuum at the heart of martial arts cinema. An entire genre, dubbed "Bruceploitation," emerged, with Lee look-alikes heading up films such as *Re-Enter the Dragon, Return of Bruce,* and the bizarre *The Dragon Lives Again,* in which Bruce Lee bat-

tles James Bond and Dracula in hell (he also teams up with Popeye). Meanwhile, Jackie Chan found himself being positioned as
the star's natural heir.

"After he died, there were so many Bruce Lees," Chan says.
"Bruce Li, Bruce Lo, Bruce Table, Bruce Chair, Bruce Telephone
Booth. Even on the poster for one of my films, it said 'Bruce Lee' in
big letters. You look closer, and it says, 'The second Bruce Lee,
Jackie Chan.'" In 1976, he was cast in a film called *New Fist of
Fury,* his first starring role in a widely released picture.

Others might have been delighted at the prospect of being
hailed as the Dragon's offspring. Chan had even taken over Lee's
old dressing room at Golden Harvest, his name supplanting his old
master's on the door. But it just didn't feel right to emulate Lee's
serious style or his clean-cut, flawless heroism. So Chan decided to
buck expectations. "I cannot follow him," he says. "When Bruce
Lee kicks high, I kick low. He looks angry, I pull a funny face. I
want to be a normal human being. He's a superhuman. I am not."

In the late 1970s came a trio of game-changing films. *Snake in
the Eagle's Shadow, Drunken Master,* and *The Fearless Hyena* not
only fizzed with invention but gave Chan an opportunity to show
off his own way of doing things. Instead of being virtually invincible, like Lee, he was treated like a punching bag, getting smacked
and kicked around with jaw-dropping frequency. Not afraid to
look ridiculous, he performed kung fu moves for *Drunken Master*
while dizzy—to look inebriated, he would hold his breath while
performing, sometimes for twenty takes in a row. For *The Fearless
Hyena,* the first film he ever directed, he dressed up like a woman
to battle one opponent before blabbering like a baby while fighting
another.

On-screen, Chan was self-deprecating, silly, a cartoonish figure
with the resilience of Wile E. Coyote. He was also endlessly inventive, treating everything within the frame as a possible weapon or
piece of gymnastic equipment. And Chinese audiences reacted
with joy, making the three films massive hits. *Drunken Master*
ended up taking in more money in Asia than *Rocky* or *Jaws.* Chan

was now the one being mobbed on the street, fans throwing pretend punches at him, paparazzi chasing him.

The sudden fame was enough to make even the ultra-disciplined Chan lose his rigor. "When I was twenty, I was already a millionaire," he says. "I cared about luxury cars, jewelry, diamonds, women, fun." He bought seven Rolexes, one for every day of the week. An entourage of strutting stuntmen accompanied him wherever he went. The Drunken Master was now also drinking for real, sometimes turning up late on set with a puffy face from the previous evening.

His ego was rising. But a reality check was imminent, in the shape of his first foray to America.

WHEN CHAN SAT DOWN in front of a Hollywood movie, he preferred it to be a black-and-white one, a Golden Age slapstick from the likes of Buster Keaton or Harold Lloyd. Still, when his bosses at Golden Harvest decided to try to break him into America, he agreed. The thought of having huge success on the other side of the world, just as he was experiencing in China, was tantalizing.

The first ominous sign came in the form of the project he was being offered. *The Big Brawl,* about a Chinese man taking on the Mafia in 1930s Chicago, was being created by many of the people behind *Enter the Dragon,* including director Robert Clouse and members of Bruce Lee's stunt team. Chan, who had fled as far as he could from the shadow of Lee, was hesitant. That feeling intensified when he was put on a plane to Los Angeles alone, Golden Harvest feeling it would encourage him to improve his English.

The trip would prove an unhappy one. Despite taking lessons at a Beverly Hills language school, Chan struggled to string an English sentence together; after weeks of ordering a burger and Coke for every meal—the only words he could remember—he was rushed to a doctor for high cholesterol. Attempting to make a day trip to the San Diego Zoo, he got lost and sat in his car, overwhelmed, until a police officer stopped and asked where he was going. "How do I get home?" Chan said. He wouldn't go on the freeway again.

Rather than being mobbed, as he would have been in Hong Kong, he wandered alone, feeling invisible. "America really scares me. It's too big," he admitted to one of the journalists he was dispatched to speak to. "But I like working in America. I get steak for $2. I eat a lot of steak."

The reporters who met him were wowed by his physical prowess. "He spends a good deal of a truly animated conversation leaping around and over the furniture," said one. But it turned out that while interviews were a decent medium for his skills, the work he was doing in Hollywood was not. *The Big Brawl* turned out to be a low-energy actioner, devoid of Chan's usual ingenuity. When the actor offered to do a flip out of a car, Clouse replied, "No, we'll shoot it as written." And another disappointment followed in the form of *The Cannonball Run,* in which Chan was cast as a Japanese driver in a Subaru GL. The part was thin, and Sammy Davis Jr. made the situation even worse by greeting his Chinese co-star in Japanese each time they met.

Chan worked as hard as ever. He even faced the American talk-show circuit, griping, "They don't give me enough time. By the time I reply, the talk-show host says, 'Thank you for coming.'" But it was all to no avail. *The Big Brawl,* made in a way alien to Chan's entire philosophy, failed to amass *Enter the Dragon* box office.

Chan went to see it alone, buying a ticket and sitting in an almost empty theater. It was the final straw. He headed back to Hong Kong, feeling the unfamiliar sting of failure, but determined to channel his frustrations in a productive direction. *The Big Brawl* hadn't worked out, but the brawls he had in his imagination were a lot more exciting.

SHAKING OFF HIS JET LAG, Chan got back to work. He directed his second film, *The Young Master,* another huge success; went to Taiwan to make *Dragon Lord,* a shoot so savage that the local hospital filled up with injured bit players; and played a small role in *Fantasy Mission Force,* in which his character is recruited for a rescue mission sufficiently dangerous that Rocky Balboa, James Bond, and Snake Plissken fail to make the grade.

But something else was brewing in his mind: an enormous epic that would sizzle with kung fu action. So excited did Chan become about this top-secret project that he refused to tell even his bosses at Golden Harvest what it would involve. "In Asia, whatever I make people follow me," he recalls. "When I made *Young Master,* the next day they make *Young Sister.* They just follow my step. So I gave no budget and no title."

The new movie, simply called *Project A,* was, in fact, a historical drama about the conflict between early twentieth-century Hong Kong coastguardsmen and a gang of pirates. A team of researchers worked to study the harbor city's history, although accuracy was often sidelined in favor of huge action beats. And for inspiration co-writer Edward Tang and Chan pored over Steven Spielberg's *Raiders of the Lost Ark,* seeing how he had paced and escalated his set pieces.

For Chan, starring as demoted coastguardsman Dragon Ma, it was the perfect opportunity to reassert his powers. Working closely with his old schoolmate Sammo Hung, who had been hired to oversee the action and play a supporting role, he performed some of his most blistering stunts yet. In a scene reminiscent of the Cairo street pursuit in *Raiders,* but considerably higher-octane, Chan rode a bicycle at high speed down Hong Kong roads, performing feats of two-wheeled daredevilry. Informed midway through shooting the sequence that *E.T.: The Extra-Terrestrial* was playing at a nearby cinema, he shot off to watch it, to make sure there was no overlap in stunts. He came back reassured that at no point did the little friendly alien leap over a ladder and back onto his bike.

Project A's high point comes when a handcuffed Dragon Ma is cornered at the top of a clock tower. Dangling from the clock's minute hand, in a setup reminiscent of Harold Lloyd's *Safety Last!,* Chan then does something Lloyd didn't—fall. All the way down from the top of the building to the ground, to land face-first on the surface of a road.

There was no way to fake it, not to Chan's satisfaction. So he decided to do it for real. Every day, for almost a week, he came to the clock tower and climbed the stairs to the top, only to call off the stunt at the last moment.

"The sun's in the wrong place," he called down one morning.

"Now there's a cloud," he said on another occasion.

Eventually Sammo Hung, who wasn't in the scene, turned up on set, glaring up at Chan.

"Goddammit, it's been six days!" he yelled. "Are you going to jump or not? Get a move on! You're blocking the whole fucking street!"

Chan jumped. Ripped through two canopies. And landed on his head, twisting his neck badly. Then, despite feeling close to blacking out, he went up and did it all over again. "Nobody can push me but Sammo Hung," he says.

Despite his reputation for invincibility, the fear he'd experienced was not uncommon. "Every stunt I get scared before. Every stunt," Chan says. "I learned to never go to the top until the last moment. If you wait up there, you start thinking, 'What happens if I break my back? What happens if I land on my head?' So many thoughts."

But for Chan, the work was worth it. And with *Project A* his gamble with his life paid off. The movie was hailed as a masterpiece, pushing kung fu cinema onto its biggest canvas yet and taking audiences on a thrill ride that could compete with anything Hollywood had to offer. That year, for the first time, Chan was nominated for his first-ever Golden Horse award—the Chinese equivalent of an Oscar—for his performance in *Project A*. At the awards ceremony, he happened to be seated next to Chuck Norris, who was being given a special trophy. Norris, who as a non-Chinese-speaker was unable to understand a word of the show, had to be alerted by Chan when it was his time to head to the stage.

The American star's films had managed to translate from West to East. Chan's had not yet succeeded in going the other way. But in just a few years, he would get another shot.

CHAPTER 5

...

MAXIMALISM

WHILE ON VACATION in Hawaii in June 1982, John Travolta paid for a ticket to see *Rocky III*. And what roared to life on the screen that evening electrified him: the kinetic flash of the combat, the aural swagger of "Eye of the Tiger," the undying gumption of Rocky Balboa. Travolta, who was going through a fallow patch at the time and had just agreed to make a sequel to *Saturday Night Fever* for Paramount, called his new agent, Michael Ovitz, and said, "We need a director who can do *that*." Ovitz, who happened to also represent Stallone, said, "Why don't we get the real deal?"

The call came in to Stallone's Pacific Palisades villa, but it was just one of many. Now the king of the action movie, with Rocky Balboa and John Rambo causing mania everywhere, the star was getting offers from all over. Most were for movies where he would once again lunge into action, gun in hand. And Stallone seemed ready to go, working out every day in the gym by his swimming pool, just west of the flower gardens, and packing his body with protein—raw fish and six soft-boiled eggs for breakfast each morning, without fail. Around his neck, replacing the diamond boxing glove that had symbolized Rocky, now hung a golden dog tag. "It's Rambo's tag," he explained. "Blood type A-positive." He had done a U-turn on the character, whose exploits had earlier seemed to depress him to the point of puking. Now, after receiving sacks of enthusiastic letters from Vietnam veterans, he announced that John Rambo was his most meaningful character.

But those waiting for a second splash of *First Blood* were going to have to wait a while longer. Because Stallone, despite all those eggs, was feeling the call of his artistic side.

Waking each day at five A.M., he would sit in his office trying to refine a biopic of his beloved Edgar Allan Poe, something he'd been working on since the 1970s, before heading off to the polo field. There were also his paintings. When he was eight years old, Stallone had created his first piece of art: a primitive man in a jungle, a kind of proto-Rambo. Now he both collected works—bronzes by Barye, sculptures by Bourdelle, endless late nineteenth-century canvases by Romantic artists—and created them. His favorite color: "arterial red." He often painted in the nude.

So maybe it shouldn't have been too much of a shock when he ended up making not the rowdy action comedy *Beverly Hills Cop* or the jungle caper *Romancing the Stone,* both of which he was offered, but two forays into heightened musical cinema, way outside his comfort zone. The first: that sequel to *Saturday Night Fever.*

Stallone's directing fee for *Staying Alive* was relatively paltry—$1 million—but he threw himself into the project, spending months working with Travolta to perfect the latter's body, just as he had reshaped himself for *First Blood.* For Travolta, the experience was an almost spiritual one. In *Saturday Night Fever,* hero Tony Manero had had a *Rocky* poster on his bedroom wall. It turned out the actor himself, eight years younger than Stallone, was just as starstruck. "Sly is gorgeous," Travolta said with a grin. "To have Sly's kind of body would be beautiful." He worked out furiously, bronzed his skin, and followed the dietary instructions laid out by Stallone to the calorie. Once a week, he flew his Cessna Citation jet from his Santa Barbara ranch to LA, met with Stallone, and took his shirt off so his fellow A-lister could inspect the goods. "If John keeps it up, I'll have to fight him in *Rocky IV,*" quipped

Stallone. An increasingly excited Travolta marveled, "People like Sly can look at a body like clay and mold it. I never thought of designing a body."

Stallone, in fact, was to design everything on *Staying Alive,* throwing out the existing script by Norman Wexler and writing his own. "The only thing we kept of the original was the title," he declared. The film became oddly autobiographical, with Tony trying to break into the entertainment business just as Stallone had. A major subplot was written about Tony's difficult father, although later cut. The spiky grit of *Saturday Night Fever,* however, was lost in a torrent of wisecracks and schmaltz. Over Travolta's initial objections, Stallone decided this would be a PG film, with no swearing.

Frequently shooting the movie in his new fur coats, Stallone focused much of his energy on the gigantic musical finale, a nearly thirty-minute performance of a musical titled *Satan's Alley* (Stallone had toyed with riffing on *The Odyssey* before choosing Dante's *Inferno* as the jumping-off point instead). The extended sequence cost more than the entire production of *Rocky* and involved Travolta, in a headband and loincloth, fighting his way out of hell. There was a giant ascending platform. There were S&M dancers brandishing whips. There was, for some reason, blood.

It was an intense bonding experience for Travolta and Stallone, who started to talk up a *Godfather Part III* in which both would star (Travolta as Michael Corleone's son Anthony) and Stallone would direct. But that never happened, and while *Staying Alive* became one of 1983's big money-spinners, critics were unimpressed by the thin love-triangle story, the gauche theatrics, the songs by Stallone's brother Frank, and the bizarre ending in which a triumphant Tony announces, "I wanna strut!" and then does just that, down a New York street. "From the several close-ups of Tony's blue-jeaned rear-end," observed Vincent Canby's review, "he seems less to be struttin' than to be cruisin'."

If *Staying Alive* elicited unwanted giggles, Stallone's next release was met with out-and-out mockery. Based on the Glen Campbell song "Rhinestone Cowboy" and set to be directed by *Rocky III* editor Don Zimmerman, *Rhinestone* teamed him with Dolly Parton for a *My Fair Lady*–esque tale of a New York cab driver who is the subject of a wager to see whether he can become a successful country-and-western singer. The 20th Century Fox film was by design a trifle, but once again Stallone seized control, not only shrinking his biceps to fifteen and a half inches but comprehensively rewriting the script by Phil Alden Robinson, the future director of *Field of Dreams*. "No offense to Mr. Robinson, who I haven't met," Stallone sneered, "but nobody could say those lines and live." His own zingers, it turned out, would include the likes of "You're thinking of shacking up with the guru of doo-doo?" as well as much innuendo about his character's "large organ" (it turns out he owns an actual church organ).

Robinson, unhappy about Stallone's meddling, couldn't keep quiet, telling a reporter, "If you take a non-housebroken puppy and put him in a nice house and he makes a mess on the floor, you don't blame the puppy—he's only doing what comes naturally. You blame the person who put him in the house in the first place." And soon Stallone had fallen out with another colleague on the film, his old friend Zimmerman. Four weeks into the eleven-week shoot, after intense arguments between the pair, Zimmerman was fired in Nashville and all his footage except a solitary moment involving a stoplight discarded. "He got overwhelmed by the logistics, the size and the pace of this project," Stallone elucidated. A new director, Bob Clark, whose *Porky's* had just made $136 million for Fox, was hurriedly flown in.

But nobody quite understood why a film about country music was becoming such a behemoth. The final budget ended up at $28 million, $4 million more than planned, and a ragged Clark, who was sleeping just three hours a night, was having as bad a time as his predecessor. Stallone, who claimed he had signed on to the project to confront his deathly fear of singing and who was mumbling his way through numbers such as "Old MacDonald Had a Farm" and "Drinkenstein," shrugged, saying, "It cost more than the three *Rocky*s combined. I don't know where the money went. I swear to God I don't know. I ask myself that every day."

The money was gone, and it wasn't coming back. *Rhinestone* made just $21 million, with reviews so stinging that Stallone pledged never to read one again. One that captured the general temperature came from Robert Bruce in the *Daily Texan:* "Stallone singing 'a-wop-bop-a-loo-wop' while playing a funeral parlor organ may sound funny, but watching it makes a good case for his being shot."

A studio insider, meanwhile, speaking anonymously a month on from release, revealed that Fox's market research had uncovered a truth that should probably have been discussed before the light turned green: "Whether it was a good film or a bad film, it couldn't have been a hit because nobody wanted to hear Sly sing."

AS HE SAT in the Beverly Wilshire Hotel in June 1984 for the *Rhinestone* press junket, gazing across at the glass skyscrapers of Century City, Stallone considered his standing in the world. "It's like Edgar Allan Poe used to say," he mused. "The worst vice a man can acquire is a bad reputation, because there's just no eradicating it. It's there forever."

There was no doubt about it: his own reputation was starting to get stained. The critics were after him. Moviegoers were proving fickle. And as for the industry itself, foes were coming out of the woodwork. When Stallone backed out of a role in the crime drama *The Cotton Club* (which ended up starring his old *Lords of Flatbush* nemesis, Richard Gere) after having demanded a rewrite to make the gangster character more sympathetic, former Paramount boss Robert Evans sent him a public letter, which read, "Your deportment in our relationship both personally and professionally I find repugnant and ill-mannered and, concerning you, most self-destructive." Even Dolly Parton, despite praising his kissing skills, would say less-than-flattering things, too. "Sly is the perfect balance of total ego and total insecurity," she said to a reporter. "I always told him he was spectacular but that he had a blind spot where compassion and spirituality ought to be."

As he fingered his dog tag, Stallone related to John Rambo: a tough loner, running through the trees, enemies on all sides. He was funny in real life, but for some reason his charisma wasn't working on-screen, and it hurt. "There were days on *Rhinestone,* let me tell you, when I'd think to myself, 'Wow, it sure was safer walking through the jungle carrying a gun,'" he said. "A lot easier."

And so back to the jungle he went.

The script for *Rambo: First Blood Part II*—or, as it was then titled, *First Blood II: The Mission*—was initially tapped out by James Cameron. As is etched in screenwriting mythology, Cameron wrote both that sequel and *Aliens* simultaneously over three months while also finishing *The Terminator,* toggling between three separate desks. Opening Rambo's second adventure with the character confined to a psychiatric hospital—"A nasty piece of machinery," the stage directions note of his physique—Cameron's story dispatched him back to Vietnam on a mission to photograph American prisoners of war who were still being held captive. This time Rambo would be proactive, restaging the war America lost. And he had a sidekick, in the form of a sleazy lieutenant named Brewer, set to be played by Stallone's new buddy John Travolta. "Got the kinda legs I like," Brewer was to say of an attractive Thai woman in one scene. "Feet at one end and pussy at the other."

As with Schwarzenegger and *The Terminator,* a lunch date was set between Cameron and Stallone to discuss the project. But it would prove to be their only meeting. Before long, the whole screenplay was being reworked by the project's star, who would grouse later that he'd inherited a draft that "took nearly 30–40 pages to have any action initiated." That was something he changed quickly, cutting much of the jargon-heavy dialogue, as well as Brewer, and getting Rambo from military prison (not the psychiatric hospital) to the jungle within seventeen pages, killing a snake only seconds after parachuting down from an Acro Commander 1121 jet.

First Blood Part II would be huge, a $25.5 million tropical thriller that swapped the redneck cops of the first film for well-armed phalanxes of Soviet and Vietnamese troops. Stallone adjusted his body accordingly. Working with Franco Columbu,

Schwarzenegger's old gym pal, who was hired as the project's "bodybuilding coach," the star jacked up his physique with awe-inspiring dedication. For eight months he trained four hours a day, devouring chicken, taking courses in archery, survivalism, and SWAT combat. The result: a chiseled edifice of musculature that made Rocky look like a slob. Co-star Julia Nickson, hired to play Vietnamese love interest Co Bao, would later joke, "It's one of the few movies I've done where the guy looks better than the girl."

Originally the picture was to shoot in northern Thailand. But Carolco's Andrew Vajna had barely arrived there on a scouting trip when he and co-producer Mario Kassar received word that Stallone had decided to look at Hawaii instead. "I said, 'Uh-oh, here we go. We're gonna end up in Hawaii probably,'" says Kassar with a laugh now. In fact, they ended up in Acapulco, Mexico, trying to shoot a high-octane action movie while surrounded by tourists. "Next to all the discos and the hotel, two and a half miles away on the left, there was a little bit of jungle," Kassar recalls. "You could finish shooting and go to Jackie O's, or whatever the bar was called. All the Acapulco things. Everybody was having fun."

That included Stallone. Driving around in a vehicle dubbed "the Slymobile," he partied so hard he acquired the nickname "the Mayor of Acapulco," despite getting in one gym session at five A.M. and another at the end of the day. But at all times he kept a close eye on the production. Director George Cosmatos, who had surely heard about the *Rhinestone* drama, fretted constantly that he would be let go. Says Kassar: "For four months I had to hold George's hand every day. I mean, bless his heart, but he drove me crazy. Every day he said, 'He's gonna fire me!' and I'd say, 'He's not firing you. Relax.'"

Cosmatos had his work cut out for him. Even with the increased budget, it wasn't easy to lay on the kind of mayhem Stallone had in mind; in the edit, explosions were repeated from different angles to eke out the production value. The heat was brutal, with only Richard Crenna free from extreme perspiration (when asked for his secret, he replied, "I won't allow myself to sweat"). The fauna was gnarly—in one shot a scorpion scuttled up Stallone's leg, prompting him to quip, "Do you have an Actors Guild card?" The Mexican authorities were corrupt, demanding bribes for the shoot's helicopters to be brought in from Texas and one general insisting Stallone have a drink with him in exchange for use of an aircraft hangar. And while ingenious use of boulders and waterfalls did make Acapulco a convincing substitute for Southeast Asia, when somebody put a pair of fake horns on a cow, to pass it off as a water buffalo, Cosmatos had to step in and wave the confused animal away. Much more seriously, in Valle del Rio, twenty-one miles north of Acapulco, stuntman Clifford Weger slipped from the top of a waterfall and died.

In spite of the chaos and tragedy, *First Blood Part II* was turning into something powerful. Jack Cardiff, cinematographer of such beautiful, elliptical masterpieces as *The Red Shoes* and *Black Narcissus,* painted the mayhem with a mythic sweep. Bullet casings rattled to the ground in hypnotic abundance; helicopter gunships dueled like giant, hulking eagles. And through it all rolled Rambo (by now it seemed ridiculous to call him John), hailed by a stirring Jerry Goldsmith score. No longer the haunted wreck of the first film, the character was now a gleaming god, torso honed to perfection, padding through frames like a jungle cat. Before, he had avoided violence. Now he mercilessly deployed it, laying waste to scores of foreign troops with compound bow, M60 assault rifle, hunting knife, and rocket launcher. In one applause-inciting sequence, he lunged out of various hiding spots, destroying his prey with the efficiency of a villain from a slasher film. Except this guy was on our side.

First Blood Part II was a new kind of Vietnam picture, one in which military power was celebrated, not apologized for—"Do we get to win this time?" was a line Stallone himself had added—and America was raised high once more. And in the summer of 1985, amid a spate of real-life headlines about international terrorism, audiences ate it up. The original had been a hit. This was something else. Merchandise proliferated: squirt guns, video games, action figures, bumper stickers ("Beware—This Vehicle Is Protected by Rambo"). The novelization by David Morrell, the original cre-

ator of Rambo, became a bestseller, despite vastly changing much
of the film's story and dialogue (at one point, Rambo waxes lyrical
about the movie *Star Wars* to the POWs). Rumors began to circulate that the US Army was putting up Rambo posters in recruiting
centers. Newspaper ads proclaimed, "Rambo—a symbol of the
American spirit." And the box office wildly eclipsed that of the
first movie, with *First Blood Part II* making more than $150 million
domestic, $300 million international.

There were detractors, those who saw the movie as buying into
the US government's new hawkish mode of foreign policy. The star
of the new James Cameron movie *Aliens,* Sigourney Weaver,
quipped "Just call me Rambolina" while promoting that film, but
the director himself was uneasy when he saw what had been done
to his script. "After *Rambo,* I'm not that interested in making a
film where people are running around shooting each other," Cameron said in 1986. "And getting into the moral complications of
saying, 'Well, just because they're wearing a different uniform from
another country, it's okay,' in order to feel absolutely lily-white and
clean about the havoc that's wrought on their bodies by high-
velocity ballistic weapons." Morrell would later complain that the
film caused liberal bookshops to pull their copies of *First Blood* off
the shelves. And Ted Kotcheff, who had turned down the chance to
direct again, was also unimpressed. "In the script of it that I read,
Rambo kills seventy-one people. This is not the character I created," he says now. "Need I say more about why I refused to direct
the sequels?"

Stallone remained unapologetic about the movie's patriotic
leanings. In *Time* magazine, in a piece titled "Rambomania," he
explained, "People have been waiting for a chance to express their
patriotism. Rambo triggered long-suppressed emotions that had
been out of vogue. Suddenly, apple pie is an important thing on the
menu." With its high-voltage impact, *First Blood Part II* was a
game-changer, boosting the action genre to the next level and giving Stallone a new sense of purpose. Plus, it had answered a question: what to do with *Rocky IV?*

Again he would look east, this time to create a villain who

would outdo even Mr. T's Clubber Lang for ferocity and bulk. A Russian monster who would not just give Rocky a run for his money but pull the franchise in a new geopolitical direction.

The problem was going to be finding a guy who could play him.

A BIG TURNING POINT in Dolph Lundgren's life—quite possibly the biggest—can be traced back to an evening in 1981. Studying at the University of Sydney in Australia, broke and desperate for cash, the twenty-four-year-old Lundgren—then still going by his birth name, Hans—had scored a job working security for two weeks at the city's Capitol Theatre. One night he had been posted outside the musicians' dressing room, along with a friend, and whenever the door swung open, he could glimpse a vast buffet of food and drink laid out. As dictated by the visiting star, Grace Jones, there were six bottles of Louis Roederer Cristal Champagne, two dozen Fine de Claire oysters on ice (to be shucked, per her command, by Jones herself), enough sashimi and sushi for sixteen people, and much, much more. Lundgren's mouth began to water.

And then the unimaginable happened. The famous singer appeared in front of the humble bouncer and invited him in.

"Immediate attraction," Lundgren summed up a few years later. "It just happened."

The relationship that sparked up that night transformed the entire path of Lundgren's life. Before then, he had been set on a career in academia; a native of Sweden, he was in Sydney to study chemical engineering. An IQ test at school had yielded an astonishing, genius-level score of 160—"That was probably before I got kicked in the head," he quips. He spoke five languages, including Japanese, and was extraordinarily well read, having stayed at home for marathon book binges as an asthmatic child. But when he and Jones became a couple, he was drawn into her wild, adrenaline-fueled celebrity world, moving to New York, partying all night at Studio 54, having his photo taken by Andy Warhol. Jones acted as both girlfriend and stylist, decking him out in outfits by Issey Miyake and Kenzo. Lundgren even dabbled in modeling, though he was frequently told his frame was too big for the clothes to fit. "I didn't feel much like going back and shaking test tubes after that," he remembers. "It seemed a bit boring."

He did win a coveted spot at MIT on a Fulbright fellowship, but left Boston before classes even started and never returned. Instead, he spent more time in New York, where he met acting coach Warren Robertson, who had trained Jessica Lange and Matt Dillon, and who encouraged Lundgren to pursue a career in Hollywood. His chance came sooner than he expected: while visiting Jones on the set of the James Bond movie *A View to a Kill*, in which she was playing villain May Day, he was asked by the director if he wanted to jump into a scene, since an extra hadn't shown up. And so, hair slicked back as a burly KGB bodyguard named Venz, the first screen performance of Dolph Lundgren, Hans no more, came to be.

It amounted to forty seconds of screen time, dialogue-free and mostly out of focus. But unbeknownst to Lundgren, another, far more significant role was being hotly discussed in Los Angeles. The producers of *Rocky IV* were facing, once again, the tricky task of finding a bane for Balboa. "How do you get any better than *Rocky III* in terms of a bad guy?" says Irwin Winkler. As Clubber Lang, Mr. T had proven formidable, both on-screen and off. "My big thing about Mr. T was that there was a warrant out for his arrest in Chicago, and we had to deal with that," Winkler recalls. "When we found out, I said, 'What happened? Why is there a bench warrant out for you from a judge?' He said, 'Well, I beat up a guy.' I said, 'Who was the guy?' He said, 'A cop.' So there was a bit of work with that—they wanted to take him back to Chicago while we were shooting."

There were no tricky situations involving law enforcement on *Rocky IV,* but instead a vast hunt for an actor who could credibly play the new nemesis: Russian heavyweight Ivan Drago, aka "the Siberian Express," a Cold Warrior with a red-hot uppercut. In keeping with the asymmetrical warfare of *Rambo: First Blood Part II*, Stallone's script envisioned Drago as dwarfing first Apollo Creed, whom he brutally slays in the ring, and then Rocky. He is everything our hero is not: monolithic, unsmiling, machine-like.

He has only nine lines of dialogue but dominates the story, the personification of Red Peril in a pair of boxing shorts. Or, as Stallone himself described the character in 1984, "the greatest fighting machine ever built—a biochemically produced Soviet fighter."

Lundgren, still a nobody in New York, auditioned. He was told, inexplicably, that he was too tall. So he sent photos of himself in fighting gear directly to Stallone. And Winkler was dispatched to New York to check him out in person. "Sly told me one day, 'Do me a favor—get on a plane and meet this guy. He's at a gym on 47th Street and Manhattan,'" says the producer. "I went to the gym and this guy was towering over me—I'm five foot ten, he was six foot six or something. Big, strong guy. He said, 'Do you think I'll be good for this movie?' What was I going to say—no?"

The final contenders for the role were Lundgren and two actual Russians. "Big, long guys," Lundgren says, "but their acting was over-the-top. They kind of did a Russian Mr. T: 'I will knock your head off!' I decided to just play him very cool. Internal. Warren Robertson told me something very clever: 'Whatever you say, just keep your eyes neutral. Don't let it show in your eyes.'"

Finally hired, he soon found himself in California, working out with Stallone for four hours a day, every day, for months. Lundgren was in good shape already—a kickboxing champion and karate black belt, he had taught Jones the martial arts she needed for A View to a Kill—but this was another level. The Stallone diet plan involved eliminating beef and dairy, and starting each day with huge spoonfuls of wild rice soaked in apple juice. The A-list star and the unknown Swede clambered into a boxing ring again and again and again, sparring as if their lives depended upon it. It was like a fantastical, if painful, dream for Lundgren, who had adored the original movie in 1976 and now found himself facing off against Rocky himself.

But the pressure was huge, too; few third sequels dream quite as big as Rocky IV. Riding the wave of Rambomania, while simultaneously haunted by the failure of Rhinestone, Stallone was bent on making this one a nationalistic, fist-pumping phenomenon, souped up in every respect. The movie would begin with the sight of boxing gloves, patterned with the American and Russian flags, smashing into each other and exploding. The single training montage of the first film had become two, with Rocky lifting rocks, outrunning cars, and climbing a mountain (a staggering 30 percent of the film would end up being montage). There was even a somewhat bizarre talking robot, gifted by Rocky to Paulie.

The retooling would, of course, extend to the climactic battle. Balboa versus Drago was to be filmed in an arena in Vancouver, where a banner of Lundgren that seemed almost the size of a football field was hung in place. Stallone brought in eight cameras, which would ultimately shoot an amazing thirty thousand feet of film, enough to create three normal pictures. There, over a fortnight in late 1984, the two men set about enacting the greatest on-screen brawl of all time, between two characters who truly hate each other.

There were light moments, as when the robot, named Sico, was wheeled in to interrupt shooting, booming at Stallone, "You want I should take care of this Russian guy for you?" But mostly it was sweaty, relentless, punishing work. Especially when Stallone decided, near the end of the two weeks, that he and Lundgren should go at each other for real. "I just let caution to the wind. We were really slugging it out for the first thirty seconds," Stallone said near the end of production. "I wanted two people like in everyday life. . . . You just lose all sense of style, proportion and distance, and you just revert to animal savage instinct."

The result was an eight-day stay at St. John's Hospital in Santa Monica for Stallone, when a blow from one of Lundgren's sledgehammer arms slammed his heart into his breastbone. Lundgren, meanwhile, sustained injured ribs and a painful jaw. Rumors proliferated of a real-life rivalry between the two, something that Stallone didn't discourage; the publicity couldn't hurt. And Lundgren was undeniably a beast, one day picking up Carl Weathers and casually tossing him three feet into the corner of the ring. "I'm calling my agent," Weathers growled as he clambered over the ropes. "I quit!"

Lundgren, declaring that "I could beat Mike Tyson. Why not? I would have to train for a while, but I could beat him," grinned his way through the feverish publicity campaign. There were *Rocky IV* jigsaw puzzles, pencils, children's pajamas, and a board game. MGM/UA vice president Bill Dennis pondered the possibility of a Rocky Balboa cologne. And there were Drago toys glowering from shelves in every kids' store. "I cannot wait to go into a department store and be surrounded by hundreds of little Ivan Dragos," Lundgren joked. "They better be well-made—especially in the face."

A new action star had been airlifted into Hollywood, one with both maxed-out brawn and a mighty brain. Celebrity may have come with lightning speed, but Lundgren wasn't the least concerned that it might ebb away. "Pretty soon my life will be a circus," he said with certainty. "I'm ready for people to start beating down my door with offers."

AS FOR STALLONE, he was now truly riding high. *Rambo: First Blood Part II* had made $300.4 million worldwide. In a strange cosmic coincidence, *Rocky IV* grossed the exact same amount. Theaters in LA and New York ran out of popcorn during opening weekend in November. *Back to the Future* aside, Stallone was front man of the two biggest movies to open in America in 1985. He was also becoming buddies with the most powerful man in the world.

Ronald and Nancy Reagan's regular eight P.M. movie nights at Camp David included screenings of *Rocky III* and *Rocky IV*. While preparing to make a radio address about the federal budget, shortly after seeing the latter, the president marveled: "It's some of the greatest fight stuff I've ever seen filmed. From experience I know how fight scenes are done, but good Lord—I can't help but think they were swatting each other." It's possible that he'd already gotten to quiz Stallone about the movie in August 1985, when the star attended an LA fundraising dinner at Reagan's invitation, or in October that year, when Stallone went to a state dinner for the prime minister of Singapore. "It's always flattering to have the highest person in the land admire your work," he had said as he arrived at the White House.

It was enough to make anyone's head spin: lifting barbells in a gym one day, lifting forks at ritzy banquets the next. And as a final success to savor, Stallone was dating a woman he had stolen away from his biggest rival.

Brigitte Nielsen was the other tall, cream-haired European in *Rocky IV*. Towering above most other people on the set—including Stallone—the six-foot-one Dane had acquired a nickname around Hollywood: "the Amazon." Impossibly glamorous and highly athletic, she had landed the title role of a major movie on her very first try, cast in the *Conan the Barbarian* spin-off *Red Sonja* after producer Dino De Laurentiis spotted her on the cover of a fashion magazine. Shooting in and around Rome in September 1984, Nielsen and Arnold Schwarzenegger began what she calls an "outrageous" affair, even though she was married and he was living with Maria Shriver. "Time was limited, so we didn't hold back," she would recall. "The set lights would barely be off before we disappeared to do our thing: we wanted time to ourselves and we wanted to try everything. And when we were alone, that's exactly what we did."

The entanglement didn't last, but Nielsen's marriage evaporated soon after. And when she arrived in New York for the start of the *Red Sonja* promotional tour, she ran into someone who claimed Stallone was staying at a nearby hotel. Harboring a longtime crush on the star, dating back from when she'd seen *Rocky* at the age of thirteen, Nielsen sent along a flirty note, plus a photo of herself. A couple of hours later, Stallone called her room. Soon they were face-to-face, talking about her divorce. "Red Sonja," he said as he stepped back out into the hall, "why don't you come for dinner with me tonight?"

And so began their roller-coaster relationship. Nielsen's was a world of wild parties and edgy photo shoots; Stallone's, despite his raucous filmography, was a more refined one. When the couple ran into Grace Jones in a Beverly Hills club and Jones greeted Nielsen by screeching "Gitte!" and burying her face in Nielsen's crotch, Stallone was lost for words. Soon the same level of control he asserted when it came to movie scripts was being applied to his personal life.

Nielsen moved into his oceanside mansion, which had every luxury one could imagine: a butler standing by at all times, fine art everywhere (including freshly commissioned statues and paintings of her), exquisite furniture. Steven Spielberg and Quincy Jones were neighbors. But she began to feel that she was paying for all of this with her freedom. Before their wedding, a star-studded event in December 1985 (the Reagans were invited but unable to attend), a document was presented for her to sign, putting limits on what she could say or do. And soon she felt she was being watched at all times—by bodyguards who dogged her every step, and by her new husband, who monitored every transaction made on her credit card.

Even her work life was now firmly in his hands. "Sylvester made sure throughout the time we were together that I was busy on his projects," she said. "I felt that he didn't want me on a movie with somebody else." So she starred in *Rocky IV*, as Drago's sadistic wife, Ludmilla, and then in *Cobra*, as a businesswoman under threat. When he did allow her to appear in something without him, *Beverly Hills Cop II*, Stallone rang up Eddie Murphy and accused him of sleeping with her.

The drama in Stallone's movies was getting ever more pumped up and outrageous. And his home life, which had until now been a peaceful reprieve from the sets, was starting to go the same way.

CHAPTER 6

...

KNOCK KNOCK

DRIVING THROUGH PACIFIC PALISADES in Los Angeles is usually a serene experience: blue sky, palm trees, cool ocean breeze. But if you were journeying through Santa Monica Canyon sometime in the mid-1980s, you might just have experienced a shock.

First you would have spotted in your rearview mirror a huge black Jeep Wagoneer speeding toward you. Then you would have heard the heart-stopping blare of a siren. Finally you would have been jolted by a booming, microphone-amplified voice with a strange accent, shouting: *"Hey! Idiot! Get out of the road!"*

It was, of course, Arnold Schwarzenegger, behind the wheel of one of his numerous vehicles. He owned a classic Mercedes convertible, a Porsche, and a Harley-Davidson motorcycle that he called "the Hog." But this one was his regular ride: a custom-built 1984 model with a colossal 6.6-liter Duramax diesel engine and an exhaust pipe the size of a Terminator's arm. Inside, it was festooned with fine leathers and reptile hides. And under the hood, near that siren, was a powerful speaker with which he could prank his fellow drivers.

"He did that to me a couple of times," laughs *Predator* screenwriter Jim Thomas. "I think he got a couple of tickets for it, too."

Schwarzenegger's first big hits had seen him deliver no-nonsense performances. The T-800 hadn't been big on mirth. Conan wasn't much funnier. But off-screen he was an insatiable practical joker, a guy for whom sophomoric humor was second nature. And as he accelerated on to his next few movies, he was finally taking command of his own persona.

It was time to get silly.

NOT THAT COMMANDO was originally designed to amuse. The two writers behind the first draft, Jeph Loeb and Matt Weisman, had conceived the somber tale of an Israeli soldier who had turned away from violence but finds himself forced back into the fray. The screenplay made its way to 20th Century Fox, and there it sat, until two sentences from the studio's chairman jolted it into production.

In early 1985, Barry Diller had only just settled into his new job at Fox, but he was as aware as anyone of the heat being generated by *The Terminator*. Schwarzenegger hadn't worked with the studio since 1979's *Scavenger Hunt,* but Diller wanted him back in the fold immediately. "This guy Schwarzenegger is a phenomenon," he proclaimed one Friday. "If you find the right movie for him that can be done for under $12 million, I'll greenlight it immediately."

His underlings scrambled into action, blowing dust off every script languishing in an inbox. That weekend, bleary eyes pored over endless pages. "They got together every script on the Fox lot that could theoretically be an action movie, and in a day and a half we read them all," says writer Steven de Souza, who had been brought in by his friend Lawrence Gordon, Diller's lieutenant. "Most of them were unmade for a reason."

Some were too ambitious; others, just impossible to get through. But one stuck out. Its very title page seemed mythic, with the word "Commando" stark against white. And though the dialogue was earnest, the premise seemed ripe for fun. De Souza started riffing on the material, and with Fox's blessing he headed to Schwarzenegger's house on Monday morning to pitch it to him.

The meeting could have gone wrong. De Souza had nothing down on paper and was still fleshing out the story as he drove his car. He only had three credits under his belt (including, rather auspiciously, a debut film called *Arnold's Wrecking Crew*). But he was also a quick-witted wiseass who thrived on flying by the seat of his pants. Halfway through recounting the story to Schwarzenegger, on his feet and acting out the combat beats, he accidentally slipped into an impression of the star.

"He gives me this Terminator look," de Souza recalls. "And I go, 'I do all the greats. . . . Want to hear my Cary Grant?' "

Schwarzenegger's glare disappeared. He chuckled. Then he stood up and told the writer, "It's a part John Wayne could play. I'll do this picture."

By Tuesday, sets were being designed, based on verbal descriptions of scenes from de Souza. And a brand-new version of the screenplay was being written to meet an insanely imminent deadline. It was March, and Diller had declared that the movie had to be in theaters on October 8. As he typed away furiously, de Souza kept thinking of a quotation from Samuel Johnson: "When a man knows he is to be hanged in a fortnight, it concentrates his mind wonderfully."

This project was hardly highbrow—it amounted to a burly man named John Matrix (no longer Israeli) bumping off one by one the bad guys who have kidnapped his daughter, until he gets to the chief villain, Bennett. But de Souza saw in it a chance to revamp Schwarzenegger's image, pushing it in a comic direction. "He had fourteen lines of dialogue in *Terminator*," he says. "In *Conan* he's basically a hick, kind of unsophisticated compared to the characters he's running around with." Here, though, he would be cool, confident, always ready with a quip. He'd even repeat his famous *Terminator* one-liner—"I'll be back"—turning it into a catchphrase.

A director was enlisted by producer Joel Silver during a party at the Playboy Mansion. "We were sitting next to each other in pajamas," says Mark Lester. "He said, 'My next movie's going to be called *Commando*. Want to do it?' I said, 'Can I read the script?' He said, 'No—if you read the script, you'll never do the movie.' " And a lead actress was found: Rae Dawn Chong, who had recently appeared in a bizarre Mick Jagger film/music video hybrid called

Running Out of Luck. As part of her audition to play stewardess Cindy, she had to perform a mortifying scene opposite Schwarzenegger in which Matrix goes through Cindy's bag and pulls out a sex toy. But Chong kept her cool, changing the line from the scripted "It gets lonely on the road" to "That's not mine!" and charming the star with childhood memories of Muscle Beach—her father had been a bodybuilder.

"Was Arnold embarrassed about handling a dildo?" she recalls of that day. "He didn't break a sweat."

ON APRIL 22, 1985, cameras rolled on *Commando* in Los Angeles. The evening before, Lester, who had been advised by Fox executives to model the film on the 1972 Jim Brown picture *Slaughter,* had had dinner with Schwarzenegger, and found him in a surprisingly fragile mood.

"Are you scared?" Schwarzenegger asked Lester.

"No," the director replied.

"I am," admitted the brawny star. "I'm petrified."

Unlike his role in *The Terminator,* this wasn't a scene-stealing villain, slipping in and out of the film. And unlike the *Conan* films, there was no real ensemble to back him up. Schwarzenegger would be in almost every scene, cracking jokes as well as skulls and having to dig deep into his reserves of charm to play a loving father.

But even the pastoral scenes that open the movie are hardly naturalistic. Matrix and his daughter, Jenny (Alyssa Milano), pet a deer, eat ice cream, and discuss the music of Boy George. "They should call him Girl George," says Matrix, unimpressed by the singer's signature androgynous look. In one astonishing shot, Schwarzenegger strides forward, a chain saw in one hand and an entire tree atop his shoulder. That image, and the whole montage that introduces Matrix, was directly inspired by the propaganda pictures of Leni Riefenstahl. "Even though they were Nazi films," says Lester, "they had some amazing filmmaking in them. It was to make Arnold seem strong and powerful, coming out of the woods."

Once Jenny is kidnapped by the cronies of a deposed South

American dictator who wants to force Matrix into carrying out a political assassination, all hell breaks loose. Matrix picks up phone booths with people inside, tosses villains off cliffs, slits their throats, blasts them to bits with Claymore mines. It was more action than Schwarzenegger had ever done before, and he took to it with glee. Recalls Lester: "He wanted to do a lot of the stunts himself, because he insisted that nobody could duplicate his body. Even down to that quick-cut sequence on the beach where he tools up with all the weapons. He said, 'My hand cannot be duplicated. It's one of a kind.' When he jammed the knife into the sheath, he cut his other hand and had to go to the hospital."

The talking scenes were the ones that scared him. His biggest chunk of dialogue came during a sequence at a shopping mall, and to make matters worse, a gaggle of Fox suits decided to visit that day of filming. They stood watching from one side of the set, gritting their teeth, as Schwarzenegger flubbed his lines again and again. "I told you not to have him talk," one of them snapped at Lester. After some debate, it was agreed that a lovemaking scene between Matrix and Cindy, aboard a flight to the dictator's lair for the climax of the film, should be cut from the film. "It was so lame," says Chong, who was relieved that the sex toy scene had also been excised. "It just didn't make sense. Who would have been flying the plane at that point?"

But if the romance element of the film had been dialed down, the violence was increasingly cranking up. The finale in Val Verde—a country that de Souza had invented—was big to begin with. Then things got crazy. "In the script, there was some plausibility," says de Souza. "The dictator is living on a private island, so there were maybe a dozen security guards. But during the shoot, Mark saw a sneak preview of *Rambo* [*First Blood Part II*] and realized how many people get killed in that. He said, 'We've got to have a bigger dick than *Rambo*. We've got to slay more people.' And suddenly there were 150 extras getting killed. It got out of control."

Lester denies there was ever direct competition: "We never had a conversation about the body count." But the mayhem he was pointing his cameras at on the grounds of Hearst Castle in California, as Matrix storms the compound, stripped to the waist and smeared in camouflage paint, was starting to resemble a Tex Avery cartoon. A stuntman would be killed, then have a false mustache stuck on and be rushed back onto the set to die again. "I was in my trailer when they were shooting those scenes, so I didn't even know the amount of carnage until I saw it in the theater," says Chong. "I was like, 'Holy fuck!' It's wild. But I was sad that they were all little brown guys getting nailed."

Schwarzenegger embraced the chaos that ensues as Matrix destroys his foes using a four-barreled rocket launcher, a machine gun, hand grenades, and even some gardening equipment he finds in a shed. In fact, the star had his own idea for a kill: inspired by a likely apocryphal World War I story he'd heard, Schwarzenegger suggested that Matrix could chop off an enemy's arm with an axe, then pick up the severed limb and slap him with it to get him to stop screaming, accompanied by the line, "Quit whining!" To his disappointment, the moment did not make it into the film.

One side effect of the jacked-up melee was that the final face-off between hero and villain ended up going in the other direction. De Souza's original vision involved Matrix and Bennett, played by Australian actor Vernon Wells, commandeering speedboats and crashing onto a military installation. "It would have been awesome," says the writer. "A knife fight on the beach, like *Saving Private Ryan,* where there's a minefield and naval gunnery ships shooting at the island."

But it didn't quite work out that way. Instead, while on a trip to Vancouver, de Souza got an urgent call from Joel Silver telling him the money had run out and that they needed a new ending, fast. De Souza tapped out a much smaller denouement, deleting minefield-based one-liners ("Watch your step!") and adding in new ones that would work in a claustrophobic boiler room. "I was making this up in my hotel room, and they were shooting it a few minutes later," he recalls. "It was like 'Let's put on a show!' with Judy Garland and Mickey Rooney."

There was zero ordnance in this new sequence: just two men coming at each other with blades. Even so, it proved a dangerous scene to film. Shooting in a basement back on the Fox lot, to keep costs minimal, Wells and Schwarzenegger circled each other for wide shots with genuine intensity. "When the director said action, I just went straight into it," says Wells. "I *was* Bennett and I was going to cut Arnold's throat. There was just no way I wasn't. And apparently Arnold decided after that that the knife had to be plastic."

It was in a moment without Wells present, though, that the film's star actually got hurt.

"There were sharp metal edges on the floor," says Schwarzenegger. "And I remember that Benny Dobbins—the stunt coordinator who did the actual fighting with me—landed on top of me. And the sharp edges dug deep inside my elbow, in my tricep, and blood was pouring down. There was, like, a chunk of meat hanging out. And we just continued fighting. This was the old days, you know? You just wanted to do the scene and not whine."

They kept shooting through lunchtime. Then, at three P.M., Schwarzenegger headed to the doctor to get stitched up again.

RECENT JAMES BOND and Indiana Jones films had also combined action and comedy. But *Commando* was so unrepentantly macho, so gleefully ludicrous, that it felt like something new. Silly deaths capped off by sillier jokes, dispensed by a man who looked like a child's drawing of somebody strong. "Let off some steam," a one-liner ad-libbed by Schwarzenegger himself in the Fox basement as Matrix skewers Bennett against a pipe, got huge cheers. As did "I lied!" as Matrix drops a minion off a cliff, breaking his promise to let him live.

"On opening night, I drove around to all the theaters to watch it," says Mark Lester. "And before he said that line, the entire audience yelled, 'He lied!' They all knew the line and I couldn't figure out how. Then I realized it was in the trailer. That line became famous even before the film came out."

In the end, speedboats and minefields proved wholly unnecessary—Schwarzenegger was the ultimate special effect.

Watching him in *Commando* was like witnessing some kind of prehistoric beast unleashed; his acts of violence, free of any bothersome emotion or consequence, yielded a cathartic secondhand high. "Schwarzenegger has become the most engaging of the new crop of killing-machine leading men," wrote the *Washington Post*'s Paul Attanasio, "partly because, outsized and inarticulate as he is, you can't imagine him functioning in civilization. How would 'I'd like a tuna fish on rye?' sound, coming from Schwarzenegger? It's easier to see him biting the tuna's head off."

Kids snuck into screenings and imitated him at school, recreating the firefights in play areas. And, with its minimal dialogue, it traveled well around the world. "There was a weird thing that came out in this book an African boy wrote," says Lester. "It was disturbing—it said the kids in this African country were watching *Commando* before they went out to battle. I felt bad when I read that. I mean, it's a movie, but they were showing it to these kids to psych them up."

For good or ill, the Schwarzenegger formula had been set. It was his third solid hit, making $57.5 million in the United States, and a path forward was clear. After wriggling out of his *Conan* contract, he grabbed on to a project destined to become even more iconic.

It began in a hot tub. Screenwriter Jim Thomas had been trying for years to get his first script, a sci-fi thriller co-written with his brother John, off the ground. For the main character, the siblings envisioned Mel Gibson. But when the project finally got traction at 20th Century Fox, it was Arnold Schwarzenegger to whom they were dispatched. They arrived for the summit at the Knoll, the 45,000-square-foot Beverly Hills house of producer John Davis's father, Marvin, a colorful character who liked to greet people with the question "How old are you and how much money do you have?" There it became apparent that they would be convening with Schwarzenegger not in the library, nor the dining room, but in one of the mansion's seventeen bathrooms, where the star sat, stogie in mouth, in a huge, fizzing tub of water.

"Naked, of course," says Thomas. "That's his sense of humor."

The unorthodox script meeting got under way. And the brothers, who had originally thought, "Uh-oh. Conan? This isn't going to work," were surprised to find he was smarter than he looked, peppering them with questions about the character. "I was delighted that he took so much interest," recalls Thomas. "I said, 'You've just done a movie called *Commando,* where you can fall off buildings and bounce off cars. But if you play this part as an everyman, then at the end when you have no weapons and this creature is about to destroy you, you can rise out of the mud and take it on like a Greek hero.'"

Ash fluttered down onto the water. And *Predator* was born.

The plot may have sounded corny—an extraterrestrial big-game hunter stalks special-forces soldiers in a remote jungle—yet this was designed to be a hard-boiled, genuinely tense affair, with an alien villain far scarier than *Commando*'s mustachioed, chain-mail-vested kidnapper. But the production immediately started running into problems. Original director Geoff Murphy, an affable New Zealander who had just made the Maori Western *Utu,* was let go as soon as Schwarzenegger joined; it turned out the two had had a bad meeting for *Conan the Destroyer,* with a Murphy wisecrack about "Conan the Librarian" rubbing Schwarzenegger the wrong way.

His replacement didn't initially strike most as an astute hire. John McTiernan, then thirty-four, had only made one film, an art-house horror called *Nomads* with Pierce Brosnan as a French anthropologist haunted by Inuit demons. John Davis thought he had the right stuff, and *Nomads* and *Predator* had a similar supernatural tinge, but McTiernan quickly began butting heads with the Thomases over their screenplay. "I could see the potential," the director remembers. "It had some stupid stuff in it that I figured I could get rid of. But it seemed fun. It was an action movie that didn't take itself too seriously. Well, the script took itself seriously, but I didn't."

As Jim Thomas recalls, "We had a real difficulty communicating with John. And then one day I realized it was a left-brain/right-brain kind of problem. He was trying to explain a character arc to us as a trigonometry syllogism. And we'd approach things more instinctively."

The main area of contention was the ending, which as written saw Schwarzenegger's character, Major Alan "Dutch" Schaefer, discover the alien's spacecraft and a mass of grisly human trophies, muttering to himself, "Even the fuckin' Nazis didn't do this." Recalls McTiernan: "It was creepy and sort of repulsive and didn't go with an adventure movie." The director also wrote his own new opening to the film, inspired by the 1961 monster movie *Gorgo*. But his efforts to reshape the narrative were initially stymied. "The studio viewed me as a kid and didn't pay attention," McTiernan says. "In fact, they got mad at me for writing it."

One thing everyone seemed to agree on, at least, was their leading man. Unlike *Conan* or *Commando,* this movie put Schwarzenegger in a team, surrounded by hulking men such as Jesse Ventura, Sonny Landham, and Bill Duke, the last of whom he'd impaled on a table leg in *Commando*. But their presence didn't diminish him; rather, as soon as the cast was assembled, he began to up his game even more, as if he was competing in a bodybuilding contest once again.

"I had to really campaign to get Carl Weathers for the movie," McTiernan recalls. "To get the studio to pay for him. Because he was a really good actor, and I knew if I put him next to Arnold in most of the scenes it would help Arnold enormously. Every time Carl was working, Arnold was over in the corner of the set, watching. Because he was thinking, 'Okay, this is my new life. And this guy knows how to do it.' I just put Carl in Arnold's way, and it worked out."

As for the dialogue, despite Thomas's "everyman" speech at the hot tub, this would give fans as many quotable Schwarzenegger zingers as they could wish for. "Knock knock," as Dutch kicks down a guerrilla's door, was lifted from the John Wayne film *Brannigan*. "Stick around" was the capper for a scene in which he pins a Communist to a door with a machete. And not even the Predator itself could intimidate him into silence—"You're one ugly motherfucker," Dutch tells the beast as they come face-to-freaky-face.

Other bits of dialogue would come courtesy of screenwriting wunderkind Shane Black, whom McTiernan embedded in the cast as squad joker Hawkins after reading his script for *Lethal Weapon,* so that Black could sharpen everyone's lines as the shoot rolled on.

IN THE DYING DAYS of March 1986, the cast touched down in Mexico for a brutal week of military training. There were enforced runs over rough terrain, red-ant attacks, and of course scorching insults, with drill sergeant Gary Goldman informing them that they looked like ballerinas. Schwarzenegger, a longtime acquaintance of pain, embraced it all.

In the meantime, McTiernan was trying not to have a nervous breakdown as he surveyed the landscape in nearby Puerto Vallarta, a beach town on Mexico's Pacific Coast. "The cameraman and I looked at each other and said, 'There's no jungle here. What are we doing?'" he recalls. "It turned out the [production] designer had a house there and got the movie moved so he could redo it."

As the crew attempted to shoot in a way that would disguise the lack of foliage, another nightmare struck. A wave of food poisoning engulfed the team, resulting in Schwarzenegger both throwing up and having diarrhea in the middle of the same jungle run, then being put on an IV drip for several days.

Then there was Sonny Landham, an actor who proved so rowdy that an enormous South American bodyguard named Hernán was hired to protect everyone else from him. "Sonny couldn't hold liquor," explains co-screenwriter Jim Thomas. "I remember one night I made the mistake of going out to dinner with him. After a few drinks he was really going on a rip about something. I got him out of there and the last time I saw him he was walking down a hallway, punching out light bulbs that were hanging down." Landham was ejected from more than one nightclub for writhing around on the dance floor, kissing women's legs. And McTiernan remembers an even wilder nocturnal event: "He rappelled out of the top floor of the hotel, drunk out of his mind at three in the morning, buck naked with his underpants on his head. He went down five floors and swung into somebody's room. He wasn't trying to hurt anybody; he was just a loose cannon, and he mostly pointed it at himself." It was only when Landham's girlfriend, an actress and Playboy Playmate named Deborah Dutch, was hurriedly convinced to fly down to Puerto Vallarta that the chaos stopped.

Finally, and most significantly, there was the issue of the monster. *Predator* was titled after its fearsome star-beast, a creature capable of making itself invisible at will, but the shoot had begun without an approved design. One Sunday afternoon down in Mexico, a monkey was put in a red suit and let loose for a camera test. "The monkey didn't work at all," rues McTiernan. "That was a nonstarter." The crew then built a giant bungee system to make it look like the alien could move at phenomenal speed, but they only got one shot for the film out of it. Most calamitous of all was the creature designed by Boss Film Studios, a peculiar-looking thing that Schwarzenegger thought resembled a lizard with the head of a duck. "It was awful," says the director now. "It came in a box, and Joel Silver and I looked at it and said, 'We are in deep shit.'"

The actor who was set to don the alien costume was a fresh-faced Belgian named Jean-Claude Van Damme, making his Hollywood screen debut. Ultimately, however, he would remain on set for just two days. "I think he was under the impression that he was going to be the hero," Thomas says. "And then he kind of erupted when they asked him to get into the suit. It was disastrous. But wearing that suit had to have been an impossible ordeal, because of the temperature." According to the writer, Van Damme was hired to take advantage of his acrobatic agility, though McTiernan scoffs at the notion: "What, so you'd have a monster from outer space come down and be a judo expert?"

Predator was officially in crisis. Van Damme was fired, and the production shut down to resolve the situation. But to the rescue came Stan Winston, the FX genius who had turned Schwarzenegger into a cyborg in *The Terminator* and who now came up with a brand-new design, creating a seven-foot-tall alien warrior (to be played by Kevin Peter Hall) with slavering mandibles (a James Cameron suggestion) and a bristling array of sci-fi weaponry. And some more good news: the studio executives, who were impressed when they reviewed McTiernan's footage so far, allowed the director to move the production to some proper, primal jungle, in southern Mexico's Palenque.

Some off-the-cuff sequences were shot to introduce the squad at the start of the movie—a destined-to-be-iconic close-up of Schwarzenegger's and Weathers's bulging biceps as they grip hands was insisted upon by Joel Silver. Then they plunged into the wilderness. Despite the physical hardships, from the intense heat to the predawn wake-up calls, the mood remained light, something that jibed with the director's intentions. "It was like playing cowboys in the woods," says McTiernan. "I saw the movie as being aimed at fourteen-year-old boys. It was meant to be simply wonderful, childish popcorn."

The Predator's fantastical armory—wrist blades, shoulder-mounted plasma cannon, self-destruct nuke—was rivaled by the heroes' own weapons, many of which were invented especially for the production to enhance the G.I. Joe feel. While Schwarzenegger wielded a relatively standard slab-sided AR-15 rifle, Richard Chaves, as Poncho, lugged around a bespoke six-shooter rotary grenade launcher, so awe-inspiringly destructive it would later be sported by Chuck Norris in the third *Missing in Action* movie. Most astonishing of all was the weapon known as "Ol' Painless," a minigun that until now had solely been mounted on helicopters. Jesse Ventura, the former wrestler tasked with hauling it through the jungle, commented that it was "like firing a chain saw."

"It was ridiculous," chuckles McTiernan. "Completely impractical as a real gun. We had to slow it down by a factor of ten or something so that you could even see the spin. And it could only shoot maybe five or six seconds' worth of bullets before the guy was standing up to his knees in shell casings. But carrying it around just looked cool."

As the Palenque jungle got shredded by pyrotechnics and ear-splitting sounds echoed for miles around, any witnesses would have been forgiven for thinking this was just another Hollywood action picture. But there was something a little subversive happening under the hood. *Predator* was a sneaky riposte to the very American idea that guns equal power: after all, there are eight good guys, all armed to the teeth, against a single enemy, but all their ammunition does them no good at all.

Not everyone on the production grasped the subtext. "One of the studio executives was really selling gun pornography," the director recalls. "He kept sending notes about it and going to the head of the studio saying, 'McTiernan should film more gun barrels!' It disturbed me. So I finally said, 'Look, I will give you so many pictures of gunfire that you won't know what to do with it all. But I'm going to put it all in one place and in the context that I set, and then I never want to hear another note from you again, okay?'"

His solution: a moment where the unit, haunted by the creature, lights up the jungle, blazing away with enough ammo to take down an army. But despite all the sound and fury, not a single shot finds its target. "Not a thing. Not a fucking trace. No blood, no bodies. We hit nothing," reports Poncho glumly. Ultimately, it comes down to Dutch, alone, unarmed, and slathered in gray mud, using a sharpened tree trunk to defeat his sophisticated foe. A wry bit of subversion for a mainstream action movie: peace through inferior firepower.

And in the end, McTiernan didn't have to shoot the ending he detested, either. "Fortunately, Arnold had another business commitment and told Joel Silver he was only going to work two more days," he recalls. "And the schedule said we were supposed to work another week and a half or something to shoot spaceships and creepy things. So I shot forty-two setups in a day, got Arnold home, and got to finish the movie pretty much the way I'd had in mind anyway."

After all the battles, the fired alien, the three A.M. hotel rappel, *Predator* was finally crawling out of the jungle.

ON SATURDAY, April 26, 1986, Arnold Schwarzenegger took a short hiatus from the shoot. He flew from Puerta Vallarta to Hyannis, Massachusetts, in a Learjet chartered by Joel Silver, arriving at his destination just before dawn. Wearing a gray tuxedo, he got in a limousine and headed to a white clapboard church. A crowd had been gathering there from seven-thirty A.M. on, some spectators even climbing trees for a better view, while a ring of off-duty police officers stood guard outside.

This was an event. After all, it's not every day you get to see the Terminator getting married.

For Schwarzenegger, it was a radical change of scenery, from sci-fi carnage to a high-society do. The reception was to take place at the Kennedy compound in nearby Hyannis Port, where there would be an oceanside buffet under three huge tents. And the wedding itself was studded with famous faces from the worlds of politics, entertainment, and sport. Grace Jones and Andy Warhol turned up incredibly late—in fact, twenty-five minutes after Maria Shriver, the bride herself, had walked down the aisle—with Jones adorned in a skintight green gown, green fur hat, and green contact lenses.

But the star, as always, took it all in stride. Grenades one day, Bellinis the next? No problem. As he surveyed the scene with his best man, Franco Columbu, he must have felt like he was now the king of not one but two worlds. And besides, married life, even with America's sweetheart, wasn't going to change him: after a brisk two-day honeymoon in the Caribbean, he was back at work in Mexico, preparing to swim in a leech-filled lagoon.

The movie was huge, as he'd sensed it would be. "*Predator*'s final scenes, with a mud-coated, primeval-looking Schwarzenegger locked in battle against the lizard, knight-like monster, are terrific— two big guys going at it in the mud," said the *Hollywood Reporter*. It grossed almost $100 million, launched McTiernan as a major director, and spawned a sequel three years later, though Schwarzenegger wouldn't return. "We had a meeting with Arnold," remembers Jim Thomas. "Our germ of an idea was that we would start in the burned-out jungle from the ending of the movie, three feet deep of ash, and then a camouflaged hand plunges down into the ash and comes up with the Predator's arm. Activates the computer and sees the demise of his friend. And at that point he knows it's Arnold and he's got his target." But this version of the sequel would fall apart over salary disputes.

Schwarzenegger's next film after *Predator, The Running Man,* would give him another Steven de Souza script and repeat the kill-and-quip formula. In fact, it would boost it to another level, turning Stephen King's dystopian novel into a pumped-up murderfest, as hero Ben Richards dispatches game-show assassins with silly names.

After cutting Buzzsaw in half with his own chain saw: "He had to split."

After throttling Subzero with barbed wire: "He was a real pain in the neck."

After combusting Fireball: "What a hothead."

The truth was, Schwarzenegger wasn't in the business to get a political viewpoint across or make people cry. "I see films as pure entertainment," he told a reporter on the set of *Predator.* "I try to stay away from films with heavy messages. I want to sell tickets, not slogans."

That sounded like a veiled shot at Stallone, the tortured artiste. And after *Predator* came out, the emboldened Schwarzenegger started to say in public things about his box-office rival that he had been telling his friends in private for some time. "He is not my friend," he said to *Playboy* in early 1988, pulling on a Cuban Davidoff cigar. "He just hits me the wrong way. I make every effort that is humanly possible to be friendly to the guy, but he just gives off the wrong vibrations." He then zeroed in on things that annoyed him. Stallone's plan to start an all-male smoking club, which Schwarzenegger claimed he refused to join, on grounds of sexism. Stallone's ostentatious gold jewelry. And, most of all, Stallone's dress sense, the polar opposite of his own studiously conservative wardrobe.

"Seeing him dressed in his white suit, trying to look slick and hip—that already annoys people," Schwarzenegger said disapprovingly. "He should have LL Bean shoes and corduroy pants with a plaid shirt. That's cool; that's how a director should look, rather than have that fucking fur coat when he directs."

The interview poured more gas on a fire that was already ablaze. The feud was being reported on at an increasingly hysterical pitch, most writers siding with the unpretentious Schwarzenegger (one *Washington Post* article referred to Stallone as a "Venusian pimp" with "the charming modesty of a steroid-crazed Napoleon"). In terms of box office and salary, his enemy was winning: Stallone had pocketed well over $10 million for *Rambo: First Blood Part II*, compared to Schwarzenegger's $2 million for *Commando* and $3.5 million for *Predator*. But there was one area besides media opinion in which Arnold had the edge. When Rambo is asked in *First Blood Part II* what brings him luck, he points to his oversized Bowie knife, with a nine-inch serrated blade, and says, "I guess this."

When John Matrix unsheathed his *Commando* blade later the same year, it was half an inch longer.

CHAPTER 7

...

THE ALIEN

DURING HIS FEW DAYS on the *Predator* set, Jean-Claude Van Damme had a brief interaction with Arnold Schwarzenegger. Sizing up the unknown twenty-six-year-old who had been choppered in to play the alien hunting him, Schwarzenegger (six foot two) looked down at Van Damme (five foot eight). "I like your belt," he said. "Where did you buy it?"

Adopting a jokily high-pitched voice, the Belgian replied, "I bought it on *San-ta Mon-ica Boul-e-vard*."

The Austrian cracked a grin and moved on.

On this particular job, Van Damme wasn't doing much smiling himself. His *Predator* experience had begun in an office on the Fox lot in Los Angeles, where he had been summoned to show off his agility. Witnessing Van Damme leaping an astonishing height into the air, performing the splits at eye level, John McTiernan had given the nod to casting agent Jackie Burch. But something had been lost in translation. As Van Damme understood it, the gig was to involve him having his face painted with makeup to make him look like some kind of extraterrestrial cat. At the effects house, however, he was presented with a bulky rubber-and-metal suit that would encase his whole head, and which took twenty minutes to put on. With its freakishly extended arms and unearthly backward knees, Van Damme was unable to jump—he complained that if he did he would break his legs—and he felt so overwhelmed by claustrophobia, as he gulped in air through a small tube, that he had to focus on wiggling his finger to avoid a full-blown panic attack.

"It didn't work for nobody," Van Damme recalls. "My feet were in the ankles of the animal, my hands were in the forearms, moving its fingers with cables, and my head was in the neck. Very difficult to run or walk. Very dangerous. Joel Silver was angry because he'd spent close to a million dollars on that outfit. But I think it was better than the new one. The mask was more like an alien face— more scary, less comic-book. The second one looked like a human on the move, like a Jamaican with that hair."

The experience was a humiliating disaster. Not least because it ended with a firing in Mexico that, according to the film's assistant director, involved Silver telling Van Damme that he wanted to run over his head with a truck fifty thousand times. But as the man who could have been the beast from Yautja Prime flew back to LA, his new job cut short, he shook it off the way he had already shaken off many disappointments.

Van Damme was nothing if not resilient.

Born Jean-Claude Camille François Van Varenberg, in Berchem-Sainte-Agathe, a small suburb outside of Brussels, he had been a pale, gawky, sensitive child, with thick glasses and a lisp. So quiet was he, even those who knew him well thought he had a speech impediment. Nobody, not even his doting parents, the owners of a flower shop, suspected a career in Hollywood awaited him. But little Jean-Claude quickly developed an obsession with films. Visiting the local cinema on Sundays with his father, Eugène, he cried during *Ben-Hur* and *Gone with the Wind,* and when he saw *Star Wars* at seventeen, he bounced up and down in his seat. "The guy in the small village working in mechanics," he was to excitedly surmise of the groundbreaking science-fiction film's plot, "and then they give him the power to be a ninja of the future."

By that point, he was already training to become a ninja himself. His childhood daydreams of being a gladiator or a pirate found fruition at the gym, as he started taking Shotoken karate lessons at eleven. But he also studied ballet, perfecting graceful twirls to go with his powerful kicks. He didn't know exactly where all this was going to take him, but he knew it would be somewhere.

After winning the Mr. Belgium bodybuilding title at age seventeen, and marrying a twenty-six-year-old Venezuelan named María, he started running the country's most popular gymnasium, California Gym. Training customers on the mat, he saw martial arts not as a way to keep fit, or even to stay safe, but as a higher calling. Kickboxing, the future star of *Kickboxer* was to say, "is like a religion. If they die in the ring, they don't care, because they believe in a second life, that the kickboxer is someone special on the side of God."

And like a Christian who feels the missionary call, the man who would become Van Damme began to realize that Belgium wouldn't satisfy him. Neither, for that matter, would gym management. He left his first marriage, informing María that he needed to roam the globe in search of stardom. He waved goodbye to his parents, who thought he'd taken leave of his senses. And, most difficult of all, he left behind his beloved dog, a black chow named Tara. Walking around a park, he identified the kindest-looking dog-walker he could see, then entrusted him with ownership of Tara.

A year later, Jean-Claude returned to check in on his old pet. But not wanting to emotionally distress her, he sported a disguise: a pair of sunglasses and a hat, like a noir movie detective. He followed the man and Tara around for three days until he was satisfied, spying on them from a distance. Now and again he would weep beneath his shades.

HIS FIRST DESTINATION had been Italy. There, at a film festival, he scampered around, approaching anyone who looked important and shouting "Look at this!" before performing high kicks and jumps in front of them. Most recipients were unimpressed, but those who showed a flicker of interest were largely investors from Hong Kong. So he headed there next, to try to break into the action-movie business. It didn't work out.

Inevitably, the former boss of California Gym decided that his salvation could be waiting for him in the actual California. So, in 1982, he and a friend named Michel Qissi headed to Los Angeles. Jean-Claude was twenty-one. He had barely any money, no work permit, and an extremely shaky grasp of the English language. But he was convinced that eventually people would be watching his gymnastic moves not with barely concealed boredom but with ardor. "I suffered many years," he says of the first half of the 1980s. "It was a long way until you see the light. You don't know when the light will come, but the light was there."

Navigating through the darkness, however, was no easy feat. He had tried his best to scratch together as much cash as possible before getting on that plane out of Brussels. "I was a pizza boy, a masseur, a taxi driver; I cleaned houses," he remembers. "I was always working and didn't touch the money, so when I came to America, I had a minimum of money." In reality, he was so poor that he ended up sleeping on beaches or in a rental car. He would drive aimlessly around Los Angeles, parking for the night wherever felt right. One time he paid for a star-maps guide to celebrities' houses, drove to the mansion of Sylvester Stallone, and tried to climb a wall into the garden, in the hope of meeting his hero. The police were called. Nonplussed by his excuse—"I just want to do karate with Stallone"—they told him to move on.

During the daytime, he would drive to the major Hollywood studios, talk his way into the parking lots, then slip posed photographs of himself—with a number for a voicemail service printed on—under the windshield wipers of the most expensive-looking cars he could find. Sometimes, on a whim, he'd follow an executive's car home, sit outside, and gaze in awe at the huge house. Thousands of these self-made flyers were attached to windshields, but they were futile: not a single message was left for him as a result.

He pondered whether his name might be the problem, changing it from Van Varenberg to "Frank Cujo" before deciding that associating himself with a movie about a rabid dog might not be the best career move. The one he settled on, "Van Damme"—the surname of a man who had given him a modeling job in Hong Kong years earlier—was better, still Belgian though not *too* Belgian, but that didn't move the dial, either.

Not that he was giving up. "I broke into Hollywood before coming to Hollywood," he explains of his sunny, borderline-deluded attitude. "I made up my mind that I would succeed. And every time I met people, they felt that vibration. If you know you have it, you'll smell like talent. And if you smell like talent, projects will come to you like bees to honey." One day Van Damme visited the Griffith Observatory, looked down at the shimmering expanse of Hollywood before him, and declared, "One day you will all come to see my movies."

The few opportunities he did win were meager. His first Hollywood role (credited as "Jean-Claude Vandamme") was as Gay Karate Man in a twenty-eight-minute affair titled *Monaco Forever*. The job called for him to drive a sports car along Mulholland Drive while attempting to seduce the lead character, and then doing a peculiar karate demonstration on the side of the road when his advances are rebuffed. His next assignment, also in 1984, was as a background dancer in *Breakin'*—he and his pal Michel donned unitards and did their best to get the camera's attention, gyrating and hopping wildly. He was particularly proud of one spectacular leap he had achieved. But when he went to see the film at a movie theater, the moment had been cut.

Despite all the energy he was pumping into his career, it was going nowhere. Then came an unlikely savior: Chuck Norris.

Back in Belgium, Van Damme had written fan letters to Bob Wall, Norris's business partner and Bruce Lee's on-screen sparring partner. And when he arrived in LA, he followed up on it, turning up at Wall's house in the hope of getting a photo with him, something he thought might make people take him more seriously. As it happened, Norris and karate champion Bill Wallace were also there that day, training. An excited Van Damme ran back to his car and returned with a *gi*, ready to join in.

"Big mistake for him," says Wall. "Now, we were in our forties in those days, he was in his twenties, but Bill and Chuck, they did brutal three-hour workouts. I said, 'Kid, whatever we do fifty of, just do five. Because you're not gonna make it.' Of course, he ignores me. We start doing pull-ups—wide, narrow, forehand, backhand. Thirty minutes later, he was puking his guts out."

Van Damme opted to sit out the rest of the Chuck Norris gauntlet—from three-minute assaults on a banana bag to sprints across a concrete tennis court, leaping over the net at full speed. But when the three hours was up, Wallace challenged him to a spar.

"And Bill just beat the shit out of him," Wall recalls. "Chuck, being a kind guy, sits down with him and says, 'Oh gosh, you know, Bill always beats all of us up.' Not true, by the way—Chuck and Bill sparred twice and Bill never wanted to do it again. And I knocked Bill Wallace out after he was world champion. But Chuck was sympathetic—that's the kind of guy he is—and found out [Van Damme] was sleeping in his car. So Chuck hired him as a gofer, even though we already had one. He kept doing the splits and coming in without his shirt on and did that for a year. Only because he was with Chuck Norris could he get away with it."

This was the pivotal moment Van Damme had been waiting for. As well as bringing Norris and Wall sandwiches, washing their cars, and sweeping the floor of their gym, he started working nights as a bouncer at the Newport Beach bar Woody's Wharf, which was owned by Norris's wife, Dianne. Norris even gave him a job on one of his movies, *Missing in Action*, as a stuntman. Suddenly Van Damme was close to the action, literally, and tantalizingly close to the orbit of notorious producers Menahem Golan and Yoram Globus, co-owners of the Cannon Group and financiers of such lurid excesses as *Breakin'* and *Missing in Action*.

"They raped and pillaged and plundered, but you couldn't get close to them," says Wall. "Their building down on Wilshire Boulevard had Israeli guards with machine guns on the roof in front. They were getting assassination attempts every day. The only way Van Damme got to know them was because he worked for Chuck."

Van Damme slowly started to make his move. In 1985 he auditioned for a film called *No Retreat, No Surrender,* performing moves for three Chinese men at a karate school. As a final round he sparred with another hopeful, knocking him out, and won the role of the movie's Russian bad guy, Ivan Kraschinsky. It may have been a forgettable *Karate Kid* rip-off (even retitled *Karate Tiger* in some countries), but the job was a confidence-booster. Around this time, he began wearing a suit and carrying around a briefcase. And then, one night in Beverly Hills, came the encounter that changed everything.

Van Damme was entering a restaurant. Menahem Golan was exiting it. As usual, the former thought with his feet. His right leg flashed up at lightning velocity, arcing around and coming to a rest two inches above the head of the head of Cannon.

"Jean-Claude Van Damme," he reminded the startled producer. "Karate guy."

Golan told him to call his office the next day. So he did—no answer. Not to be put off, Van Damme headed to Wilshire Boulevard anyway, bringing along Michel Qissi. There the duo from Belgium waited for seven whole hours before managing to talk their way into Golan's executive suite. Without hesitation, Van Damme whipped off his shirt, stretched himself between two chairs in the splits position (legend would later suggest he also broke entire bricks on his head, though it's unclear how he got them through security), and began to talk. "I'm fucked. I'm hungry. I've got an accent. They say I'm stupid," he spieled. "But I'm an action guy who can do special things with my body. You can buy me with a piece of bread."

Then came Van Damme's closing gambit, delivered with a simplicity that the producer of *Ninja III: The Domination* might appreciate: "I'm a young Chuck Norris. Maybe one day a Stallone. So, what do you say?"

The tough Golan remained unimpressed. But then he was informed by Qissi that Van Damme was playing the villain in the upcoming sci-fi movie *Predator*. For the first time, he regarded Van Damme with genuine curiosity. If this guy was co-starring with Schwarzenegger in an expensive Fox film, surely there must be something to him.

He and Globus signed up this hungry newcomer—whom Golan referred to as "Gene-Claude Van Damme"—for a string of films, for which he would be paid a pittance. The first of them: something called *Bloodsport*.

GIVEN THAT ITS star's casting originated with a half-truth, it's apt that *Bloodsport* was itself seemingly woven from a series of fabrications. The movie began with an interview in the November 1980 issue of *Black Belt* magazine, in which martial artist Frank Dux outlined the bizarre story of a top-secret fighting tournament in which he had taken part. Taking place once every five years, this shadowy "kumite" saw combatants from around the world battle, often to the death. According to the twenty-four-year-old Dux, he had already won the kumite, using a formidable technique called Dim Mak (Death Touch) taught to him by his sensei, Tiger Tanaka.

"All of which was BS," says Sheldon Lettich, *Bloodsport*'s screenwriter. "It turns out that Dim Mak came from some phony martial arts guy named Count Dante, who used to advertise himself in comic books as 'the world's most dangerous man.' There was no Tiger Tanaka that trained him—that was the name of the ninja master in the James Bond novel *You Only Live Twice*. And I think 'kumite' was another term he picked up from somewhere. A lot of this stuff was hatched within Frank Dux's feverish imagination. Except where Tom Clancy came up with a character named Jack Ryan who has all these macho adventures all over the world, Frank Dux invented a character but named him Frank Dux, and said, 'He won the Medal of Honor in Vietnam. He was in the CIA. And he was the first Westerner to win the kumite.' All made-up stories. But they sounded great."

Lettich had the idea of turning Dux's far-fetched tales—which to this day Dux continues to insist are authentic—into a screenplay. The title, *Bloodsport,* came from a word Dux dropped in conversation one day. And Golan and Globus pounced on the idea, excited by the fact that the *Black Belt* article would legitimize this film, setting it apart from any other martial arts movie out there. The phrase "Based on a true story" would appear in the opening credits, although *Black Belt* editor John Stewart later said he regretted running such an unprovable story. "Not that Cannon really cared if it could be proved or not," says Lettich. "They didn't give a shit about stuff like that. It was just one more element we could add to the advertising."

The film, costing about $1.5 million, would be shot in Hong Kong, just as *Enter the Dragon*—another movie about a shadowy tournament—had been fifteen years earlier. Van Damme was relieved: he still didn't have a green card to work in America. Already exhausted by an intense three-month training program, he threw himself into everything asked of him in the role of Frank Dux, whether it was performing his trademark side splits in the Lions Pavilion at Victoria Peak, battling his martial artist co-stars, or smashing a brick with the raw power of Dim Mak, screaming as his hand crunched down. "I didn't like the title at first," Van Damme says. "But what I put into it as a karate boy and the experience was fantastic. I put in everything I've got, and it was pure passion."

The first viewing of it, however, would prove a calamity. After sitting in the screening room at Cannon to watch the first cut, Lettich exited the building onto Wilshire Boulevard, ashen-faced. "It was horrible," he recalls. "I saw it with Jean-Claude and Frank Dux and a few others, and we were totally in the doldrums after we saw it—the movie just did not work. I don't remember details. All I know is I thought, 'Wow, this is really a travesty.'"

The irascible Menahem Golan, meanwhile, who had discovered that "Gene-Claude Van Damme" was not in *Predator* after all, was going berserk. He hated the film, and specifically hated its star: in meetings, when the name came up, he would scream, "Van Damme is *poison*! He's never gonna make it!" Golan refused to greenlight a sequel to Chuck Norris's *Lone Wolf McQuade* on the grounds that the package included Van Damme, insisting it should feature Michael Dudikoff, a real star, instead. And he decreed that if *Bloodsport* even came out at all, it would go straight to video.

The movie languished in purgatory for fourteen months. But Van Damme was not going to give up. He went right back to driving limousines—*Bloodsport* had only earned him $25,000. And he talked himself into Cannon's cutting room, persuading editor Carl Kress, veteran of *The Towering Inferno,* to let him rework the fight scenes. As Kress and Van Damme snipped away, one focusing on the talking stuff and the other on the kicking, the latter took the opportunity to rummage through discarded footage for *Breakin',* delighted to find his excised acrobatics. "It looked like a rabbit was trying to take so much attention away from the camera," he would later report with glee. "You see a guy going 'BOING! BOING! BOING!' in the air. . . . I was eating the screen with that fantastic jump."

Despite the recutting, things looked pretty hopeless for *Bloodsport.* But Van Damme and Michel Qissi, who had also scored a small role in the film, decided they would just go ahead and promote it themselves. They flew to the Milan Film Festival, where they hyped it up to some Malaysian producers. Impressed by the two relentless Belgians, the producers bought the rights. And the film proved a hit in the East. Then it came out in France, where Van Damme did the splits on the Champs-Élysées and broke through there, too.

Impressed despite himself, Menahem Golan had no choice. He reluctantly informed his star, "Van Damme, the iron is hot."

IT'S DIFFICULT TO pin down exactly why some action stars shoot into the stratosphere and others remain grounded. What did Jean-Claude Van Damme have that, say, Brian Bosworth, Jeff Speakman, or Olivier Gruner did not?

There were his legs, of course. A pair of precision-engineered torpedoes, honed by a combination of karate and ballet, that could flash out at alarming velocity. While Schwarzenegger, Norris, and Stallone lumbered through films, the slim, 203-pound Van Damme pirouetted through them like a lethal pixie. His trademark move, aside from the splits: a lightning-quick scissor kick. Often, his producers would come to claim, the action had to be slowed down in postproduction in order to be viewed properly by the human eye.

There was his sex appeal. Even before he was famous, he had

been the subject of frequent indecent proposals, from women and from men. While chauffeuring two inebriated women in a limo around Los Angeles, he declined their offer of a blowjob—not out of professionalism but because he didn't find them attractive. When he did a stint as a masseur, a male client had suddenly whipped off his robe (Van Damme told the guy, "Buddy, that's it. I'm leaving"). In the context of a brutal action movie, his boyish good looks and charm stood out.

And then there was his relentlessness. If *Bloodsport* had bombed, chances are Van Damme would have licked his wounds and regrouped. Sooner or later he would have emerged again.

Bloodsport, however, did not bomb. On opening weekend in the United States that February, Van Damme and Sheldon Lettich, by now good friends, returned to the apartment Van Damme was renting on Riverside Drive in North Hollywood. The answering machine began beeping, alerting them to new messages. "And this thing is just beeping and beeping and beeping," says Lettich. "It won't stop. And though it had a limit of fifty beeps, there was an overflow. There were that many people calling him to congratulate him and probably to offer him film roles. It felt particularly good to be able to politely throw that back in Menahem's face. He hated the movie so much, and here it was, making more money than *Missing in Action 3,* Cannon's big movie at the time."

It made its budget back that opening weekend, and cruised to $50 million when it opened nationwide. Decades later it would achieve a peculiar honor when Donald Trump, in a 1997 *New Yorker* interview, singled it out as one of his favorite films—"an incredible, fantastic movie"—before revealing that he got his son Eric to fast-forward through the dialogue to get straight to the action.

Van Damme, meanwhile, was finally where he had dreamed of being all these years. That day at the Griffith Observatory, he had told the Los Angeles Basin, "One day you will all come to see my movies." It had happened, even if one critic called him "a muscular Brussels sprout." Unfortunately, lacking the business acumen of the star to whom he was most often compared, Arnold Schwarzenegger, Van Damme had gotten himself tangled up in a string of contracts for low-paying jobs, meaning he would make an average of just $70,000 for his next seven films.

Regardless, he was on his way. Visiting the set of *Red Heat* shortly after the release of *Bloodsport,* his new clout allowing him to wander onto studio lots without worrying about being thrown out, Van Damme accidentally sat in a seat designated for Schwarzenegger. When the Austrian returned from the scene he had just finished, he frowned at the intruder.

"I like your belt. Where did you buy that belt?" Van Damme quipped, repeating Schwarzenegger's words from the set of *Predator* back to him.

Schwarzenegger broke into a smile of recognition. Then he laughed. Last time he'd encountered the Belgian, Van Damme had been a nobody. Now he was worthy of sharing his seat.

CHAPTER 8

...

FOREIGN POLICIES

ON MONDAY, July 1, 1985, Ronald Reagan sat down in the Oval Office to make a critical speech. Two weeks earlier, TWA Flight 847 had been seized by terrorists between Athens and Rome, and the hostages—including dozens of Americans—taken to Lebanon. It had been the biggest crisis of Reagan's White House tenure so far. But ultimately it had been resolved peacefully, thirty-nine hostages freed and on their way home to the States without the use of force. In an address to the nation, Reagan, in a dark suit, crisp white shirt, and blue tie, was to read strongly worded remarks, including the dramatic threat "Terrorists, be on notice . . ."

As technicians in the room prepared for the broadcast, though, Reagan was asked to test the microphone in front of him. And he said something not written on the teleprompter: "Boy, I'm glad I saw *Rambo* last night. Now I know what to do next time."

The comment, leaked and quickly disseminated throughout the nation, was proof that even the president wasn't immune to the power of Stallone's on-screen rampage of revenge. And in turn it bolstered *Rambo: First Blood Part II*'s box office: one marketing executive at TriStar Pictures estimated that these sixteen words may have added $50 million to the sequel's gross.

Then again, nobody should have been too surprised that the sight of Rambo cutting swaths through Russian hordes had quickened Reagan's pulse. He and Stallone had shared a bowl of pop-corn way back in 1981, during a White House screening of *Escape to Victory,* and the actor and the actor-turned-politician had im-mediately clicked. A photograph of Reagan even appeared early in *First Blood Part II,* smiling down from the corner of a shot like an official sponsor. After seeing the movie, the president sent produc-ers Andrew Vajna and Mario Kassar a different photo of himself, in jogging gear, holding a placard that read "Rambo Is a Republi-can."

Reagan's ascendance tangled up movies and politics in unprec-edented ways. For one thing, he had been a Hollywood star him-self, hitting his peak with the 1942 drama *King's Row,* in which his legs are amputated by his lover's angry surgeon father. (Reagan recycled his most famous line in it, "Where's the rest of me?," for the title of his 1965 autobiography.) He had even taken the odd ac-tion role, such as the grim-jawed captain in a crummy submarine thriller titled *Hellcats of the Navy.*

When he triumphed in the 1980 presidential election, the en-twining with Hollywood continued. Reagan was shot by a man obsessed with the film *Taxi Driver* in 1981, yet appeared at the Academy Awards the next day, via a prerecorded video message, as he lay recuperating in bed. He failed to read the briefing book be-fore a crucial summit of world leaders in 1983, telling his exasper-ated chief of staff, "Well, Jim, *The Sound of Music* was on last night." When his anti-ballistic-missile program, announced the same year, was criticized by Senator Ted Kennedy as "reckless *Star Wars* schemes," Reagan responded by telling reporters, "The Force is with us."

It was not Oscar contenders or sci-fi adventures, however, but action movies that became synonymous with the fortieth POTUS. The years before he took office had felt much like a typical 1970s film—morally complicated, gloomy, subdued, with America as the tormented protagonist undergoing an inner crisis. But Rea-gan's administration would tell a new story, simpler and brighter. Taking his lead from the indomitable loner heroes of films such as *Death Wish* and *Dirty Harry* (Reagan would even become Dirty

Ronny in 1985, telling Congress to "go ahead, make my day"), his moves as president became increasingly dramatic demonstrations of strength, as if he were still starring in a rousing movie and charging toward the third act. Many cheered him on. Others were dismayed. Opponents included Michael Rogin, a professor of political science at Berkeley who warned that Reagan was deliberately oversimplifying situations and demonizing foes, saying, "The film fantasies make the violence easier to handle."

As Reagan bombed Libya, escalated the Cold War with the Soviet Union, and invaded the Caribbean island of Grenada, a new nickname for him was coined: "Ronbo." And just as the president looked to Rambo and Co. for inspiration, many of the creators of 1980s action spectaculars saluted him right back.

CHUCK NORRIS WAS one of those keeping an eye on Washington, DC. He declared himself to be "a big Ronald Reagan fan," explaining, "I'm not so much a Republican or a Democrat; I go more for the man himself. I want a strong leader, and he is a strong leader."

Among the many things Norris liked about the president was his attitude toward the Vietnam War. In August 1980, at the beginning of his first presidential campaign, Reagan had stood up at a Veterans of Foreign Wars convention in Chicago and said, "They told us for nearly ten years that we were the aggressors bent on imperialistic conquests . . . It is time we recognized that ours was, in truth, a noble cause."

Norris concurred. While he thought Vietnam had been mishandled, it was in the sense that America hadn't gone in hard enough. "If you don't want to win the battle," he told a journalist, sounding like one of his hard-boiled characters, "don't get involved."

The subject was more than just rhetoric for him. His brother Wieland had been killed in Vietnam in 1970, while on patrol at a US enclave called Firebase Ripcord. So when in the early 1980s producer Lance Hool brought Norris a script set in Vietnam, the star decided he could use it to honor his younger sibling. He and Hool shopped the project around, getting no after no. Finally they got a yes from Cannon Films, which already had a Vietnam script of its own kicking around. Impressed by Norris in a way they had not been by Van Damme, Golan and Globus signed him up to a five-film contract and greenlit both of the war pictures, to be released as *Missing in Action* and *Missing in Action 2.*

The first was set during the conflict itself, with Norris's character, American POW Jim Braddock, tormented by his Vietnamese captors. One torture scene called for Braddock to be hung upside down from a tree, a sack placed over his head, and a ravenous rat placed inside it. After a violent tussle, it would end with the reveal that Braddock has bitten the creature to death, rather than vice versa. "They were getting ready to do this scene, and I see all these mountain rats in cages," remembers Norris. "I say, 'Where's the fake rat?' No one says anything. So I say to the director, 'How are you going to do this scene?' And he says, 'I haven't really thought about it that much.'"

Norris faced a choice: cancel the scene or have an actual rat killed and placed inside his mouth (the American Humane Association had clearly not been invited on set). But he didn't see it as a choice at all. He ordered the animal killed, bit into its bulbous, furry corpse, and was hoisted up for the scene, shaking to simulate a struggle while fake blood poured down the rope.

"The blood is coming down into my mouth, mixed with the saliva of the rat, I'm shaking all over, and finally I'm about to throw up," Norris says, shuddering. "All I can taste is this rat in my mouth and I'm thinking I've got the bubonic plague from doing this with a mountain rat. But the scene was good."

Norris's wife, Dianne, refused to kiss him for a week.

If that shoot wasn't harrowing enough, Norris almost immediately had to head back to the Philippines for the second film, in which Braddock returns to Vietnam after the war to rescue missing-in-action American soldiers from a prison camp that few believe exists. This time Norris would be accompanied by a pre-fame Jean-Claude Van Damme, who had been recruited as a stuntman for the project. "I actually met him at Chuck's house the day before they left," says James Bruner, the film's writer. "We sat on the stairs and had an hour's conversation. I don't know if he actually did any stunts, but he got an offer to do *Bloodsport* while in the Philippines and left. And Chuck wasn't happy about him leaving the production. At least he got a nice vacation."

This film was more action-packed than the other, with Braddock taking the battle to his enemies, storming the jungle with only a slovenly black-marketeer named Tuck (M. Emmet Walsh) and a bulletproof boat for backup. But despite Norris's heroics on-screen, even he was powerless when local gangsters raided the production's remote camp one day. "They recognized me, so I was signing autographs as they're holding me up," he recalls. "They got my autograph, took all my money, and left. At least they didn't shoot anybody."

After a total of five months, the two films wrapped. But back in America, only one of them was proving to be as impressive as Cannon had hoped. The studio decided to switch the two around, releasing the sequel first in November 1984. The one with the rat was hastily retitled *Missing in Action 2: The Beginning* and put out in March 1985.

Rumors still persist that Cannon stole the idea for *Missing in Action* from James Cameron's treatment for *Rambo: First Blood Part II*, which had been written back in 1983. (Ironically, Rambo's call sign in that film is "Lone Wolf," not far from Lone Wolf McQuade.) Bruner, for one, denies it: "The thing that started all of this was the book called *Mission MIA* by James Pollock, an ex–Delta Force guy. A lot of people read it, including Chuck, and that's what gave them the idea for doing an MIA picture. I mean, I didn't know anything about Cameron having a [Vietnam] project." Others, meanwhile, would throw flak at both films for portraying the Vietnamese as diabolical monsters, holding Americans captive years after the war, when there was no evidence to suggest this was true.

"The MIA movement was a fetish of the American political right," says director Oliver Stone, who spent much of the 1980s battling to get *Platoon,* a more complex examination of the conflict, off the ground. "Which I think was completely played out for political reasons. They never discussed the Vietnamese and the suffering of those people. *Rambo* 1 is actually a good film—I read the book and actually was thinking about writing [an adaptation] at one point. It degenerated in the second and third one into this madness of the POW movement."

Norris was unfazed by this type of criticism—at the time, he said of *Platoon,* "If you want all that realism, if you want to be depressed, you can watch the news at night"—or the usual barbs from professional critics, which seemed to have gotten sharper now that he was tackling a hot-button topic. The subject of MIAs was a big one in America's heartland—none other than Clint Eastwood had helped fund a Vietnam POW "rescue mission" in 1983, which yielded no results—and *Missing in Action* did well, making $23 million from a $3 million budget. "It was talked about a lot," says Bruner. "Maybe not in New York and Los Angeles, but the rest of the country. It was a very emotional thing—when we went to see the picture, people were standing up and cheering at the end in the theater."

It was still very much a Chuck Norris vehicle, full of ludicrous action, wanton shirtlessness, and bizarre moments (he is introduced watching a Spider-Man cartoon, before getting angry at a news bulletin about himself and kicking the TV to smithereens). But it also did something new, tapping into the sense of injustice held by a large swath of America.

The man with the beard had sorted out Vietnam. Now for the rest of the world.

THE HEIGHT OF NORRIS'S critical acclaim came with 1985's *Code of Silence.* Written for Clint Eastwood, the Orion Pictures film featured a few lunk-headed lines, such as "If I want your opinion, I'll beat it out of you," but otherwise it was surprisingly naturalistic, the tale of a Chicago cop named Eddie Cusack (aka "Stainless Steel," because he's so squeaky clean) facing down a Colombian drug gang. Director Andrew Davis, born in Chicago himself, set out to achieve the unlikeliest thing: verité in a Chuck Norris vehicle. "I was trying to keep Chuck a little more real," says Davis now. "In terms of surrounding him with real people, so the environment felt a little more honest than some of his cartoonish Vietnam movies."

Dennis Farina, a character actor who worked cases as a real-life Chicago police officer when he wasn't on set, played the hero's partner. John Mahoney, later the Emmy-winning star of *Frasier*, was cast in a small role as a tech wonk teaching Cusack how to use a new police robot. "John had a lot of technical things to say and blew his lines a couple of times," Davis recalls. "And Chuck said, 'Where did we get this guy?'"

The action was kept gritty and lo-fi—Norris did almost all his own stunts, at one point hanging on to the roof of a speeding train. And even though the climax does involve Norris teaming up with the aforementioned robot, PROWLER (Programmable Robot Observer With Logical Enemy Response), *Code of Silence* went on to garner the best reviews of Norris's career. Unlike *Missing in Action*, this one impressed even New York and LA.

"There's a scene where he quietly, awkwardly tries to comfort the mobster's daughter, and it rings completely true," wrote a surprised Roger Ebert, who had previously dismissed Norris's career as "a series of grade-zilch karate epics." He went on to conclude: "It may be the movie that moves Norris out of the ranks of dependable action heroes and makes him a major star."

Norris even received a letter from Burt Reynolds praising *Code of Silence*. "The best compliment I can give you is that I'm extremely jealous," Reynolds wrote. "Just remember, you're only as good as your last film, so be very careful with what films you pick." But Norris's next choices would fail to boost him onto the A-list. While Davis went on to work with a major studio on *Under Siege* and *The Fugitive*, Norris returned to Cannon for a series of outlandish movies, repositioning him as a one-man slaughter machine taking down America's foes. The Middle East–set *The Delta Force* (1986) and South America–set *Delta Force 2: The Colombian Connection* (1990) could have been worse: before being let go from the latter, Michael Winner wrote a script that featured Norris karate-fighting in a kilt. But they also might have been better if an early casting idea had worked out. "Originally the [first] movie was going to be Chuck Norris and Charles Bronson," says James Bruner, who by now was Norris's go-to writer. "I was unbelievably excited—it was going to be probably the biggest thing." Posters featuring the two stars were even created by Cannon. But Bronson dropped out due to a commitment to star in the HBO movie *Act of Vengeance,* and the first *Delta Force* proved only a mild hit, with the second a downright flop.

The films still hit the spot in some quarters. Reagan may have wished for Rambo to intervene in the Flight 847 hijacking, but in fact he got Norris's Major Scott McCoy, with *The Delta Force* virtually reenacting the incident, resolving it with violence rather than diplomacy. It even got a White House screening, which pleased Norris. "Bob Dole and all the senators came to see the movie," he recalls. "They were getting ready to have a bill passed in the Senate that they had to vote on, so Pete Wilson said, 'Chuck, we're not gonna be able to stay through the whole movie.' But when they got up, Bob said, 'Just a minute . . . just a minute.' He was so engrossed. Even when he finally got up and was at the end of the aisle, he stayed there and watched the end of the movie. The minutes said that they were late for the vote because Bob Dole was watching *Delta Force.*"

If conservatives loved the power-affirming scenario the series played out, not least the part where Norris shoots missiles at some Arabs from a souped-up motorbike, others saw it as jingoistic and hawkish. That went for *Braddock: Missing in Action III,* too, with the *Washington Post* writing, "We could say this is mind-bogglingly insulting, lowest-common-denominator-style filmmaking, that it's gratuitously racist and violent and just plain dumb, but then wouldn't that be stating the obvious?" The apotheosis of Norris's flag-waving fantasies, though, is *Invasion USA.*

With Cannon lavishing on it a $12 million budget, gargantuan by Norris standards, it is a pure, pumped-up slab of gun-toting madness. And, amazingly, it began with its star sitting down to flip through an issue of *Reader's Digest*. Norris came upon an article positing that America could be full of secret Communist agents plotting the nation's downfall. It made him anxious. And so he decided that a movie should be made to wake people up to this grim possibility. *Invasion USA* was to see Florida swarmed by an army of Latin American terrorists hell-bent on bringing the state— and all forty-nine others—to its knees. "I know it's going to happen," Norris warned darkly at the time.

James Bruner worked with Norris and director Joseph Zito on the story, which started far smaller than it ended up. "The original script was going to be Chuck teaming up with his father, who lived in a retirement park in Florida," he says. "And then it just blew up into this whole giant thing." Norris's character, retired counterterrorism agent Matt Hunter, became an Everglades-based alligator wrestler (the star claimed he spent weeks training with the beasts on a farm, though no actual wrestling made it into the film). Hunter also has a pet armadillo. "Zito took me on a location scout, which really let me expand the script," Bruner recalls. "I remember sitting in a bar in Florida with Zito and us eating alligator tail, which is actually very good. And that's where we came up with the idea of the armadillo."

Matt Hunter, a stone-cold badass equipped with double denim and hip-mounted Uzis, was designed to feel mythic. And the action had to match. It remains the only Chuck Norris film to feature a squadron of tanks, as the Communists storm Miami, while for another scene an entire street of houses was detonated with TNT. "We blew them up for real!" says Bruner. "They were going to bulldoze them to extend the Atlanta airport runway. So they said, 'Sure, do what you want.'" An entire $5 million of the budget was spent on a sequence in which three hundred terrorists go head-to-head with two thousand National Guardsmen on the streets of Atlanta. "It's a battle like in *Gone with the Wind*," enthused Norris at the time. "One of the best action battle scenes that's ever been done so far."

There would be no *Gone with the Wind*–style critical raves for *Invasion USA*. Its dystopian vision of evil foreigners (at one point, an all-American family putting up their Christmas decorations are the targets of a rocket-propelled grenade) and incoherent plot (twenty minutes of exposition were cut due to what was deemed a subpar performance by Melissa Prophet as a reporter) were too much for even recent Norris convert Ebert, who called it a "brain-damaged, idiotic thriller." Vincent Canby wrote that though Norris "seemed on the verge of becoming a kind of benign Clint Eastwood character, he loses all credibility in this awful film." So much for New York and LA. Though, in a strange turn of events, *Invasion USA* became an underground sensation in Romania, with bootleg videos of the film passed around and helping to fuel the 1989 uprising.

"They use the poster, to this day, in Romania when they protest against the government," says an amazed Bruner. "Ultimately, action movies are about freedom. Overcoming evil, in whatever form it may be. To find out that was one of the inspirations for them to become free, it was really nice. Never in a million years would I have expected it."

And despite all the ultra-violence, in 1986 Chuck Norris became an icon to children, too, with the animated series *Chuck Norris: Karate Kommandos* going on air for five episodes. "I don't like having to resort to violence," a live-action Chuck told tiny viewers at the end of one episode. "It's always my last option."

The dual Uzis were nowhere to be seen.

SYLVESTER STALLONE also got his own cartoon series in 1986. *Rambo: The Force of Freedom* saw the character, who had begun as an R-rated cautionary tale about the consequences of combat, jetting around the globe with a squad of allies, battling General Warhawk and his terrorist organization S.A.V.A.G.E. (Specialist-Administrators of Vengeance, Anarchy and Global Extortion). Stallone did not participate in the cartoon; instead, Neil Ross, who had also recently lent his voice to Monkeywrench in *G.I. Joe*, delivered a loose impression of the star. It lasted sixty-five episodes, with decent ratings, until it and the accompanying toy line were halted after a backlash spearheaded by Peggy Charen, president of watchdog group Action for Children's Television.

"The problem with Rambo as a doll is it's a doll for children," Charen said. "Whereas the movie is not a children's movie—it's a movie for adults."

By the second half of the 1980s, Rambo had come to dominate conversations all over the world, from playgrounds to city halls. In 1986, Soviet cultural leaders held a press conference denouncing *Rambo: First Blood Part II,* calling it "horrible" and "warnography." The same year, a Russian film called *Solo Voyage* was released, about a Rambo-like Soviet commando who mows down evil Americans with bullets and grenades. In the United States, meanwhile, the character was mentioned in hearings in Congress, by the president himself, and of course in almost every development meeting in Hollywood. Was the character a symbol for peace? Or was he pro-war? The debates raged. Jay Kesler, in the Christian journal *Transformation,* even made the comparison that *First Blood Part II* had seemed to hint at: "I fear the United States is on the verge of saying, 'Give us Rambo!' We would rather have him than Jesus Christ. He is offering so much more of what our national psyche craves."

Stallone was perturbed by some of the allusions he read in the press. "I find it incredible, every time some local atrocity happens where a man puts on fatigue pants and takes a rifle and goes into a shopping center, it's 'Rambo murderer slays three,'" he complained in an interview. "Rambo doesn't kill innocents." He dismissed the fact that in 1985 a seventeen-year-old in Missouri who had seen *First Blood* half a dozen times put on camouflage gear and attacked his neighbors with a kitchen knife and pistol. "If it wasn't Rambo it was going to be another fictional character, which he would use as his—I don't know—primer cord."

Perhaps the accusatory headlines helped slow Stallone's return to the Rambo well. Instead, he made *Cobra,* a ludicrously dark cop thriller in which his Lieutenant Marion Cobretti—even dirtier than Dirty Harry—cuts pizza with a pair of scissors when he's not blowing away perps. He made a family drama featuring competitive arm-wrestling, *Over the Top*, about a trucker trying to connect with his son when he's not forcing people's biceps into surrender. But by 1987, those voices yelling "Give us Rambo!" were too loud to ignore. And so the globally iconic crimson headband, which had even recently been adopted by soldiers in the Salvadoran army, came out of storage. For his third adventure the character would go to Afghanistan, where a current, real-life war was being waged between the ill-equipped, malnourished Afghans and the all-powerful Russians. Stallone's lethal alter ego would be parachuted in to help defeat the Soviets.

Rambo III would quickly become a set strewn with conflict itself. Mere weeks into the shoot in Israel, director Russell Mulcahy, his cinematographer, and several others were fired for not aligning with their star's vision. On a baking-hot Saturday afternoon, British second-unit director Peter Macdonald was ushered to Stallone's trailer and asked to take over the film.

"Sly took me in this great big double-decker bus and told me he had always wanted to start working with me," remembers Macdonald, who had choreographed the action on *First Blood Part II*. "I thought, 'Well, that's amazing. Because last time I worked with you was three years ago and the phone hasn't gone since.' It was the usual American bullshit, you know. I had no wish to do it, because it was in such turmoil. It really wasn't going to be a lot of fun. But I had my whole crew out there, all my mates. And if I said no, then I would go, they would probably bring in an A director from America, and they'd all lose their work."

Macdonald took a half-hour walk in the scorching Israeli heat to think it over, weaving between the trailers parked up for the $63 million production. Then he returned and told Stallone and the producers he would do it, on two conditions. First, he wanted Rambo to become more vulnerable, not an unbelievable superhero. Second, he wanted to add humor to the super-solemn script.

"Of course, they agreed to everything," the director says. "And then once we started to shoot, they forgot what they agreed to."

DURING PREPRODUCTION FOR *RAMBO III,* Stallone had flown on a private jet to Denmark with his wife, Brigitte Nielsen. They had checked in to a five-star hotel. And all hell had broken loose.

"There was a huge left-wing demonstration against Stallone, Reagan, and American militarism," says Sheldon Lettich, who was co-writing the script with the star at the time. "Hundreds, maybe thousands, of people were outside his hotel room, shouting and chanting slogans. Then somebody spray-painted graffiti on his plane. I got a call from him after; he was very shaken up. And he said that he had called Reagan personally and said, 'Hey, can you send over some Secret Service agents? Can you check the plane for bombs? Can you send some guys with dogs?' Which they did. Because of the *Rambo* movies, Stallone became this symbol of American militarism. The left, throughout the US and Europe, disliked and even hated him."

The presidential conversations continued once the movie started shooting, the star sometimes ringing the man he called "Ronnie" from the set and talking foreign policy with him, clad in full Rambo gear. "One day I got quite angry," Peter Macdonald remembers. "I said, 'Where the fuck is Sly?' They said, 'He's on the phone to the president.' I thought it was the president of Carolco, so I said, 'Well, tell him to put the fucking phone down and come here and talk.' I didn't realize he was talking to Reagan, not Andy Vajna or Mario Kassar."

The Hollywood icon and the Hollywood president had more in common than their political views. They both received regular death threats. They both were escorted by bodyguards wherever they went. And they both had access to a formidable arsenal of weaponry. On *Rambo III,* Stallone had more than ever: M203 grenade launchers, AK-47s, mortars, flamethrowers, tanks, anti-aircraft guns, attack helicopters, and of course Rambo's iconic knife, which had been lengthened by another two inches, thus outdoing Schwarzenegger's *Commando* blade. After assaulting a Russian with his fists on *Rocky IV,* Stallone would now bring hellfire down on the Soviets, waging a war in front of cameras that Reagan felt unable to wage in real life—though the Afghan rebels were being sent billions of dollars secretly through the CIA's Operation Cyclone.

For Macdonald, who didn't harbor strong political views, it was a case of simply making it through the shoot with sanity intact. "I was hanging on by my fingertips," he admits. "It was like hanging off a cliff, thinking, 'Am I gonna fall this time?'" Incredibly, it was his first film as a director, and he was kept awake at night by visions of somebody dying in the skirmishes he was orchestrating, like the crew member who had plummeted from the waterfall on *First Blood Part II*. His mantra, whenever testosterone levels spiked too high, was "It's just a fucking film!"

One of the tensest days came in Arizona, where two hundred enthusiastic Civil War reenactors were drafted for a cavalry charge sequence. It was a surreal sight, a sea of men behaving like they were actually going into battle. "This guy dressed as a Civil War colonel came up and saluted me and said, 'I've got the men ready for your inspection,'" recalls Macdonald. "I thought, 'What the hell's going on?' These guys would have paid us, basically. We did the first big shot, tracking for about a mile with these horsemen and thirty explosions and bodies flying up in the air. At the end I looked back and said, 'Jesus Christ.' It was like a war zone. Then they all got up and started saluting each other. Behind the colonel a stretcher went by with a body on it, and this guy with a cracked bone saluted from the prone position and said, 'I'll be back as soon as I can, Colonel. I'm sorry I let you down.'"

In Israel, there was another close call, this time involving Stallone. At the end of a long day, while filming a shot involving a Stinger missile and some tanks (an ambulance was on standby perpetually, just out of shot), the star's hair caught on fire without him realizing it. Macdonald burned his hand putting out the blaze. "It could have gotten out of control, because his hair and body were so greased up," he says. "It could have ended up like one of those Buddhist monks who sacrifice themselves. I couldn't tell him, so I had to pretend I was patting him on the back. He looked at me very strangely, because I'd never done that before."

Attempting to direct Stallone was, by this point in the star's career, an extreme sport. George Cosmatos, on *First Blood Part II* and *Cobra,* had rolled over on every argument, so much so that crew members nicknamed him "George Comatose." Macdonald knew he was on thin ice, with Stallone so quick to fire people that the director stopped learning new people's names until they'd lasted a week. While Stallone would later claim that Russell Mulcahy was booted off *Rambo III* for hiring insufficiently intimidating "third-rate male models" to play Rambo's Russian foes, Macdonald remembers it differently. "Sly was walking through the bazaar set and started pointing at guys, saying, 'They don't look right.' And I suddenly realized that the ones being pointed at were all about five foot ten and over. In other words, anyone above him." Another day, during playback of a cut-together sequence, two editors sitting next to Macdonald had vanished by the time the lights went up. "One of Sly's entourage was this Mafia enforcer or something from New York. He said to me, 'Oh, don't worry, Peter, they're history.' I never, ever saw them again. They could be floating around in the Red Sea, I don't know."

Attempts to add more laughs and make Rambo more human were, in the end, fruitless. If anything, the character became more cartoonish than the actual cartoon Rambo, cauterizing a major wound with gunpowder and shooting down a Russian chopper with his compound bow, but with barely a flicker of humor (asked what a blue light does, Rambo replies, "It turns blue"). Macdonald did win one battle, at least: keeping Rambo's child sidekick, an Afghan child named Hamid, played by nine-year-old Doudi Shoua, alive to the end of the movie.

"This kid was annoying; he could drive you crazy," says the director. "But he was full of life and energy. I'm doing a tracking shot with him and Sly with quite a bit of dialogue, and Sly gets his lines wrong. The kid picked him up and told him the right line. Now I'm looking at Sly and thinking, 'This is not going to work too well.' "

Stallone and his entourage skulked off. A short while later, a producer approached Macdonald and said, "Sly's had a great idea. The kid's got to die."

"In the film or in reality?" replied Macdonald.

After holding firm, and cautioning Shoua not to meddle again, lest his character be targeted by a compound bow, the director got Hamid's termination reversed and the sequence back on track.

"I thought it was quite funny," he admits now. "A nine-year-old going to war with the world superstar. 'The kid's got to die.'"

IN THE END, world events worked against *Rambo III*. As the tumultuous shoot stumbled on, the morning newspapers proclaimed a new era of peace: glasnost. "Gorbachev and Reagan are meeting and everyone's shaking hands," Macdonald recalls. "And then every day I'd go and kill thirty fucking Russians. The producers and Sly never really believed that perestroika was happening. That there could be friendship between the good American and the dirty Red."

Reagan, Stallone's ultimate hype man, stepped in to boost the release. "In a few weeks, a new film opens: *Rambo III*," he announced at a congressional fundraising dinner in May 1988. "You remember in the first movie Rambo took over a town. In the second, he single-handedly defeated several Communist armies. And now in the third Rambo film, they say he *really* gets tough." The high-powered audience tittered at the odd scenario: a sitting president making up his own tagline for an action movie. Then they howled at Reagan's punch line: "It almost makes me wish I could serve a third term." But when the actual film arrived in theaters on May 25, despite making a decent $189 million, the Soviet-slaughtering epic already felt like a relic, and a glum one at that. "*Rambo III* has the hardware, but it doesn't have the heart," concluded Roger Ebert. Not that Stallone—who pronounced in an interview, "I'm all for glasnost"—was considering making this the last crusade for John Rambo. He revealed that he was already considering other real-world war zones to drop the character into, favoring Panama.

The inner struggle between sensitive artist and action god seemed to have been won: Stallone even admitted that he had finally given up on his Edgar Allan Poe screenplay, since audiences wouldn't buy him with a quill. "What's he gonna say? 'Yo! Quoth the raven! Yo! Poe!'" he joked, making light of abandoning his passion project. And he even suggested a team-up for his two famous creations, seemingly at total peace now with both.

"We find out that Rambo had a brother, and it's Rocky Balboa. And they meet and we do like a Hayley Mills split-screen," he pondered. "We could keep this baby going on forever."

CHAPTER 9

...

THE GREAT ONE

THEY WERE LED IN, like lambs to the slaughter.

It was an early afternoon in 1986 when four men in white robes and black belts entered an empty soundstage on the Burbank lot of Warner Bros. Before them lay a large mat, around which the studio's top executives, dressed in suits and ties and holding sandwiches, sat cross-legged. Facing them, alone and grim-faced, stood their adversary.

His dark hair was slicked back. He wore an open-necked white shirt and baggy black pantaloons. His feet were bare. His name was Steven Seagal.

As the chatter in the room dropped to a hush, Seagal strode to the center of the mat and lifted a butcher's knife. Looking around solemnly, he pricked his thumb with the blade. After showing his audience the blood, he smeared some on his face. Then he screamed something in Japanese—nobody in the room knew quite what—and, on cue, his four adversaries rushed toward him, their own hands gripping knives.

The event, not exactly an ordinary lunchtime at Warner Bros., had been arranged by the studio's president, Terry Semel, as a showcase for the unknown Seagal's fighting prowess and charisma. Seagal had been recommended to Semel by Hollywood super-agent Michael Ovitz, who employed Seagal's services as a personal trainer. If he excelled, the plan was to build a series of martial arts movies around Seagal, despite his total lack of acting experience. If he failed to impress, he would quietly return to his life as aikido master at a fifty-member dojo, ten miles east of the studio in Sherman Oaks.

But mere seconds after Seagal's scream, it was clear he would not be teaching aikido again. The melee was one-sided, to say the least, and the spectators' mouths dropped open, sandwiches forgotten, as they watched him send his opponents flying. Before long, the mat was littered with bodies and colored with a dramatic streak of blood. Bowing to the Warner Bros. bigwigs, Seagal exited without saying a word. "The demonstration was quite miraculous," reported a giddy Semel. "I'm no martial-arts expert, but he had the ability to send these guys up in the air so effortlessly."

"We were all blown away," marveled another executive, more used to looking at budget reports than at lightning-fast neck strikes. "We'd thought that he might be a star, but that show really convinced everybody."

The mayhem, of course, had been meticulously planned in advance. Ovitz had instructed Seagal to deliver "blood and shock," with the four black belts handpicked by Seagal and told what to do. One of them, Mark Mikita, later told *Spy* magazine, "I still can't believe that those guys at Warners didn't know that it was a rehearsed demonstration. It shouldn't have fooled anybody. Seagal could not toss me or anyone else in the air unless we were in on it."

But it mattered not. At the age of thirty-four, off the back of that violent illusion, Steven Seagal was about to become famous.

EVEN IF THEY WERE now convinced that Seagal could credibly be pitted against an entire army, the Warner Bros. suits didn't know much else about their new acquisition. But that's the way he liked it. Even before he got the opportunity to storm Hollywood, Seagal conjured a cloud of mystique around himself, nurturing myths but rarely confirming facts. Everything about his background was hazy, going right back to his earliest years: while he said on a TV show that he grew up in Brooklyn, his mother told *People* that he was raised in Michigan and California. Then there were his years in Japan. Almost exclusively wearing all-black attire and gold jewelry, Seagal liked to speak of his years as a *gaijin* (outsider) in that country, studying under a legendary sword master, and tell oblique mythic stories, one of which concluded with the punch line "The monk said to her, 'Is that so?' "

Some of the stories about his Japanese years sounded like myths, too. Like the one about a mysterious white dog appearing one day at his dojo. "He just wouldn't leave," Seagal recalls. "So I fed him and he used to stay at the front of the *genkan,* which is the front there. He stayed for maybe a week. Then one night he started barking. I came out and the front of the dojo was on fire. And I thought, 'Wow, that's great. He kinda saved me.' And then the next day he was gone."

Lethal and mystical, like a cross between Dirty Harry and the Dalai Lama, Seagal fascinated those who crossed his path. Not least actress-model Kelly LeBrock, who said of first meeting him in Japan, "He reminded me of an alien." On their first date, he gave her acupuncture. Soon after, LeBrock was under his spell, embarking on a relationship with this man who claimed he was the reincarnation of a seventeenth-century monk. "When I met Steven, I thought he was the biggest liar I ever met in my whole life," she explained. "As you get to know him, you realize there is never a lie from his mouth."

The two married (she was Seagal's second wife, after the Japanese daughter of an aikido master) and started a life together in Los Angeles. Driving around town in a vintage Rolls-Royce, he began to train people in Hollywood in the ways of martial arts, breaking Sean Connery's right wrist while sparring with him for 1983's *Never Say Never Again.* (A decade later, Connery claimed the injury still hurt each time he put that hand in his pocket.)

Seagal started becoming what he termed a "guru" to extremely powerful people in the industry, including Ovitz. Those who made the pilgrimage to see him at his Tenshin Dojo, a humble building furnished with Japanese art on the walls and a small wooden altar, were impressed by his solemn air, his collection of mysterious herbal teas (one, he claimed, contained dried lizard parts), and his allusions to past altercations. "Many, many different kinds of people came to discredit me, kick ass, or kill me, and it never lasted more than a few seconds," he said once of his days in Japan. "I'm not the one who got hurt or carried away."

Here, it seemed, was a genuine tough guy in a city full of pretend ones, and influential men in LA loved his half-told tales. "When you look at him, you see danger," Terry Semel told a *Los Angeles Times* reporter. Arnold Kopelsen, the Oscar-winning producer of *Platoon,* pondered, "Maybe it's this [Eastern] training that creates a strength of character you don't find in a Stallone. Arnold [Schwarzenegger] has a tremendous strength of character, but not the sense of mystery that Steven has." Tony Ludwig, president of Imagine Films, said, "The closest person I've ever seen that carries himself with the same kind of stature is Mikhail Baryshnikov. Steven is smooth, powerful and has this don't-mess-with-me presence. It's almost as if he's a manufactured human being."

Whispers circulated around town—that this shadowy, six-foot-four guy had been a bodyguard for South African bishop Desmond Tutu, that he was now running security for Steven Spielberg, that he was a CIA recruit, a wet work specialist. Had Seagal actually left corpses in his wake? It seemed possible, though he kept details hazy.

"I am reticent to get into that," he says these days of his bodyguarding career, "but I will say that I did do special security operations for some kings and queens and monarchs. Some important people." He did, however, confirm that he worked ops for "the Agency," shrugging off those who noted the lack of evidence by pointing out that the best spies are those who cannot be proven to be spies.

So potent was the aura around him, in fact, that he was to instantly become the front man not only of a big-budget action picture, but one based on the story of his own life.

At least, the story he told.

—

DIRECTOR ANDREW DAVIS was entirely unaware of Seagal when he began developing his fifth movie. His follow-up to Chuck Norris vehicle *Code of Silence* was, at that point in time, titled *Out,* a story about dirty cops on the San Francisco waterfront stealing TVs off ships. Davis was thinking of Jon Voight for the lead role. Then he got a call out of the blue from executives at Warner Bros., summoning him to a restaurant to meet someone else.

"Who's Steven Seagal?" Davis asked, confused.

"Just meet him," he was told. "We think he may have some potential."

So he went to lunch, sat down opposite a poker-faced man in black with zero acting credits, and was told, "I saw *Code of Silence,* and I'm picking you to direct my first movie." Davis was taken aback, but also impressed. "Steven was very thin, and he was handsome," he recalls, "and we talked about politics, all the crap that was going on with the Reagan administration lying and all the stuff that we're doing, selling firearms illegally during Iran Contra." Seagal hinted at deep corruption he was aware of within the US government, something that piqued the director's interest. And, after insisting on a screen test for Seagal—trial sequences for *Out* were shot in Chicago, making use of LeBrock, who had tagged along, as a scene partner—Davis made a radical decision. He called the project's producer and told him he didn't want to make *Out* after all. He wanted to make a movie about Seagal.

"The guy said, 'You're crazy. It's a go picture. Why change the script?'" says Davis. "I said, 'There's a better movie, whether this guy's full of shit or not. The story he tells about going from Detroit to Japan and working for the CIA? Let's make a movie based on that.'"

And so *Out* became *Above the Law,* about Nico Toscani, an ex-spy turned Chicago police officer, who uses the aikido expertise he picked up in Japan to expose a CIA conspiracy involving narcotics and human rights violations. Although Seagal didn't do the actual writing—that was taken care of by Davis, plus *Alien* co-writer

Ronald Shusett and novelist Steven Pressfield—he hovered over the story, pointing out when some small detail was off. Of a scene in which a rogue operative injects a foe with a chemical truth serum, Seagal insisted, "That's not made up. That's something that really happened." His passion for the project was almost fevered; for him, *Above the Law* clearly wasn't just an entertaining yarn—it was something akin to spiritual atonement. In an interview, he explained, "The whole motivation behind me doing this film was my trying to make up for all the things I've seen—and done. I'm tired of us trying to destabilize governments, prop up dictators, and get involved with drug smugglers and crooks."

As the production wound on, Davis was introduced to some of the furtive figures from Seagal's past, including Gary Goldman, a forty-six-year-old mustachioed army veteran, whom Seagal referred to using the code name "Carol." Goldman claimed, with the same vagueness employed by Seagal, that the two had gone on several "missions" together, one of which involved the recovery of "some items that were someplace they shouldn't have been." He spoke highly of Seagal's "capabilities."

The director, however, wasn't entirely convinced. "It gets complicated," Davis says, "because there were people he brought around who *had* been doing some things in the Golden Triangle, you know, and weird things. And I think he appropriated some of their stories. With one of them, they got into it pretty badly: you know, 'You're ripping me off. You're screwing me.' But at that point he was okay. He was accessible. His ego wasn't through the roof. He hadn't made it yet."

At the time, Davis rolled with the autobiographical angle, telling press on the Chicago set that "what we're really doing here with Steven is making a documentary." Albeit a documentary with a body count. As the $8 million, nine-week shoot rolled on in 1987, Seagal—wearing the same all-black ensemble he favored in real life—had input into bouts of combat, one of which features an eyeball-gouging, that left even hardened stuntmen feeling shaky. Far from feeling giddy at his sudden status as a Hollywood leading man or the half a million dollars he was being paid for the role,

Seagal was frequently annoyed—by technical issues or the feeling he was being rushed in his quest to reveal intelligence community misdeeds to the world. "If we only had a little more money and some more time," he griped, "we could really do this right."

The violence, he kept telling Davis, had to feel real. Because it had to match what he'd seen with his own eyes, and possibly inflicted with his own limbs. The action Seagal executed for *Above the Law*—looking as grumpy on-screen as he did off it—was hard-hitting as hell. "You guys think you're above the law," he growls at one point. "Well, you ain't above mine." Cue an alleyway machete duel and a bar fight that compels one character to say, "Stop this motherfucker—he's crazy!"

Nobody, including the execs who had been dazzled by that initial performance, knew for sure if Seagal would connect with audiences. In fact, Bob Daly, the CEO of the studio, had no faith at all, telling Michael Ovitz before the film's release, "Michael, you really screwed me on this one. I ran this movie last night, and it's terrible." Some at rival studios scoffed at the unprecedented experiment, or repeated an urban legend that Seagal was the product of a *Trading Places*–esque bet between Ovitz and other Hollywood power brokers after Ovitz claimed he could turn anyone, even his personal trainer, into an A-list star.

Seagal himself, however, never betrayed nerves. Surely that white dog in Japan hadn't saved his life just for him to fail.

DALY'S FEARS, it turned out, were misplaced. The time was right for a brand-new action star—Schwarzenegger and Stallone had lost their novelty factor, while Warners' in-house bruiser, Clint Eastwood, was still playing gun-toting cops but nearing sixty. And when *Above the Law* hit movie theaters in April 1988, it punched through. Hyperbolic pull quotes were seared across the one-sheets. "Steven Seagal is a dazzling combination of Bruce Lee and Arnold Schwarzenegger with a dash of James Bond," raved syndicated journalist Judith Crist. TV reporter Pat Collins proclaimed, "Steven Seagal is a one-man lethal weapon with high-voltage sex appeal." *Playboy* cautioned, "Make room for Steven Seagal. He streaks through the movie like a state-of-the-art missile."

The buzz was building. "When we tested the movie, the scores were through the roof," remembers Andrew Davis. "He wasn't a WASP-y, blond-haired, Redford-looking guy. Kids of color loved his martial arts and the fact he had an attitude. He was an action star they could relate to. Though it was funny—one of the executives at Warner Bros. said at that point, 'I wish we had a star in this movie.' Meaning they realized they had a movie that, if Mel Gibson were in it, would have been really huge."

As it was, *Above the Law* made $18.7 million, pretty good for a Hollywood *gaijin*. Seagal's manufactured air of mystery, which had mesmerized people in person, seemed equally convincing on giant screens. It may have helped that he behaved the same in interviews as he did in the film. "He speaks with a hushed, conspiratorial purr, as if he were worried that a tiny man hidden under the floorboards might be taping the conversation," one reporter wrote, conveying the general sense that Seagal carried with him dark, redacted secrets. And the act extended to his opinions of his fellow action stars, whom he spoke of with contempt, as if they were children playing at being tough guys, while he, Steven Seagal, was the real deal.

It started with Bruce Lee. Seagal—who claimed to have known Lee, to have trained with him, and even to have taught him a few things (to the disbelief of many, given that when Lee died in 1973, Seagal was only twenty-one)—disparaged the *Enter the Dragon* star on several occasions, sniffing in one article that while Lee's films were "watchable," they were "exceedingly lacking in story . . . [and] just about how many fights you can get in." This drew the attention of Bob Wall, Lee's old friend, who claims that in a pre-fame interview Seagal referred to Lee as a "110-pound rice bandit."

"It said in the article that he owned Tenshin Dojo—so I called information, dialed 411, and got him on the phone," says Wall. "I said, 'Master Seagal, you don't know who I am, but my name's Bob Wall and I'm going to come and kick your ass. I don't want to embarrass you in front of your students, so I'll come at midnight. And I'm gonna bring an ambulance because I'm going to beat the living fuck out of you.'"

Seagal, according to Wall's telling, threatened at this point to shoot him on sight if he saw him. "So I said, 'Well, that's bad news for you,'" Wall recalls. "'I'm an ex-army sniper. And I'm better with guns than martial arts and I'm damn good in martial arts. You're gonna play guns, I'll come over with a gun and we'll see how that works out for you.' He said, 'You're crazy!' and hung up on me."

Wall's mood did not improve when he read another interview in which Seagal disrespected his best friend and business partner, Chuck Norris. "I shouldn't say this," Seagal pronounced, "but I despise being compared with him in any way, shape or form. I wouldn't mind being compared to anybody but him." While Norris, as genial in real life as he was unforgiving on-screen, shrugged off the insult, Wall was apoplectic. Finally, when Seagal issued a challenge in *Black Belt* magazine to fight to the death anybody who believed they could beat him, Wall assembled a group of martial artists—dubbed "the Dirty Dozen"—who would take him up on his dare. While a death match never came to pass, Wall would remain red-hot about the star. "Seagal's a little teddy bear," he says. "If he broke seventeen arms in a movie, it grossed $17 million. If he broke twenty arms, it grossed $20 million. But, you know, he couldn't break his grandmother's arms for real."

Seagal did not stop there. Next to be belittled were Schwarzenegger and Stallone, with a comment that his *Above the Law* hero was "not a cartoon character like you find in films which have gratuitous violence without much of a story, like the *Commando* type of movie . . . The Rambo type is limited to me as an actor and in terms of telling a story."

But his strongest ire was reserved for Jean-Claude Van Damme. The two men had risen together, their first films as stars coming out just a month and a half apart in early 1988, but Seagal was unable to stomach any comparison. The first shot was fired on *The Arsenio Hall Show,* after Seagal, having articulated his desire to make a film about toxic waste that would be a cross between *Three Days of the Condor* and *Terms of Endearment,* was asked, "Do you know Van Damme?"

"No," Seagal replied, maintaining eye contact with Hall.

"You've heard of him?"

"Mmm-hmm."

Nervous laughter from the audience and from Hall.

"What do you think of his work?" Hall nudged.

"Can we change the subject?" Seagal answered, with a grin more disconcerting than his glare. "I just promised all my mentors I was going to be a good boy." Then he immediately broke that pledge, asserting that Van Damme wasn't, in fact, the martial arts champion he claimed to be. "There are an awful lot of people who say that's not true."

Word got back to the maligned Belgian, of course, but Van Damme remained composed. "I don't know if he changed since he became a so-called Buddhist," he reflects, "but Steven Seagal early in his career did talk bad about me with no reason. Said I was a fake, did the same to Stallone. He should not do that. It's not needed to speak bad about somebody you don't know. I was one of his first fans—when I saw *Above the Law,* I said, 'That guy's gonna go far.' People make fun of him because he's overweight; I believe that's a physical problem. But I've got great respect for Steven for his charismatic face."

DESPITE ALL THE SHIT-TALKING, there was—apparently— a gentler side to Seagal. When Pam Grier, one of his co-stars in *Above the Law,* was diagnosed with stage-four cancer in 1988, Seagal was one of the few people who came to her bedside. She would later call his kindness "truly amazing." As he embarked on his next two projects, however, there would be little room for sensitivity or sweetness. Instead, they would be machine-tooled to reinforce his image as the toughest motherfucker on the block.

Since he'd arrived in LA, when not sending people careening across a mat he'd been scribbling away at screenplays. "I came to

America in 1985 to write," he says. "I started writing and people kept saying, 'Steven, we like your stories.'" But even after the success of *Above the Law,* he failed to get his script *Pandora* off the ground. Perhaps this was due to the controversial subject matter: the story posited that the AIDS virus had been created by a renegade wing of the CIA. Seagal would have played a scientist unraveling the conspiracy, aided by a doctor played by Kelly LeBrock. It was announced as a Warner Bros. project but stalled out. Instead, Seagal and his wife ended up starring together in *Hard to Kill,* with LeBrock now not a doctor but a nurse.

Above the Law's documentary-level verité was absent in this follow-up. For one, Seagal's character name was Mason Storm (at one point the film was titled *The Seven-Year Storm*). For another, the plot is splendidly silly. Seven years after being shot by the henchmen of a powerful politician, LAPD cop Storm comes out of a coma, complete with one of the fakest-looking beards in cinema history, and vows revenge. LeBrock's nurse, who has been sneaking peeks at his privates, takes Storm to a ranch that is handily equipped with a dojo and training center. There, while contemplating a single clue—the phrase "You can take that to the bank," uttered by the shadowy figure he was on the trail of almost a decade earlier— he has a breakthrough. The villain is now a senator, and conveniently using the same phrase in TV ads. "I'm going to take you to the bank, Senator Trench," Storm rages, alone in a bedroom. "The blood bank."

As well as introducing Seagal's iconic ponytail to audiences around the world, *Hard to Kill* cemented his image as a yin-yang badass: both serenely mystical and grimly unstoppable (even on a stretcher). At one point he sits atop a mountain peak as an eagle shrieks; at another he mocks the size of a villain's penis. In one scene he says, "First learn how to heal people to be great." Later he intones, "Fuck you and die."

That dichotomy applied off-screen, too. The monk-loving martial artist feuded with director Bruce Malmuth over the shooting of the action scenes, as well as being excluded from the editing process. "We had a bad director who didn't understand the process of directing very well," says Seagal. "It wasn't a war between the two of us, but I will say there were some battles. I just don't think that was a good movie at all." And on his next film, *Marked for Death*, he clashed with the writers, Michael Grais and Mark Victor—renowned in the industry for their *Poltergeist* screenplay with Steven Spielberg—over how much he had contributed to the final script. Ultimately, Seagal got out his calculator and called the *Los Angeles Times*. "I figured it out," he told them. "I rewrote 93% of their script."

Seagal, to the surprise of nobody who knew him, was taking control. Not just of what was being shot—surely the incongruous image of a white horse escaping captivity in *Hard to Kill* could only have come from him—but how it was being shot. After having his nose broken on the set of *Above the Law* during a torture scene, he had proclaimed, "I should have my own people in here, doing the stunts." And so, more and more, he was hands-on with the action, bringing in his own crew of hardened stuntmen, hand-picking every weapon used, and orchestrating the most vicious melees he could imagine: wrists snapping, backs breaking, skulls split by swords. During the filming of one combat sequence in *Marked for Death*, in which Seagal's DEA agent John Hatcher faces down the henchmen of a Jamaican drug lord named Screwface in a department store, even professional stuntmen got freaked out, prompting stunt coordinator Conrad Palmisano to come up with an eyebrow-raising solution. "A bunch of Black guys are attacking him in the scene, so I got a bunch of his Asian stunt team painted black," remembers Palmisano, an event that surely would not be permitted today.

Brutal action. Triple-word titles. The ponytail. Whatever it was, something was working. *Hard to Kill*, despite Seagal's personal distaste for it, made $59 million from an $11.5 million budget, becoming the sixth-highest-grossing martial arts film in history. And *Marked for Death*, also released in 1990, made only a million dollars less. The gamble by Warner Bros. had paid off, and now the other big studios were looking hard at this newcomer, too. Tom Sherak, the head of marketing at 20th Century Fox, who had wooed Seagal away from Warners to make *Marked for Death*, said, "It was a gut feeling that the marketplace was thirsty for a hero, that it was looking for someone to fill the Arnold Schwarzenegger gap. Arnold is the king of that genre, but he is going on to other things. . . . We had a feeling Steven Seagal was that hero."

Seagal may only have been paid $1 million for *Marked for Death*, a fraction of the paydays going to Schwarzenegger and Stallone, but he was now unmistakably on the map. His dedicated fans were coming up with monikers for him—"the Brickster," "Lord Steven," "the Great One"—though none, it has to be said, rival the magnificence of "Mason Storm." In a position that would give anyone a big head, Seagal was developing a huge one.

"Yeah, I could deliver an Academy Award performance," he said in late 1990, in a *Los Angeles Times* article titled "Steven Seagal Wants His Oscar." Gold statues had been a fixation for him since early on in his career: the opening scene of *Hard to Kill* is set on Oscar night 1983 and littered with references to the event ("Come on, guys, I'm missing the Oscars," his hard-boiled cop mutters on a stakeout, presumably keen to get home to see *Gandhi* pick up Best Costume Design). Around the same time, Seagal wrinkled his nose at descriptions of him as an action star. A better parallel, he offered, would be Spencer Tracy, who played a one-armed jujitsu expert in the 1955 thriller *Bad Day at Black Rock*. "Would you call Tracy a martial-arts guy because he did that?" he asked.

More incredibly still, the black-clad neck-snapper was beginning to talk about trying his hand at comedy. It seemed impossible to imagine him rasping wisecracks that didn't immediately result in somebody's elbow pointing in a direction it shouldn't. Even so, as the 1990s dawned, Seagal was laughing all the way to the bank—and this time, it wasn't the blood bank.

CHAPTER 10

...

WELCOME TO THE PARTY, PAL

IT WAS AROUND TEN-THIRTY P.M., LA time, when the hand-cuffs were slapped on Bruce Willis's wrists. All evening, music had been blasting from his Hollywood Hills mansion, the thumping bass lines of Diana Ross songs and jams from his own recent debut album, *The Return of Bruno,* echoing around the canyons and per-meating the walls of nearby homes. This was nothing new—the thirty-two-year-old Willis loved to party, and as usual he had a crowd of friends around, dancing and swimming in the backyard. But on this Memorial Day in 1987, enough was enough. Eventually a neighbor called the cops. Four LAPD officers drove up the wind-ing road to Willis's door and rang the bell. Nobody heard them. They yelled over a fence. Still no response. Finally they walked around the back of the house, spotted an open glass door, and en-tered the party.

Willis had been in the pool when the squad cars arrived. Now he hopped out and steamed into the house, soaking wet, barefoot, and wearing only a pair of slacks. "What the fuck are you doing here without a warrant?" he snapped at the officers, launching into a torrent of cursing. "Why are you saying 'fuck' so much?" replied one of the cops. "What is this, courtesy class?" Willis barked back. "This is how I *talk;* I'm from New York." Soon his arm was being cranked up behind his back as the officer cuffed him. His left collarbone, which he'd broken in a skiing accident in Idaho two months earlier, broke again, causing him to yell in pain. In the ensuing chaos, Willis's brother Robert and three of his friends were arrested, too.

"All we were doing was *dancing*. It was fuckin' Memorial Day—how are you supposed to celebrate it?" he said a year on, unrepentant. "My lifestyle just didn't coincide with the lifestyle of my neighbors." Willis claimed that after he was escorted out of the house that night, he never returned to it again.

The burgeoning movie actor—he had just finished shooting a hectic rom-com called *Blind Date* opposite Kim Basinger—had a penchant for trouble. He had been suspended from his New Jersey high school for participating in what he called "the annual riot," a tradition in which students ran wild around campus. In his formative years, he had regularly streaked down the main street of his town in only sunglasses and sneakers. He was an accomplished brawler; his welder father, David, had told him, "If you get into a fight, fight to win." And even in Hollywood, trouble kept finding Bruce. Not long after that ill-fated pool party, while shooting his second movie, *Sunset,* in which he played cowboy movie star Tom Mix, a man in an LA club repeatedly called him "faggot" because of the hat he was wearing. Willis's arm pulled back for a punch, but this time somebody else's fist connected with the man's head first.

Yet in November 1987, just six months after his Memorial Day arrest, Willis was being handed a police badge (#881). In a strange reconfiguring of that May evening, his new movie would see him playing a cop arriving at a party that goes wrong, a New Yorker in trouble in LA on another public holiday. And this time the experience would end not with humiliation but with very possibly the greatest action movie ever made.

DIE HARD was going smoothly enough, until it came time to cast the damn thing. To avoid having a big star try to bend the story around his image, producers Lawrence Gordon and Joel Silver had spent a long time developing the 20th Century Fox thriller before deciding who should play the hero. They were very happy with the work done by original writer Jeb Stuart and then his successor Steven de Souza, and fully expected to draw an A-lister without trouble. Except, it turned out, nobody wanted to step into the shoes of NYPD detective John McClane. Nor did they want to do the scenes where he was barefoot.

Clint Eastwood passed. He scrawled on the cover sheet of his *Die Hard* script that he didn't understand the humor. Instead, he made *The Dead Pool,* his fifth and final appearance as "Dirty" Harry Callahan, in which he is pursued by a bomb-laden remote-control car.

Richard Gere passed. Having recently toured Central America on a humanitarian mission, the practicing Tibetan Buddhist was looking for roles that challenged him spiritually. *Die Hard* did not fit the bill. "The Dalai Lama guy was like, 'How can I do a movie where I kill anybody?'" remembers Gordon. For his next project, Gere picked *Miles from Home,* about debt-ridden farmers in the Midwest.

Burt Reynolds passed. He would spend the festive season of 1987 shooting his part for the TV special *A Beverly Hills Christmas,* reading a holiday story alongside Jimmy Stewart and Lucille Ball.

A dozen other names were linked to *Die Hard,* depending on whom you ask, though Gordon strenuously denies that an offer was made to Frank Sinatra, then seventy-two years old and, according to Hollywood lore, contractually obliged to be asked since the film was a loose sequel to his 1968 film *The Detective.* Those names include—but are not limited to—Arnold Schwarzenegger, Charles Bronson, Harrison Ford, Al Pacino, and James Caan. Whoever did or did not say no, one thing is certain—nobody said yes. "All the possible action people turned it down," Gordon says. "We had a good script, but we could not get anybody to play John McClane."

Something about the role was scaring people off. It might have been the fact that, although he does incredible feats as he attempts to prevent European villains from taking over the Nakatomi Plaza skyscraper in LA, the hero is a long way from John Rambo or John Matrix. Rather than resolve to take the villains down himself, he first tries to call in the LAPD. He runs away from skirmishes and wriggles through air vents. Oh, and his wife has left him. "James Caan told me directly, 'You know, I read the script and this guy's running away for the first twenty-five pages. I just didn't have the perspective at the time,'" remembers de Souza. This was something brand-new for the genre, and Caan and his movie-star ilk feared it. "In the context of these 'roid-rage, superhuman heroes we had at the time, which I helped contribute to," de Souza says, "this character seemed like a pussy."

The producers were running out of options. And so they went back to a guy they'd approached even before Gere and Eastwood: Bruce Willis. Gordon had been impressed, as had millions of people across America, with what Willis was doing in the smash ABC show *Moonlighting*, snarking up a storm opposite Cybill Shepherd as private detective David Addison. Willis hadn't been able to seriously consider taking *Die Hard*, since the show was taking up so much of his time and energy. But suddenly, serendipitously, Shepherd announced that she was pregnant. The show was to go on hiatus for eleven weeks, making Willis available. Gordon campaigned for him again, despite the actor having little action experience beyond some high-altitude, ladder-based escapades in the *Moonlighting* pilot.

Die Hard's director, John McTiernan, had major reservations; after all, *Blind Date* had terrible word of mouth. "Bruce went and did his television character, and on a big screen it didn't work," McTiernan says. "Once the audience could see Bruce, closely and in higher definition, they didn't like him. They didn't like the smartass thing." But there really wasn't any other choice. And nobody knew this more than Willis's agent, Arnold Rifkin, who decided to hike up Willis's asking price to a staggering $5 million.

As Gordon recalls: "We were told, 'Take it or leave it. If you don't close the deal by Friday, he's gonna go to Japan and do some commercials.'" Aware that if this fell through, the movie would likely follow suit, the producer rushed to the office of Fox chairman Barry Diller, who didn't like action movies and wasn't wild at the prospect of making *Die Hard* in the first place. "It was a brutal meeting," Gordon says. "I told him, 'We got Bruce Willis for $5 million.' He said, 'What? Are you out of your fucking mind?' So I proceeded to tell him that *Die Hard* was ready to shoot, and if we did not do this deal, Fox was going to have no action movie at all for a whole year. It was not a pleasant meeting. But much to his credit, he said, 'Okay, make the fucking deal.'"

It was an incredible amount to pay a guy with only two proper movie roles under his belt, plus two bit parts (Man Entering Diner in *The First Deadly Sin* and Courtroom Observer in *The Verdict*). Willis, who had failed to secure the Mahoney role in *Police Academy* not long before, couldn't believe his luck when the outrageous sum was approved. It wasn't even a role he was particularly eager to play—not like he'd gone after a part in *Full Metal Jacket* a year before, being so big a Kubrick fan that he sat annually through a double bill of *Dr. Strangelove* and *A Clockwork Orange*. A bookworm (he had read Tolkien's *Lord of the Rings* trilogy an estimated fifteen times) and no lover of the action genre, Willis had recently turned down *Lethal Weapon* on the advice of his then girlfriend, who thought it was too violent. Still, with this kind of payday, he'd have as many bullets fired in his direction as Fox thought fit.

"They're going to laugh you off the screen," *Moonlighting* creator Glenn Gordon Caron warned Willis soon after the *Die Hard* deal was locked. "That's a Schwarzenegger movie."

"Oh, Glenn, it doesn't matter," the actor replied with a smirk. "They're paying me so much money that even if it doesn't work out, I'm okay."

DIE HARD had started with a man named Roderick going to see a movie in 1975. Novelist Roderick Thorp, a burly, bald former private investigator best known for his novel *The Detective*, bought a ticket for *The Towering Inferno*, sat through 165 minutes of Paul Newman and Steve McQueen trying to save a large ensemble cast of tanned celebrities, and then went home and had a horrific nightmare. Just as the image of a Terminator rising from flames first came to James Cameron in a bad dream, so Thorp that night imagined a lone figure trapped in a high-rise, fleeing men with guns. He expanded the image into a 1979 sequel to *The Detective*, *Nothing Lasts Forever*, in which a retired NYPD officer named Joe Leland has a very bad Christmas Eve inside the forty-story headquarters of a company called Klaxon Oil. After battling ten invading German terrorists, he drops their leader, Anton Gruber, out of a window, though his daughter dies in the process, too.

It got good reviews, with the *Miami Herald* even anticipating the inevitable big-screen adaptation ("*Nothing Lasts Forever* is truly a one-man show that would require an actor of Sinatra's stature to do it justice") and saluting the cleanness of its high concept ("The building is sealed off; the gang is in an impregnable position, except for Leland, the one-man army, who hides on the top floors above them"). Yet the book would bounce around Hollywood for most of a decade without drawing much interest. Finally a young executive named Lloyd Levin, who worked for Lawrence Gordon, discovered and began championing it. Gordon brought in screenwriter Jeb Stuart. And over two and a half months, Stuart turned Thorp's dense first-person prose, which featured its hero monologuing at length on CB radio and offering long sections of exposition about Klaxon Oil's sideline in arms dealing, into a screenplay.

Much changed, starting with the title. Where *Nothing Lasts Forever* conjured up images of a James Bond movie or Rock Hudson melodrama, *Die Hard* left little doubt as to what to expect. At John McTiernan's behest, the ten terrorists became ten thieves masquerading as terrorists; it would allow them to shake off the novel's fug of solemnity and make it a caper instead. The earnest dialogue and flat supporting characters became similarly zesty, even more so once Steven de Souza was brought in for a pass.

And then there was the hero, no longer Joe Leland but John McClane (it had been "John Ford" in early drafts, after Stuart saw a mural of the Westerns director on the Fox lot). Stuart had already made him younger than his sixty-year-old literary equivalent, but originally envisioned him as suave and sophisticated, with a slick sports coat. This would have worked for Richard Gere, but once the un-suave Bruce Willis was official, McClane was retooled all over again. "I worked with what Bruce was," says McTiernan. "We had to work out: what are the circumstances in which you can like this man?"

Overhauling the script, they leaned into Willis's working-class roots—in his pre-acting days he had been a truck driver and a security guard at a nuclear power plant—and his man-of-the-people charm, honed while working as a bartender in New York, famous for his bone-dry martinis and signature cocktail, Honey I'm Home (the ingredients for which Willis has never divulged). McClane would now begin the movie by declining an invitation to sit in the back of a limousine, getting in the front with the driver instead. He wears a white A-shirt under his flannel shirt, like a stevedore. And beneath the bravado, the grins, the "Yippee-ki-yay, motherfucker," is a guy who's scared shitless.

McTiernan, who saw *Die Hard* as akin to William Shakespeare's *A Midsummer Night's Dream* (albeit with fewer fairies and more C-4), envisioned McClane as a wounded soul. "The secret is that he doesn't like himself," the director says. "He thinks he's a loser. His wife thinks he's a loser. And he's just doing the best he can. He's being a smartass to rise above the pain. And Bruce being a smartass in that circumstance becomes an act of heroism. The audience can like him for it." Adds de Souza: "Vulnerability became a feature, not a bug."

And as the hero changed, so did the villain. A generic heavy was transformed into the polar opposite of a beat cop: designer suit, superior sneer, citations from Plutarch ("Benefits of a classical education"). Hans Gruber—Anton no more—was becoming an action-movie equivalent of the arrogant, expensively dressed bankers to whom Willis once served martinis. Albeit, thanks to the casting of Alan Rickman and the citrus-sharp dialogue, Gruber was a villain so fun that you'd actually want him to walk away with $640 million in bearer bonds, if it weren't for the guy in the A-shirt.

"It's like that cartoon about the mouse looking at the eagle and giving him the finger," McTiernan says, summing up the two opposing forces. And on November 2, 1987, the mouse and the eagle entered Nakatomi Plaza for the first time.

———

BEFORE *DIE HARD,* Bruce Willis hadn't exactly been a gym guy. His preferred environment was a nightclub, not a weight room. And for the past year he had been the public face not of a dietary supplement but of a product named Seagram's Golden Wine Cooler, an alcoholic beverage that quickly became dubbed "Bruce Juice" after a string of high-profile, Willis-starring TV commercials. ("Seagram's Wine Cooler!" he caterwauled in one, using a bottle as a microphone. "It's wet and it's dry!")

But in October 1987, a month before *Die Hard* shooting commenced, Willis started a strict regimen of exercise. He also stopped drinking and began attending AA meetings at Cedars-Sinai Medical Center. The party animal was cleaning up his act. And he was soon glad he had, because his very first shot on his very first night on *Die Hard* was to set the pace.

The parking garage at Fox was five stories high. Willis, arriving directly from the *Moonlighting* set across town, was whisked to the top. As he waited, rubbing his hands together and wearing only a pair of black trousers, a white firehose was looped around his bare midriff, a Heckler & Koch MP5 submachine gun hung via a strap from his neck, and a viscous gel slathered over his exposed skin.

"What's this for?" Willis asked of the gel.

"That's so you don't catch on fire," a crew member replied.

Shortly after, he leaped from the ledge onto an airbag far below, recorded by four cameras. As he did, large plastic bags of gasoline were detonated, unleashing a fireball that blew Willis, he claimed, right to the edge of the bag. "When I landed, everyone came running over to me and I thought they were going to say, 'Great job! Attaboy!'" the actor was to recall. "And what they were doing is seeing if I'm alive because I almost missed the bag."

Willis laughed as he rolled off the airbag. His new girlfriend, Demi Moore, who had come along that evening to see what his new job entailed, did not. As he came to tell it, it was then revealed to him that the jump had been scheduled early in the shoot so that reshoots wouldn't be required if something went wrong and they needed to recast. McTiernan, however, brushes aside the notion. "We didn't do anything dangerous with Bruce. He loved doing it. Movies are a manufacturing activity, and you don't get your workers hurt, period. But that night made it so that he could imagine the real circumstance, and could really say, 'Holy shit, this is fucking crazy!' "

As the shoot ricocheted between Fox soundstages and the 710,767-square-foot edifice that was Fox Plaza, the studio's corporate headquarters, which had areas free for filming, those words may well have been looping around the actor's mind. Juggling *Moonlighting* and *Die Hard*, Willis was run ragged from the beginning: one day he confided to the former's showrunner, Glenn Gordon Caron, "I have no idea what's going on." Certain Fox executives, watching early dailies with frowns, had little faith that Willis's cocksure performance was going to win over audiences. And there was tension between him and McTiernan, who had gotten on well with the musclemen of *Predator* but was struggling to connect with this everyman action star.

"We were all movie people, and he didn't trust us any more than he trusted anybody else," says the director. "He's very, very talented, but also very sensitive. . . . Not the sort of man who could have a genuine, intimate, emotional conversation." Things came to a head toward the end of the first week, when Willis refused to follow the blocking that McTiernan had charted out for an elaborate shot, telling him and the producers, "No, I don't think I'd stand there." Things got heated, until finally the reason became apparent. "It turned out he was afraid someone would see that his hair was thinning," says McTiernan. "We were reblocking for that! We just started laughing. We said, 'Bruce, it's our job to make you look good.' Maybe on television it's more cutthroat than that or people don't pay attention. But the whole reason the cameraman and I were there was to make this man look good. And not just physically good, but emotionally, in all the ways you can conceive of."

The situation gradually improved. Willis, who headed to Las Vegas with Moore three weeks into the shoot and ended up getting spontaneously married at the Golden Nugget hotel, began to

loosen up. Shooting on the top floors of Fox Plaza (the idea of filming in an abandoned skyscraper in Houston had been nixed early
on), the star started to throw wisecracks around both off camera
and on it. He liked to perform comedy bits for the actors playing
the bad guys ("C'mon! Tough crowd!" he'd yell, between takes of
snapping their necks); wriggling through a tighter-than-intended
mocked-up ventilation shaft as the cameras rolled, he improvised
the immortal line "Now I know what a TV dinner feels like."

And, crucially, Willis committed to not only the beleaguered
cop's bravado but his vulnerability, too. "I wanted to find the honesty, the soft side," he said shortly after the shoot wrapped. "I
mean, can you relate to Rambo? Do you have any connection with
this guy?" The best example of Willis's approach was a scene in
which McClane, stripped to the waist and equally emotionally
bared, picks glass out of his feet before relaying a message for his
wife, Holly (Bonnie Bedelia), to an LA cop outside the building
(Reginald VelJohnson). Willis spent ten minutes alone refining
McClane's desperate monologue, imagining what he would tell
new wife Demi Moore if he thought he might never see her again.
"It was something I found looking inside myself," he said.

The tender self-surgery scene, a far cry from the one in
Rambo III where Stallone matter-of-factly stuffs gunpowder into
an open wound, was shot two different ways: once with Willis sob-
bing as he talks, once without. It gave them scope to pull back in
the editing room if they thought they'd gone too far. Ultimately,
though, they'd opt for the version with the tears; Willis would later
call it his favorite scene in the movie.

DELICATE EMOTIONAL SCENES were all well and good. But
Die Hard was an action movie and would have to compete the next
summer with the likes of Schwarzenegger's *Red Heat,* Eastwood's
The Dead Pool, Connery's *The Presidio,* and *Rambo III.* Though
confined to a single building, the action had to feel huge. And that
old *Predator* team of John McTiernan, Lawrence Gordon, and
Joel Silver was determined to deliver.

In the past, they had unleashed hell in a remote jungle in Mexico. Here, they were doing so slap-bang in the middle of Los Angeles, waging war on the sterile streets of Hollywood itself. "To shoot an action film in Century City, that should have been impossible," marvels Gordon. "Marvin Davis, who owned 20th Century Fox, owned the *Die Hard* building—that was the only reason we were allowed to shoot there."

Incredibly, the production blew up an armored SWAT tank on the steps of Fox Plaza, a mostly functioning office building. And one evening two Vietnam-era Huey helicopters thundered above the chichi Avenue of the Stars, posing as FBI choppers for a sequence in which Gruber's crew set the Nakatomi roof ablaze. "I had to go to Marvin Davis to get him to call Zev Yaroslavsky, who was the city councilman for that area, to get permission for it," Gordon says. "Supposedly a man had a heart attack in the hotel near there because they saw the helicopters coming down the street firing, and thought he was under attack."

Inside the building, the mood was similarly stressful. Before the shoot, McTiernan, de Souza, and cinematographer Jan de Bont had walked through Fox Plaza floor by floor, blueprints in hand, assessing how they could eke out maximum tension from the architecture. The set pieces they were now conjuring up were tightly choreographed and blisteringly intense: bullets blasted through boardroom tables, smash-mouth brawls turned into tumbles down stairwells, a giant ventilation fan became a spinning death trap.

And despite his exhaustion from pulling double duty during the shoot, Willis nailed each moment of grimy, desperate action, whether throwing C-4 down the elevator shaft and incinerating two villains on the third floor or evading more of them during a gunfight on the thirty-fourth. (Ronald Reagan would take an office on this floor soon after, leading to an FBI inquiry when an advance party found debris and discarded shell casings littering the ground nearby.) "I like taking risks," Willis said. "And in my everyday life I don't get the opportunity to ride on the top of elevators, to jump off a roof, to fight with [former ballet star] Alexander Godunov. Those things don't come up very much."

They hadn't come up much, either, for Alan Rickman, an English stage actor making his film debut with *Die Hard*. At his audition taping, casting agent Jackie Burch had needed to show Rickman how to hold a gun because he was gripping his prop Heckler & Koch with a limp wrist. He may not have come off as intimidating then, and he was so shy during filming that he barely socialized with anyone except Bonnie Bedelia, his on-screen hostage and off-screen lunch friend. But when the cameras rolled, Rickman was magnetic. Just as Willis infused McClane with his own rough South Jersey wit, so Rickman kept adding bits of elegant mischief to his performance, such as the moment when the robber baron steals a morsel of Christmas food from the Nakatomi buffet. And despite Gruber largely avoiding the mayhem, he did perform one iconic stunt. Where Willis had plummeted twenty-five feet on his first day on the film, the British actor found himself dropped forty feet on his final one, similarly suspicious of the timing.

"I did three takes, at three o'clock in the morning," Rickman recalled in 2015. "It was my very last shot on the film. Now, I wonder why."

MANY INSIDE 20TH CENTURY FOX felt that *Die Hard* was a folly: a trashy run-and-gun action flick with a TV star. Hollywood at large watched as it ran over budget and over schedule, whispering about how much it was going to cost not just Fox but the whole town; because of Willis's $5 million fee, every certified film star was hiking up their own asking price, too. And Fox's marketing department flew into a panic as the July 15 release date rushed up and the film's original poster proved deeply unpopular with the public. "They had a giant shot of Bruce and a little building, and it tested the lowest of any poster they'd ever tested," says Gordon. "So they rejiggered it so it's a big building and Bruce small." Not a good omen for the $5 million man. "The newspaper ads didn't even say his name," recalls de Souza. "His fans had turned on him because of the feud he was having with his co-star on *Moonlighting*. And then at the same time, somebody who worked for Bruce, scraping barnacles off his boat, drowned. There was just a lot of bad press. All over the country, when the trailer played, as it said 'Bruce Willis,' the audience would either laugh or boo."

Still, inside the core group finessing *Die Hard* into shape, there was a sense of quiet confidence. An internal screening, with an audience of just fifteen in a Fox screening room, propelled the viewers to the edge of their seats. "Everybody was stoked," de Souza says. "Even with 'Shot Missing' cards, even with a temporary score, even with Alan Rickman falling onto a blue airbag—you could see the bag below him—we knew it was lightning in a bottle." And the first sneak preview for the public, in Mountain View, California, got a standing ovation. "The helicopter landed on the pad," says Gordon of that night.

When it started to screen for critics, some were unimpressed. "Manipulative, cold, sexist, too long and often badly acted," opined one newspaper review. Roger Ebert, weirdly fixating on the portrayal of a deputy police chief, dubbed it "a mess." But far more hailed its surprising smarts ("The filmmakers even have the wit to play the 'Ode to Joy' when Hans finally walks into the opened vault," wrote Caryn James in the *New York Times*) and punchy, imaginative action ("Before long you're pummeled into six-track, 70 mm shell shock," gasped Jim Emerson for the *Orange County Register*). And at public screenings people went wild for the wily mouse, screaming, "Bruuuuce!" as Willis slipped intact from one seemingly fatal scenario after another. Even a seven-months-pregnant Demi Moore, at another preview, excitedly squealed aloud at the stunts that had made her blanch on set, leading a critic seated nearby to snipe, "If she keeps this up, her water's gonna break." Willis's regular-Joe appearance intensified the tension considerably. "Bruce is not imposing. You don't meet him and go, 'Whoo!'" says Gordon. "It really worked for the film, 'cause you believe he may not make it."

Die Hard became the biggest action movie of 1988 in the United States. Rickman's agent was flooded with offers, beseeching the actor to play more debonair ne'er-do-wells. McTiernan had succeeded in making his actors look good, and accordingly was in hot demand to do the same for others. "Steven Seagal tried hard to get me to do a movie with him," the director remembers. "We shared an agent for a while, and my agent started saying, 'Will you please go to lunch with him?' So I did. But I just didn't want to make that Steven Seagal kind of junk, those fascist movies."

As for Willis, who was by now sporting a beard for his next role, a Vietnam veteran in *In Country,* his status as an A-lister was suddenly rock-solid—$5 million was starting to sound like a bargain. Two weeks into *Die Hard*'s run, a new poster was put out, with his face front and center. With his money, he treated himself to a new wardrobe of clothes and some cars, including a couple of Mercedes-Benzes and a '66 Corvette, which he was busy restoring. "The '66 was the best Corvette made," he explained. "The new Corvette is a piece of shit."

He—and *Die Hard* itself—had the attention of everyone in Hollywood. The movie would have a seismic impact on the action genre as the 1980s turned into the '90s, its simple but brilliant formula inspiring one major production after another. As for Willis, this lean, unimposing, harmonica-playing David was suddenly haunting the hulking Goliaths who had ruled the 1980s.

Sylvester Stallone visited both the *Die Hard* set and the LA premiere, sizing up the competition. It's unknown what he made of Gruber's namechecking of Rambo in a list of products of a "bankrupt culture." As for Arnold Schwarzenegger, who guffawed through a screening of the movie at Fox, not least at the moment when McClane exclaims, "They have missiles, automatic weapons, and enough plastic explosives to orbit Arnold Schwarzenegger!," he happened to be dining at Ivy at the Shore in Santa Monica one evening, soon after *Die Hard* came out, when Willis walked in.

"Know why you'll never be an action star?" Schwarzenegger called out to Willis across the room, loud enough that everyone in the restaurant could hear.

"No, Arnold, why?" Willis replied.

Schwarzenegger flexed his biceps. Pointed to it. Then announced in his thick Austrian accent: "Toothpick arms."

CHAPTER 11

· · ·

SUPERCOPS

JACKIE CHAN WAS BACK in Hollywood. And he was having another terrible time.

First, he had been roped back in for 1984's *Cannonball Run II,* shooting in Arizona, California, and Nevada, with co-stars including Frank Sinatra (in his last-ever film role), Dean Martin, Shirley MacLaine, and an orangutan. Again, Chan was playing an unnamed Japanese engineer—it's unclear whether Sammy Davis Jr., also back again, had figured out that Chan was actually Chinese— and this time he was stuck inside a Mitsubishi Starion, next to hulking Bond villain Richard Kiel. Confining Chan inside a car for weeks on end was not a particularly good use of his talents. And the end result stank. "*Cannonball Run II* is one of the laziest insults to the intelligence of moviegoers that I can remember," Roger Ebert's review said scornfully. "Sheer arrogance made this picture."

At least on that one Chan got to mingle with some showbiz legends. The US film he would make next, *The Protector,* was an even more miserable experience. Raymond Chow, the boss of Hong Kong studio Golden Harvest, was behind this second attempt to break Chan into America, lining up the film especially for this purpose. The logline sounded straightforward enough: a Chinese cop transplanted to New York has to rescue a woman from drug lords.

But the ingredients in this dish were badly matched. On one side was the director, James Glickenhaus, purveyor of dour, grindhouse-ish fare such as *The Exterminator* and future films *Frankenhooker* and *Basket Case 3: The Progeny*. On the other was Chan, who liked his films clean and his action meticulous, not to mention funny.

They did not gel. "I just didn't want to make another ha-ha, chop-sockey, Jackie Chan film," Glickenhaus would say about the experience. "His idea of martial arts I just thought was stupid, a joke." He did not like Chan's Hong Kong movies and had no intention of making a film that looked anything like them. Glickenhaus comprehensively locked the star out of the creative process, then got to work stuffing scenes with naked women, blowjob jokes, and lewd language. At one point Chan's character, Billy Wong, says the line "Give me the fucking keys!" while commandeering a boat, the first time Chan had ever used that curse word on-screen. Billy also shoots a villain while urinating, and goes to a brothel with his cop partner, played by Danny Aiello.

It was the unhappiest Chan had ever been on a set. This attempt to cast him as a womanizing, solemn Clint Eastwood type was far from the image he had been cultivating in the East; even worse, he wasn't allowed to spice up the fight sequences, which were being shot in three days apiece where he would have taken twenty. While there was some inventive stuff in the film—harbor parkour and a brawl on a construction crane—Chan got so frustrated with the squandered potential that one day he walked off set, only to be forced to return to avoid legal trouble. "A cold-blooded killer type did not suit me," he would lament. "I didn't have any say in this role or the film."

The Protector flopped. And once again Chan boarded a plane back to Hong Kong, angry and embarrassed with this attempt to turn him into Dirty Jackie. "Let's just say I can walk down most streets in America without fear of being recognized," he told a reporter unhappily around this time. He felt his talents had been thoroughly wasted in this quest for global acclaim. Critics who had been tracking his career agreed, including Mel Tobias, who wrote,

"Golden Harvest wants to think big, but they introduced Jackie Chan small and B-grade. These movies were idiot movies."

Ever the perfectionist, Chan's first action was not to banish *The Protector* from his mind but to try to salvage it. He underwent the humiliation of asking Glickenhaus for permission to redo the film—the director allowed it, on the proviso that Chan's cut would never play outside of Asia—then shot extra fight footage and painstakingly reedited the film to remove the topless women and curse words. He was protecting his image, as far as he could, from *The Protector*.

Haunted by Glickenhaus's sneer, though, Chan would go further to show him the right way to do things. Much further.

AT ONE POINT early in *The Protector,* a furious police captain dresses down Chan's character, ending his tirade with the words "You had to be a big hero—Billy Wong, supercop." The word "supercop" stuck with Chan. In time he would use it for a film title. But for now he would simply do his utmost to bring a literal representation to the big screen.

Police Story was another action-packed movie about a detective. But this one was born under Chan's hyper-exacting gaze, with him once again in full control. And it was a direct riposte to the aggravating experience he'd just been through. "That film made me angry," says Chan. "I say, 'I'll show you.' And that's how I make *Police Story*."

It started with a walk around Hong Kong, Chan noticing more and more gleaming skyscrapers going up around the city. He rushed home, called his writer friend Edward Tang, and told him he wanted to do a film where all the action revolved around glass. In his mind, Chan could already hear a sweet symphony of shattering panes. He and Tang made a list of the wildest images they could imagine, then constructed a simple story around them, about a cop on the trail of a criminal kingpin. That cop—in an indication that this was the actor's most personal film yet—was named Chan.

Both Chans would prove relentless: the fictional one in his pursuit of his quarry, and the real one in his pursuit of the ultimate action rush. Aided by his stunt team, he went about turning every image on his list into reality. An entire hillside shantytown was constructed, then flattened by a car chase that blazes through it, the vehicles bouncing and lurching through a derby of destruction. Later in the same sequence, Chan hung off the side of a speeding double-decker bus via a pink umbrella, like Gene Kelly in berserker mode. And when that bus was finally halted, two stuntmen flew from the top deck, landing on the asphalt below. That last one was an accident; while they were supposed to land on a car, the bus braked too hard. But Chan kept the camera rolling and completed the shot.

Manic energy courses through *Police Story*, even in the dialogue scenes—Chan has a cake thrown into his face on three separate occasions. But his craziest idea was saved for the end. The climax unfurls, naturally, in a shopping mall, a vast emporium of smashable surfaces. And so the stunt crew making the film, which by now they had nicknamed "Glass Story," took over Wing On Plaza, a mall in Kowloon that agreed to let them in at night, as long as they were cleaned up and out by nine-thirty A.M. Chan installed display cases made of special breakthrough glass he'd ordered from America, which was twice as thick as the usual kind, to make stunts look more real. It had the side effect of sending dozens of stunt players to the hospital, the wounded being carted over throughout the night. "Anything less would not have the same effect," decreed Chan, no matter how many new cuts and bruises there were at dawn.

Being Jackie Chan, he wasn't going to make anyone do anything he wouldn't. In fact, he was saving the most dangerous stunt for himself. He called it a "superstunt," so extreme was its conception. As the boss gangster scurries away at ground level, five stories up Chan would leap onto a metal pole festooned with Christmas lights and slide eighty feet down, finally smashing through six hundred pounds of glass onto the marble floor. The risk level, already high, soared even higher when the lighting director announced that the lights couldn't be powered with batteries—they'd have to be plugged in.

Chan—sleep-deprived from shooting not only *Police Story* but another action film, *Heart of Dragon,* simultaneously—nodded. He might have been feeling nostalgic for that simple *Project A* fall, which had almost killed him but at least didn't involve electricity. A member of his stunt team silently approached, hugged him, and slipped a Buddhist prayer paper in one of his pockets. Then, shouting two words—"I die!"—Chan jumped the eight feet to the pole. Fifteen cameras rolled and two hundred extras gawked as he slid down, the bulbs of the lights sparking, shattering, and burning all the skin off his fingers and palms. All the way down he screamed. Upon impact, blood running down his face and glass shards jutting out of his torso, he shot to his feet, bellowed, and started thumping a hapless stuntman until he was dragged away. "I'd lost my mind—it was as if I'd gone mad," Chan recalled. The makeup and wardrobe teams were loudly weeping; everyone else applauded.

Another star would have let himself be shuttled off to the hospital, along with the night's other casualties, to have his singed palms and dislocated pelvis seen to. Instead, Chan gulped down a beer, got into the back of a car, and headed to the studio where *Heart of Dragon* was being shot, at a time when most people in Hong Kong were having their breakfast.

But when he arrived and reached for the handle to open the car door, he found he couldn't. His hands were shaking too much.

POLICE STORY began a high-voltage streak for Chan. The movie blew up in Asia, grossing massive amounts in Hong Kong, South Korea, Taiwan, and Japan. The last of these had fallen particularly in love with Chan—*Police Story* opened there first—and in the mid-1980s he toured the country regularly to promote his Japanese-language pop albums, performing songs such as "I Stop the Heart Pain," "OK I Love You," and "Iron Man, Soft Feelings." This was the softer, romantic side of Chan, which fans lapped up. When a rumor spread in 1985 that the star was engaged, one Japanese woman threw herself in front of a bullet train. A year later, another fan turned up at the Golden Harvest offices, expressed her dream of bearing his child, then drank a vial of poison. There were other deaths, too, and Chan, who had been secretly involved with Taiwanese actress Joan Lin for many years, was shaken. "I'm very scared," he would admit, "because I have a responsibility with all my fans. I cannot say, 'Now I have a girlfriend, now I getting married, now I have a son.' How many people die?"

There would, therefore, be no flirting in Jackie Chan pictures. He made a solemn pledge in an interview: "Until my pictures become as popular in North America as they are in Asia, I will continue to play men who are indifferent to women." There would be no politics or social commentary, either. Instead, he leaned into what his fans did want: wanton mayhem, albeit the bloodless kind.

As with *Police Story*, he came up with outrageous images, then did whatever it took to bring them to life. A hot-air balloon on which he would land, having leaped out of a plane far above (*Armour of God*). A collapsing house he would stand in front of, outdoing Buster Keaton as it smashed down around him, leaving him untouched (*Project A Part II*). A kinetic battle incorporating the equipment in a children's playground (*Police Story II*). He would scamper through every environment, be it a tribal temple or an inner city, facing down Rottweilers (twenty of them!) and leopards, narrowly avoiding grievous bodily harm at every turn and weaponizing whatever was around him. And through it all he would keep grinning like a cheeky little boy, stopping only to wince when something went wrong, as it often did.

Something went wrong, for real, on the set of *Armour of God*. It was the most routine of action beats: a leap from a roof onto a tree branch, from which he would swing down to a forest floor in Yugoslavia. But on the second take the slippery Chan magic failed him and he plummeted sixteen feet, landing headfirst on a rock. With eight hours of surgery needed to plug the hole in his skull, it was the closest the professional death-defier had come to paying the bill. He suffered a brain hemorrhage, broke his nose and jaw, and lost a few teeth and most of the hearing in his right ear. Chan still views footage of the mishap regularly to remember how lucky he was.

"I watch it to remind myself, because that accident changed my life," he says. "I was in hospital asking myself, 'What have I done? I do nothing. I spend money fooling around, jewelry-shopping.' It used to be that I would think, 'I'll do this tomorrow.' Now, whatever I do, I do right away."

Despite the near-death experience, he was happy: even if Hollywood didn't want him, he was beating Western action heroes at their own game. Chan loved to mention that while *First Blood Part II* brought in $3.5 million in Hong Kong, *Armour of God*, also released there in 1986, made $5 million. "I think I am far better than him—I dare say it straight to his face—because I can do things he can, but he can't do things I can," he said of Stallone in 1988, before deriding the action in *Rambo III*. "We see the cave explode and then there he is, appearing on top of another hill. Really, Rambo?"

Little did he know that over in Los Angeles, Stallone was keeping an eye on Chan's work, too. Albeit with a more favorable opinion. In particular, the American was hypnotized by *Police Story*, and particularly an action beat near the beginning involving that double-decker bus, which Stallone thought would work just great for one of his own in-development projects.

In the early 1990s, Chan's Hong Kong office received a phone call. It was from somebody working for Stallone, inviting him to the LA premiere of *Cliffhanger*. Chan was taken aback; the two stars had never met or even exchanged words. "You're joking," he said to his assistant when she told him the news. But she wasn't— Stallone was even sending an assistant to Hong Kong with two plane tickets so that he could escort Chan back. Excited but confused, the Chinese star headed to the airport.

"I wondered why he'd invited me, but couldn't come up with any answers," he recalls. "I wondered what I should do if I got there and something felt off, like if he didn't know who I was. With my bad English, I wouldn't be able to explain myself. I'd have to just run away."

Chan's trepidation, though, stemmed more from the fact that he was heading back to the country that had roundly rejected him twice before. Would it go any better this time?

ONE PERSON WHO wasn't having any trouble mustering up attention in the United States was Dolph Lundgren. It had all changed for him suddenly. In fact, it had happened within the course of exactly ninety minutes, the run time of *Rocky IV*.

The world premiere was held at Westwood Village in LA on November 21, 1985. Lundgren had put on a white tuxedo and slicked back his hair, now grown out from Ivan Drago's severe flat-top cut. He and Grace Jones got in the limo that had been sent for them, then stepped out onto the red carpet, on which celebrities (Rob Lowe, James Caan, *Diff'rent Strokes* actor Gary Coleman) shared space with a full-blown marching band. Lundgren braced for an onrush; he was, after all, the movie's flashy new villain. But when the photographers started snapping, it wasn't him they were pointing at but his girlfriend. "People kind of shooed me out of the way to take pictures of her," he remembers. "It was like, 'Who's this big guy? Get out of my way.'"

Jones and Lundgren entered the building, beneath a façade that read, in giant red letters, "Stallone—*Rocky IV*." They took their seats. The film played. And by the time the credits were rolling, there was a charge in the air that hadn't been there before. "The movie was so powerful, I was just staring," Lundgren says. "The lights came up and everybody was looking at me. And then we walked out and people were taking pictures of me, almost instead of her. It was a crazy experience. It just blew me off my feet."

He looked humongous on the screen, like Frankenstein's monster with boxing gloves instead of bolts. Lundgren noted that the few times he had smiled as Drago had been edited out, but instead of being repulsed by him, fans of the series—which by now was pretty much everyone—couldn't get enough.

Jones, on the other hand, was shaken. The nobody she'd met in Australia—the man she referred to as "a gentle giant"—had been transformed into somebody else entirely, an A-list movie star. The power balance had changed, and the relationship imploded six months after that premiere. While there had been turbulent periods and dramatic incidents—on one occasion, an enraged Jones had cut up and burned a pair of Lundgren's trousers—they had been a good match. But there was no getting through this. "It was Hollywood that tore me and Dolph apart: the place, the industry, the bullshit," Jones wrote in her memoir. "Out of nowhere, the ego that Dolph didn't have before, he now had." The final straw came when she stormed the Sunset Marquis, the hotel where Lundgren was staying after touring the world for *Rocky IV,* with two female friends and a gun in her hand, banging on the door of his room and screaming. If nothing else, it was a breakup for the ages.

That world tour had seemed as bizarre as his homecoming: six months doing interviews and appearances as *Rocky IV* rolled out across the globe. "Suddenly I went from being this Swedish kid riding to the gym and hitting the bag to facing two hundred Japanese journalists and trying to explain the Cold War policy of the United States," he says. "I was also being perceived as this Russian killing machine—that was a bit strange."

Lundgren was enjoying his new fame—post-Jones, he had women throwing themselves at his 6'4" frame. One newspaper even printed a rumor that he had been offered $14 million to star in a porn flick. "I wish. I would have taken it," he laughs now. "I think in the eighties I was shooting my own porn for free. Fortunately, it never got out anywhere."

But he was also smart enough to know that he had to act quickly to develop his image: so far, he was associated only with villainy. Now was his moment. In front of him was Hollywood, and he would break it.

First he had to present his real self to the public. Not a glowering Russian killing machine, but a relaxed, sun-loving dude. And so was born the fitness video to end all fitness videos: *Maximum Potential.* Posing in front of an American flag, Lundgren opens the video by languidly philosophizing in a lifeguard tower about the human body, while surveying a beach that appears to be occupied only by nubile young women. Then, as electro music kicks in, he bursts into action, running in slow motion down the shore. Over the next hour, he dispenses fitness wisdom from the ancient Greeks, contemplates the meaning of self-motivation, works out in a gym to The Sluggers' "Perfect Man" as fog from dry ice swirls behind him, and teaches those nubile young women how to stretch in front of palm trees. It's as far from Drago's brutalist training routine as could be.

One person who wasn't enjoying it was Quentin Tarantino, whose first-ever screen credit was as production assistant for the video, alongside fellow future director Roger Avary. "The cinematographer was really, really mean to me," Tarantino recalls. "I remember going down to Venice Beach and there's this grassy area where Dolph Lundgren is going to do these exercises, with people behind him following along. And there's just an acre of dogshit, all over this small area of grass. So me and Roger have to clean it up, all right? We're scooping up the dogshit and the crew is fucking around, and me and Roger are going, 'This is literally a shitty job.'"

THE VHS TAPE OF *Maximum Potential* moved units, but it was the big screen Lundgren was more concerned about. How would he follow up the enormous *Rocky IV*? He was a Fulbright scholar who could speak five languages, and part of him wanted to develop into a serious actor. The scripts pouring in, though, were invariably of a less cerebral sort. Usually his character took his shirt off by page ten, if he started with it on at all.

Lundgren was philosophical. "There are two sides to the film business—the intellectual side and the box-office side. But I must start with the box-office side," he said, aware that it was a good move to give the crowds what they were baying for. And out of the stack, *Masters of the Universe* looked the most likely to succeed. Based on the extraordinarily popular line of Mattel toys, of which He-Man ("the most powerful man in the universe") was the most sought-after, it would also draw on one of the most successful animated shows of the 1980s. Even better, with its fantasy world and barely clothed colossus of a hero, the project had strong echoes of *Conan the Barbarian,* Arnold Schwarzenegger's breakout starring vehicle. Cannon, the studio behind *Masters of the Universe,* saw an opportunity to turn Lundgren into the new Arnie, and invested $22 million, their biggest-ever budget.

At first the actor wasn't sure. "I thought it was a joke when I was offered the part," he confessed on the promotional tour. "I remember thinking, 'Oh yeah, right. This is exactly what I need to finish off my career before it's even started.'" But despite He-Man barely having a name, let alone an arc, plus the fact he'd have to trade lines with a latex-faced dwarf named Gwildor, Lundgren hopped on board. "What is more important? Having the love of 20 million kids, which I'll have after *Masters* is released, or having the respect of 20 critics by being in a thinking film?" he reasoned. Lundgren bulked up to his heaviest-ever weight—250 pounds— and threw himself into a grueling seven months of filming.

With a personal trainer, a speech coach, a drama coach, and a "creative advisor," he worked as hard as he ever had. "I was walking around pretty much wearing a G-string for six months, showing every molecule on my body. I couldn't eat anything," he recalls. And his new physique drew plenty of attention even before it had been immortalized on-screen. "It was all muscles and a few leather straps, right?" laughs Lundgren. "Between takes this hot little girl comes up to me eating a popsicle. She's like, 'What are you doing here?' Well, it was Madonna. And she was really checking me out. I didn't recognize her at first. Nothing came about—I think I sent her flowers one time when I was in Cannes after that, hoping something was gonna happen, but it didn't. You can't win 'em all."

Despite all the star's focus, though, the role of He-Man remained as thin as it had been on paper, with the hero eclipsed by a scenery-chewing Frank Langella as antagonist Skeletor. And one evening, while performing his own stunt, Lundgren nearly had a serious accident. "I jumped out of a window onto this platform— a three-story drop," he remembers. "And it was late at night and somebody screwed up. As I'm jumping through the air, I notice that the special fold-up crash boxes aren't there. I don't know, somebody fell asleep or something. The good old eighties."

Behind the scenes, the energy was even more chaotic, with the budget being slashed by Cannon, leading to script pages being torn out seemingly at random. "It was a challenging film to make, but not because of Dolph," says Edward Pressman, the producer trying to re-create the *Conan* magic. "It was a first-time director, and it took forever. Also, Mattel didn't want to risk hurting their great product—they felt if we made a bad movie it would destroy their company. So it took three years or so to get Mattel to go along. And by that time the toys weren't selling anymore."

Indeed, *Masters of the Universe* flopped, making just $17 million back from the $22 million investment (not to mention the hugely expensive promotional campaign). An indication that the swords-and-sorcery genre had lost its luster, it was also a major jolt to Lundgren's confidence: he'd played an American icon and been rejected. "Right now, there are only three actors who can do A-class action films—Stallone, Schwarzenegger, and myself," he said at the time. But was he right?

His next move seemed to be a step back: he played another glowering Soviet bruiser in *Red Scorpion,* as if retreating into the shadow of Drago. It didn't work, with the *New York Times* scoffing, "His heaving chest actually communicates more emotion than his mumbling lips." And so he recalibrated. For his next few films, Lundgren went smaller and grittier, playing cops in modern-day milieus. For 1989's *The Punisher,* he dyed his hair black to play the Marvel Comics vigilante Frank Castle, a former undercover detective who lives in the sewers of New York City, emerging only to fling skull-embellished throwing knives at mobsters. *I Come in Peace,* released as *Dark Angel* outside of the US, made that look like cinema verité: it pitted Lundgren's Houston cop Jack Caine against an extraterrestrial drug dealer bent on injecting humans with heroin so he can extract their endorphins.

"I come in peace," insists the nefarious alien in the finale.

"And you go in pieces, asshole," replies Jack Caine.

Both films have gone on to become minor cult classics, but at the time neither was a hit. "I was really upset," Lundgren admits now. "I was trying to move into a new space. *Dark Angel* was the first time I played a regular guy who had a girlfriend and things like that. I'd had dark hair to get away from the blond kid. I kind of had to just toughen up and keep moving forward." He kept plugging away, hoping to hit the motherlode once again. It wouldn't come with 1991's *Showdown in Little Tokyo,* which saw him play another supercop, teaming up with Bruce Lee's son, Brandon. But one of the negative reviews did make an interesting comparison.

Lundgren, said *Variety,* "could easily be Van Damme–marketable, if only he'd devote as much attention to quality control as he does to pectoral development."

As it happened, within a matter of months he would be teaming up with Van Damme himself. And the results, in the words of Jean-Claude himself, would be "100% pure beef."

CHAPTER 12

...

FUNNY OR DIE

IN 1988, a pin badge started to appear at comic-book conventions. Emblazoned on the round cream surface was a famous face wearing an M1 combat helmet, straps undone. Stamped across it were two words in blood red: "SGT. ROCK."

Anybody who saw one, or fixed one to their lapel, knew it in their bones: a new Arnold Schwarzenegger event movie was coming.

The first clue had been dropped in the end credits of *Predator*: a glimpse of Shane Black's Hawkins reading a *Sgt. Rock* comic book (specifically, issue 408, containing the tale "So Long, Scribbly"). It was a cheeky wink from producer Joel Silver, director John McTiernan, and star Schwarzenegger, the three of whom were planning a new adaptation of the long-running serial. Arnie would be Frank Rock, the granite-tough leader of Easy Company, a fictional World War II US Army infantry unit, who perpetually has his lucky charms—two belts of .50-caliber ammunition—slung over his shoulders. No matter that with Schwarzenegger's accent he would sound more like the guys they were fighting than his fellow grunts, soldiers with names like Hot Head, Bulldozer, and Worrywart. Steven de Souza, who had been hired to hammer out the script, reconfigured Rock as a German who had fled his homeland after his family was killed by Nazis.

The ingredients were in place for a thundering war epic, pitting Schwarzenegger against Hitler. Locations were found. The star had costume fittings. Badges were mass-produced. But *Sgt. Rock* ended up being sunk, rather implausibly, by a member of Monty Python.

"It was just a pile of shootouts and stuff, so I had to jack it up and add a story," remembers McTiernan. "I was gonna steal the plot of a [1958] movie called *Imitation General*. Rock had this problem where he's only a sergeant and people won't listen to him. And in order to organize this defense of a mountain pass, he needs a general. There aren't any generals around, but there's this English cook, who the American guys think sounds like a general. I wanted him to die as a hero, living up to his role. So I went and tried to talk John Cleese into it."

The director and Silver headed to Deauville, France, where Cleese was attending the annual film festival. There, having stormed Normandy like Frank Rock in the comic book story *The Lost Battalion*, the duo tried to persuade Cleese not to let their blockbuster expire. It was to no avail. "He was very polite, but as far as he was concerned, we were just a couple of thug American action-movie makers," says McTiernan. "If he'd seen *Die Hard*, I think he probably would have signed up. But he judged us on our reputation. It would have been delightful—John Cleese would have had so much fun making fun of Arnold and vice versa. That was the whole essence of the movie."

Demoralized by Cleese's rejection, as well as a disagreement between Schwarzenegger and Silver over where to shoot that rocked the production, McTiernan abandoned *Sgt. Rock*. And though it would linger in Hollywood for years—with both Schwarzenegger and Bruce Willis intermittently orbiting it—it never would become a reality. For Schwarzenegger, its implosion may not have stung too much. At this point in his career, he was less excited by the thought of being another tough guy with a funny sidekick than by the notion of being the funny guy himself.

After a string of iconic ass-kicking roles, his mythos was in full bloom. Journalists still didn't know what to make of him, writing about him as if he were not a member of the Screen Actors Guild but a beast from Greek lore. "Start with the head, a huge microwave-size block accessorized with white teeth that look like stumps of chalk," said one. "The neck is huge, crawling with bulging arteries. Then there are the hands: massive things that can aptly—no hyperbole here—be compared to canned hams." Another, after breakfasting with Schwarzenegger, gasped: "He's got muscles they haven't even catalogued yet. He looks in profile like a relief map of Colorado. He looks like an X-ray of a complicated phone line. He's America's Chest."

Schwarzenegger was no longer so much a person as an idea. So in-demand was he that even his old foe Dino De Laurentiis was now begging him to sign a ten-picture deal. His parking space at World Gym near Venice Beach had been upgraded to a slab of terrazzo marble, with his name chiseled into it and bouquets of roses left by admirers propped up against it. Even Schwarzenegger seemed slightly dazzled by what he had become, speaking about himself in the third person. "Arnold is as defined as ever," he told a nodding reporter. "But I'm just not as big anymore. It's just not necessary."

His canny business brain knew that he could no longer get bigger by expanding. Instead, it was time to reduce. First, he shook off that bulk, losing ten pounds. More crucially, he decided to get rid of the violence—at least for now. He had won over the men and the boys. But women were not flocking to see *Commando* or *Predator*.

It was time to pump up his fan base.

THE OPPORTUNITY HE'D been waiting for came quite suddenly, while he and Maria were on vacation. On a ski slope in Snowmass Village, Colorado, a celebrity haven outside Aspen, Schwarzenegger bumped into the director Ivan Reitman. "You're the *Ghostbusters* guy, right?" he boomed across the snow. "You know, I could be a Ghostbuster too."

The encounter lasted just forty seconds, but it made a big impression on Reitman. "He was telling me, 'I can do comedy,'" says the director. That evening, the two men, Robin Williams, and their wives got together in front of a log fire. As the flames flickered, Schwarzenegger drew on comedy tips he'd been given by Milton Berle, the Borscht Belt legend, whom he had first met at his engagement party. There Berle had made him laugh by going up to a weedy-looking man in front of him and saying, "Arnold, thank you so much for inviting me."

Remembering Berle's key lesson—pause before the punch line—the action star killed. And once back in LA, Reitman happened to run into Danny DeVito at a screening on the Disney lot. The idea of pairing the two actors in a comedy popped into the director's head—and wouldn't leave. "I kept saying, 'We should develop something for Arnold and Danny. There's something about their energy, beyond their size. That New Jersey version of DeVito would be interesting against the Teutonic strength of Arnold.'"

The search was on for a concept. Two of the writers invited to pitch were the young British duo William Osborne and William Davies, who had just flown into LA from the United Kingdom looking for work. "We were like these little terriers," Osborne recalls. "We went down to Redondo or Zuma, one of those beaches, sat there, and batted around ideas. And then Will came up with the basic concept for *Twins*."

The idea, hatched under the California sun, was initially called *The Experiment*. The starting point was a genetics trial that results in two wildly different brothers: one a physically perfect and pure-souled Adonis, the other a dumpy dirtbag. And back at Warner Bros., the sun-dazed Brits unveiled it to a rapturous reception. "As the pitch went on, they all started to laugh and nod," says Osborne. "Ivan kept picking up the phone and saying, 'Can you come in here?' And more people would come in. By the end of the meeting there were all these people in there, nodding and laughing."

As the writing process geared up, Osborne and Davies were encouraged to poke as much fun as they liked at Schwarzenegger's macho image. His character, Julius, wears ridiculous clothes, apologizes to villains after hurting them, and is needled relentlessly by

DeVito's Vincent, who terms him (accurately) a "230-pound virgin." "Arnold is the most confident man I've ever met," says Reitman. "And as a result, he's game for anything. There was no ego going on." Confirms Osborne: "We were absolutely given free rein to point out that he is a rather strange version of the perfect human being."

Twins broke away from the kill-and-quip mode of Schwarzenegger's previous movies, focusing on the interplay between the two stars, plus a sweet romance between the timid Julius and a young woman played by Kelly Preston. For a shot showing Julius's post-orgasm face—a huge, goofy grin—Schwarzenegger allowed Reitman to direct his face, in detail. "As an athlete, he has pretty good control of his body in a way that most of us do not, including his facial muscles," says the director. "I was able to get that shot exactly the way I wanted." And the two men worked to subdue Schwarzenegger's bad habits. "We would have sessions where I would talk about how he spoke," Reitman explains. "I said, 'You have a tendency at the end of each paragraph to hammer it home with the use of your eyebrow. I've never seen so much eyebrow-acting since John Belushi.' This film was about being as naturalistic as possible."

Laughter often rang out on the *Twins* set, not least when Schwarzenegger sang "Yakety Yak" on an airplane, something witnessed by a visiting Clint Eastwood. But not everyone was convinced it would translate to a box-office triumph. Screenwriting giant William Goldman, when drafted in to help with the script, had one day announced to Osborne and Davies, "Gentlemen, what we're doing here is washing the garbage. We can wash it as much as we want, but it won't get any cleaner." The Universal top brass were more polite, but far from gung ho. "Everyone said, 'We should pay less for Arnold in a comedy than we would for him in some version of *The Terminator*,'" says Reitman. "'Because he's never done a comedy before.'"

Instead of being upset by this lack of belief, Schwarzenegger used it to his advantage, suggesting an unprecedented deal in which

Sylvester Stallone spars with boxing legend Muhammad Ali on stage at the 1977 Oscars, where *Rocky* would pick up three awards, including Best Picture. While Stallone failed to win one himself, the film catapulted the struggling actor into a new, glitzy world. (PictureLux/The Hollywood Archive/Alamy Stock Photo)

After multiple setbacks, Stallone struck gold again in 1982 with tortured Vietnam vet John Rambo, an instantly iconic character. Despite its dark subject matter, *First Blood* became a smash hit, inspiring ever bigger and bloodier sequels. (Allstar Picture Library Ltd./Alamy Stock Photo)

Arnold Schwarzenegger, in the mid-1960s, flexes on Muscle Beach in Santa Monica, California. The Austrian bodybuilder was relentless in his drive and limitless in his ambition. (Hulton Archive/ Getty Images)

Back in Los Angeles, in 1987, a now astronomically famous Schwarzenegger casually surveys a wall of his own face. When asked why he came to America, he'd once replied, "To make money." (Peter Read Miller/*Sports Illustrated* via Getty Images/Getty Images)

Chuck Norris faces down Bruce Lee, the original king of martial arts cinema, in 1972's *Way of the Dragon*. Although Norris's oeuvre would be largely derided, he was a formidable fighter who had a close friendship with Lee. (Concord Productions Inc./ Golden Harvest Company/Sunset Boulevard/Corbis via Getty Images)

A young Jackie Chan, in 1975, shows off one of his sprightly killer kicks. The Hong Kong dynamo brought comedy and wild athleticism to the action genre. (Keystone Press/Alamy Stock Photo)

"I'm an action guy who can do special things with my body," pronounced Jean-Claude Van Damme, a Belgian black belt with sex appeal and an impish sense of humor. Here, in 1988, he demonstrates his signature move: the splits. (Patrick Robert/Sygma/CORBIS/Sygma via Getty Images)

Rocky IV saw the boxing saga venture into geopolitics, with Dolph Lundgren's Russian machine Ivan Drago slaying Carl Weathers's apple-pie hero Apollo Creed before facing Rocky himself. The film turned Lundgren into an overnight A-lister. (Steve Schapiro/Corbis via Getty Images)

With 1984's *Missing in Action*, Chuck Norris gave the Vietnam War a happy ending for America, nearly ten years after the fact. While many cheered the series, one critic would label it "gratuitously racist and violent and just plain dumb." (AJ Pics/Alamy Stock Photo)

Stallone and wife Brigitte Nielsen pose with Ronald and Nancy Reagan at a White House state dinner in 1985. The fortieth president was so enamored with the star, and his view of American greatness, he namechecked his films in speeches and called Stallone frequently. (Maidun Collection/Alamy Stock Photo)

While other action heroes struggled for years, the mysterious and ice-cool Steven Seagal—pictured in 1990 with then-wife Kelly LeBrock—was elevated to instant stardom by Warner Bros. His ascent was dogged by whispers of bullying, criminal connections, and rampant misogyny. (Paul Harris/Getty Images)

Sensitive and vulnerable, Bruce Willis's John McClane in *Die Hard* transformed the action-movie landscape. A wave of imitators would follow, though only the original would transcend the genre, even becoming a holiday-season perennial. (© 20th Century Fox/AJ Pics/Alamy Stock Photo)

Stung by his failure to break through in the United States, Jackie Chan returned to Asia more determined than ever to make blisteringly breakneck action movies, like 1986's *Armour of God*. (Courtesy Golden Harvest Company/Ronald Grant/Mary Evans)

Schwarzenegger, eager to expand his horizons beyond shoot-'em-ups, successfully teamed up with Danny DeVito in 1988's *Twins*. The odd-couple comedy not only proved he could make the world laugh but earned him more money than any other film. (© Universal/Courtesy Everett Collection)

Stop! Or My Mom Will Shoot had the writers and director of *Twins* behind it, and co-starred Estelle Getty at the height of her *Golden Girls* fame, but proved an unfunny fiasco for Stallone. (AJ Pics/Alamy Stock Photo)

Having punched a rattlesnake, Van Damme bites off its rattle and rigs a booby-trap with it in 1993's *Hard Target*. While his on-screen duels became ever more excessive, behind the scenes he was battling another foe: cocaine addiction. (AJ Pics/Alamy Stock Photo)

Environmental thriller *On Deadly Ground* saw Seagal not only star but take on directing duties, to calamitous effect. After takes, he would serenely declare, "Wasn't that the best thing you ever saw?" (© Warner Bros./Courtesy Everett Collection)

Schwarzenegger, Willis, and Stallone (plus Minnie Mouse and Demi Moore) hype up their corporate alliance, Planet Hollywood, in 1994. It would burn bright before floundering in the late 1990s. (Ron Galella, Ltd./Ron Galella Collection via Getty Images)

Chan, finally accepted and lauded by Hollywood, picks up an honorary Oscar in 2016. Beside him: Stallone, his longtime champion and occasional imitator of his stunts. (Robyn Beck/AFP via Getty Images)

Lundgren, Stallone, Schwarzenegger, and Van Damme on a Paris red carpet for *The Expendables 2* in 2012. Joining forces after years of bitter rivalry, the action titans of the 1980s and '90s survived endless carnage to see themselves revered as big-screen icons. (Antonio de Moraes Barros Filho/WireImage)

he would take no salary at all, in return for 20 percent of the movie's gross. Reitman and DeVito followed suit, taking smaller back ends.

It turned out to be a very, very profitable move. Schwarzenegger and DeVito got people laughing even before the film began, with a one-sheet that saw them clad in identical suits and sunglasses—a titan and a titmouse. "When that poster went up on Sunset in November of '88, it was just so obvious what the joke was," says Osborne. "It really sold itself." DeVito had quickly clicked with Schwarzenegger on set, where the pair called each other "Low Forehead," and riffed on the theme in interviews. "He's like a tree. It's like holdin' on to a moose," he quipped, revealing that another poster, featuring Schwarzenegger with the words "Danny DeVito" over his head, had led to DeVito being asked if he had launched his own fashion line.

Twins was, in the end, humongous. Bigger than *The Terminator,* bigger than *Predator,* bigger than *The Running Man.* And bigger than its seasonal comedy competitors—*The Naked Gun, Scrooged,* and *Dirty Rotten Scoundrels.* The number-one film in America, it made $112 million domestic and $216 million worldwide, netting Schwarzenegger an astonishing sum, likely in the region of $40 million. When he ran into Universal boss Tom Pollock shortly after, the executive pulled out his pockets in a pantomime of despair. "You robbed me blind! You fucked me!" he moaned at Schwarzenegger. The star just flashed a blinding smile.

He had crossed over. Even his mother-in-law and others in the staunchly anti-gun Kennedy clan, who had largely refused to see his previous work, loved *Twins.* "Finally they can see one of my films," Schwarzenegger said, "because no one is getting shot in the head." Says Reitman: "Maria Shriver was thrilled with the movie—she said, 'Finally, people are understanding why I married him!' She later said, 'I don't think he would have been the governor of California had he not made that movie.' Because it opened him up to Californians, and whoever voted for him, the idea of who he really is, as opposed to this kind of gun-toting tough guy."

It was official: Schwarzenegger was funny. According to the data, funnier than Bill Murray or Steve Martin. Now anything was possible.

MIDWAY THROUGH THE *TWINS* SHOOT, as the production shot near LA's iconic Grauman's Chinese Theatre, Reitman had spotted a poster for *Rambo III*. Instinctively, he steered Schwarzenegger toward it and they ad-libbed a scene in which the star considers Stallone's grim, bandana-bedecked face, compares their biceps, and then chuckles in mild derision, waving his rival away like no threat at all.

The meta moment got huge laughs from crowds over Christmas 1988, but it's unlikely to have made Stallone any less grim. Their rivalry was, that year, burning hotter than ever. At the start of 1988, *Playboy* ran Schwarzenegger's interview mocking Stallone's "fucking fur coat"; to another reporter, Arnold derided his foe's security detail ("I think a lot of times this bodyguard stuff is a show"). In February, a story by Wendy Leigh ran in the United Kingdom's *News of the World* tabloid, alleging that Schwarzenegger was secretly pro-Nazi; Leigh later claimed that her source was Stallone, and that he paid for her legal fees when Schwarzenegger sued. (Stallone denied these allegations through his lawyers.) In September, according to the *New York Post*, Stallone and his entourage entered a bar, saw a picture of Schwarzenegger on the wall, and demanded that the owner take it down.

There were attempts to broker a truce, even to put them together in a film. But nothing stuck. Schwarzenegger claimed that Stallone had offered him the villain role in *Cobra* but that he turned it down: "I didn't think I would be done justice, so I stayed away from it." And when Carolco, which had a deal with both stars, arranged a sit-down with both men and director John Hughes for a project named *Bartholomew vs. Neff,* it was an uneasy affair. "Everybody was kind of tense," remembers Mario Kassar. "I managed to get them to come to my house, but the whole thing was, 'Who's coming first and who's coming second?' It was a very funny screenplay, about two neighbors who hated each other and are always doing bad things to each other. But after the meeting, everybody went their own way. It was history."

Then there was *Duke and Fluffy*. Purchased by Carolco after an intense bidding war, the action-comedy script told the story of a loyal mutt and a feisty feline who fall into a machine designed by their scientist master, are transformed into humans, and then team up to retrieve him from criminal clutches. Schwarzenegger signed up to play the dog-man, Duke. Bette Midler was in the picture to play the cat-woman, Fluffy. John McTiernan, John Hughes, and Robert Zemeckis all flirted with directing it.

"Animal movies were popular," says Rick Gitelson, who co-wrote the screenplay with Eric Freiser. "But nobody had done animals turning into people. We thought it was a great way to do an action movie." Schwarzenegger met the writers at the Rose Café in LA's Venice neighborhood to share his notes on the latest draft. "It was brief: 'I like your script. I want to do this,'" Gitelson recalls. "We played with some dog characteristics—if he saw a squirrel, he would chase after it—but that was fairly minimal, other than for little gags. We didn't have him panting."

Alas, the sight of Schwarzenegger pursuing squirrels with Terminator intensity never came to fruition. Nor did it get made with Stallone, considered by Carolco as either a replacement Duke or the lead bad guy. If it had brought the pair of them together, it would surely have qualified for being the unlikeliest peace parley in Hollywood history.

Stallone's interest, however, was an indication that he, too, was becoming increasingly eager to lighten his image. Perhaps he, like Schwarzenegger, recognized that the excess-in-all-areas 1980s, where no amount of carnage seemed too much, was giving way to a more merciful decade. Reagan's hawkish days were drawing to a close; George H. W. Bush, in a 1988 speech accepting his party's nomination, called for a "kinder, gentler" nation. Stallone's box office was reflecting this trend. *Rambo III* had seen him kill seventy-eight people on-screen—a personal record—yet had underperformed. His next release, *Lock Up,* a prison-hellhole picture pitting

Stallone against a gimlet-eyed Donald Sutherland, also failed. Schwarzenegger, during an interview with the *Los Angeles Times*, took pleasure in pointing out its wimpy box office, crowing, "Sly's movie didn't open. It will do $25 million max. . . . Is it true that audiences had booed the trailer?" His prediction was accurate: *Lock Up* would make a total of $22 million.

Stallone was also going through a rough patch at home. Rumors had swirled around his marriage to Brigitte Nielsen: that he had commissioned statues of the pair of them in the nude, that he had bought her $3,000 worth of wigs from a Manhattan boutique, that she was having an affair with either director Tony Scott or her female secretary. One day, in a fit of rage, Stallone thew a thirty-pound weight through a crystal dining table he had had especially commissioned with an image of Nielsen's face etched into it. And then, early one summer morning in 1987, Nielsen loaded her clothes into suitcases and left their Pacific Palisades villa, never to return. "It became a prison for me," she later said of that house. "I couldn't go on living like some kind of robot."

At the time, Stallone released only a terse statement confirming that the power couple, once dubbed "Beefcake and Cheesecake," were separating. But he was to add a line of dialogue to his buddy-cop comedy *Tango & Cash* that revealed his true feelings. In the middle of a prison escape—with that and *Lock Up,* Stallone was doing a lot of escaping from prisons in 1989—Kurt Russell's Gabriel Cash asks Stallone's Ray Tango if he's stopped for a Danish and coffee. Tango replies, "I hate Danish." His ex-wife from Rødovre was clearly still on his mind.

Tango & Cash would, in fact, be a turning point of sorts for Stallone, featuring glimmers of self-deprecation. "Rambo is a pussy," he quips early on, mocking his iconic character just as Schwarzenegger had in *Twins*. He paid tribute to Jackie Chan, the clown prince of action, by restaging the bus stunt from *Police Story* for the opening sequence, with a truck instead. "Glad you could drop in," he tells two villains as they plummet to the asphalt. Unlike his cop in *Cobra*, this guy has a sense of humor, even if his one-liners need some work.

But if there were more laughs than usual in the film, the making of *Tango & Cash* was not always a party. One day, Jack Palance, the legendary tough-guy actor who had been hired to play rat-sniffing drug baron Yves Perret, was sitting with Peter Macdonald, the *Rambo III* director who had taken on second-unit duties for Stallone's latest, watching the star perform a scene.

"It's not the way he should play that," Palance growled, displeased by Stallone's choices. "He shouldn't do it that way."

Macdonald, inclined to cause mischief when he saw an opportunity, replied, "Well, I've worked with Sly three times now, and one thing he enjoys is input. If anybody has input about his performance, he welcomes it."

Palance took the bait. He headed over, waved until he had Stallone's attention, then acted out the correct way of performing the scene.

"I wish I could have taken a picture of Sly's face," Macdonald says now with a laugh. "After the scene was finished, he came over and went, 'What the *fuck* was he on about?' "

Tango & Cash was almost as plagued by trouble as *Rambo III* had been. Cinematographer Barry Sonnenfeld was fired, not long after being told by Russian director Andrei Konchalovsky at a footage review, "It should be ugly and dirty and gritty and hard to look at. This looks like a pussy lit it." Stallone hired a buddy as his stand-in and ended up bantering with him between takes, meaning production had to pay for a stand-in for the stand-in. And firing after firing after firing occurred, with Sonnenfeld, Konchalovsky, and many others all being summarily forced to leave. "When you're in a car with a bad driver," Macdonald says, "you can't grab hold of the steering wheel. You've just got to close your eyes and hope for the best."

Though the movie wasn't exactly a comedy, it did have monster trucks, Kurt Russell in drag, and many other things that don't usually feature in a sober drama. And when it made over $120 million, an emboldened Stallone decided to abandon solemnity entirely.

Hence *Oscar,* a film that would win not a single Oscar.

———

"HAVE YOU EVER MET SYLVESTER STALLONE?" asked Disney chairman Jeffrey Katzenberg.

"Well, he killed me once," replied John Landis, quick as a flash.

The reply, though unexpected, was not inaccurate. Before *Rocky*, in 1975's *Death Race 2000*, Stallone's homicidal character had backed his car over a mechanic played by Landis, at that point a stuntman for hire. Since then, the director and the star had not crossed paths, but they were about to, because Landis was at this point desperate to find a leading man for his new comedy, a remake of a 1967 French hit.

Originally, *Oscar* was to star Al Pacino as Angelo "Snaps" Provolone, a New York gangster in the 1930s who endures a very hectic day, full of mistaken identities and mislaid suitcases. Landis had given Pacino two comedies to watch as prep: *His Girl Friday* and the less well-known *One, Two, Three,* starring James Cagney as a Pepsi-Cola rep in Cold War Berlin. Pacino studied Cagney's rat-a-tat verbal rhythms, the way he spat out lines like machine-gun fire, while the back lot at Universal turned into Depression-era streets.

Then Pacino dropped out. He had decided to make *Dick Tracy* with Warren Beatty instead.

"We were paying him something like $2 million for five weeks," says Landis. "And Warren for two weeks was gonna pay him $5 million. Insane. He says, 'I can't do both movies, because they're both gangsters.' I said, 'Al, please don't do it.' Anyway, he did it." Minus its A-lister, *Oscar* was teetering, despite its superb supporting cast: Chazz Palminteri, Kirk Douglas, Tim Curry, Marisa Tomei. So when Katzenberg suggested Stallone, a man not known for his lightning-fast cadence, Landis shrugged and agreed to meet him. "Sly was funny, and he wanted the role, and he was a monster movie star," the director says. "I think I talked myself into it. I mean, if I agreed to have him, the movie would go. If I said no, the movie would stop."

It went, but Stallone's first pure comedy since *Rhinestone* wasn't a great match for his talents, requiring him to hustle relentlessly around a mansion set, upstaged by a succession of scene-stealers. "He worked hard and there are several moments in the movie where he's not bad," Landis reflects. "But Sly thought that whenever he yelled, that was funny." When the high-energy farce test-screened in early 1991, reaction cards put an end to any wishful thinking that this would prove to be another *Twins*. One viewer scrawled in pen on their card: "Why didn't he take his shirt off and kill anybody?"

"I thought, 'We're fucked,'" Landis admits.

Oscar lost money, but the embarrassment wasn't enough to scare Stallone off comedy. Far from it. For his next movie, he would commit to a ludicrous high-concept idea. And this time he seemed hell-bent on capturing the *Twins* magic for himself. He brought on the director of that movie, Ivan Reitman, as producer. *Twins* writers William Osborne and William Davies were hired to redo the original draft, by Blake Snyder. And Stallone would pair himself on-screen, as Schwarzenegger had done, with a diminutive comedy star. One precisely the same height as Danny DeVito: 4'10".

Stallone and Estelle Getty, the sixty-eight-year-old front woman of the long-running sitcom *The Golden Girls,* were about to make *Stop! Or My Mom Will Shoot.*

On paper, it made some kind of sense. Just as Schwarzenegger had made himself a strongman in chains in *Twins,* neutering his muscleman image, so Stallone would emasculate himself for laughs. In *Stop!*, his tough-cop hero would be forced to contend with his worst nightmare—his elderly mother moving in with him. Tutti vacuums at three in the morning, forces him to eat a nutritious breakfast, even walks in on him while he's in the shower. "What'd you do to my gun, Mom?" Sergeant Joe Bomowski moans when he realizes his mother has stumbled upon his Taurus PT 99 and cleaned it with bleach.

But where *Twins* deconstructed an action star's image to delightful effect, this just dropped an irritating sexagenarian into a generic, *Cobra*-style thriller. "Sly is the funniest man: he's witty, he's clever, he's erudite," says William Osborne. "But even at readthroughs, he was kind of locked into his image. You were always fighting that—'Oh, Stallone doesn't do this' or 'Stallone wouldn't say that.' He and Estelle, who was brilliant and a real trouper, they never really gelled. So, it was a great shoot to do, but a lot of the time you were standing there, sucking in your lips, thinking, 'This scene is just not working.' "

Twins had cost under $20 million, minimizing the action and focusing on character beats. This movie, on the other hand, flung money around with wild abandon, desperate to please Stallone's bombast-loving fans. A huge art gallery was built and filled with pop art, to be destroyed for the opening of the movie, before the entire sequence was scrapped. Six weeks were spent in Santa Rosa shooting the climactic chase involving a truck and a plane. And in July 1991, to celebrate Stallone's forty-fifth birthday, a lobster buffet was served. "I remember we were down on Skid Row, right by the LA train station," Osborne recalls. "There were supermarket-trolley bag people going past us, looking at us sitting there eating lobster. It was just so strange."

Reitman says he tried to stop *Stop!* before it was too late, making a desperate call to Universal chief Tom Pollock. "About a month before shooting began, because Tom was my friend, I said, 'Look, I don't think this is gonna work. Save the money,' " he recalls. "And for a moment Tom killed the movie. Then Ron Meyer, who was Stallone's agent, called up and said, 'I'm going to sue you guys, every which way.' And Tom caved. Later, Stallone got mad at me; he said, 'You didn't give me the A-game!' I said, 'Look, it was just the wrong one for you.' I don't know if he knows that I tried to kill it."

Stop! Or My Mom Will Shoot ended up costing $45 million. Despite his pushback against the writers, Stallone had strained to amuse—for a dream sequence he had even donned a giant diaper. The script fired back against Schwarzenegger with its own meta jesting ("I'll be back," Tutti says, grimacing at a villain, causing Joe to respond, "Cops don't say that, Terminators say that"). The results, though, which closed with a freeze-frame of Stallone forcing a grin, proved borderline unwatchable. "When you watch

Twins, you can see that Arnold is happy making it," Osborne says. "When you watch *Stop! Or My Mom Will Shoot,* all you see is Sly not feeling comfortable. I don't think he was ever comfortable making it."

The fact that it actually made decent money—$70.6 million— was small comfort. It was a farrago ridiculed in every newspaper and film magazine in the land. "There isn't a laugh in this movie. Not a single one, and believe me, I was looking," reported Roger Ebert. "*Stop! Or My Mom Will Shoot* plays as if it were a pilot for a sitcom that wasn't sold in 1975," said Vincent Canby. But the most damning critique was by Stallone himself, venting his feelings years later. "The worst film I've ever made by far," he pronounced. "Maybe one of the worst films in the entire solar system, including alien productions we've never seen. A flatworm could write a better script than *Stop! Or My Mom Will Shoot.*"

One can only imagine the words he used to express himself when he learned that he had been tricked into making the movie by his nemesis. Schwarzenegger had in fact been sent the script, thought it was poor, and decided to have fun with his foe, leaking word around Hollywood that he was desperate to play Joe Bomowski himself.

"He totally went for it," Schwarzenegger was to gloat. "A week later I heard about it: 'Sly is signing now to do this movie.' And I said, 'YES!' "

The last laugh belonged to him.

CHAPTER 13

DOUBLE IMPACT

ON A BAKING-HOT DRIVEWAY in the San Fernando Valley, two hulking Rottweilers snapped to attention. The guard dogs, one male, one female, advanced out of their kennel, heading toward the figure settling into a lawn chair just outside the ranch house. Then, one on either side, the creatures nestled their jaws on their owner's thighs.

Jean-Claude Van Damme smiled and lit up his morning cigar.

Generally, when he woke from his customary four or five hours of sleep a night, his mind was buzzing with ideas for movies. His life was, he liked to explain, 90 percent movies. The other 10 percent he couldn't account for. And so, in the early 1990s, Van Damme's days tended to start with him sitting in that chair, lighting up a stogie (an expensive, illegally imported hand-rolled Cuban), sipping English breakfast tea (very milky, three sugars), patting the heads of his menacing pets, and thinking about the perfect shot, the perfect line, the perfect kick. "I can come up with script up the wazoo when I'm like that," he explained.

When the cigar had been extinguished and the cup was empty, it was time for a workout. His new Chatsworth home hadn't come with a gym, so Van Damme had one built: a 2,500-square-foot fitness palace that was, at his command, perpetually chilled to sixty-one degrees Fahrenheit. Inside it, he pirouetted from one item of brushed-steel fitness equipment to another, perfecting his biceps or thighs, for a total of three hours each day. "I'm so flexible, smooth, a dancer, and I never get hurt," he exclaimed one day to a visiting reporter. Then, stroking his jaw and gazing at it in a mirror: "Look at my face! It's smooth, like a baby."

In that room, which the star's fourth wife, Darcy LaPier, referred to as "the dungeon," it would have been hard to miss that face. Not only did that mirror span from floor to ceiling and wall to wall, but framed magazine covers and posters reflected Van Damme's gleaming grin and pert muscles behind him as well. It was a temple not only to his current physique but also to everything that body had carried him through so far. A monument to success, up the wazoo.

HIS EGO WAS, nobody would deny, enormous. But there were other, more agreeable elements to his personality, ones that had carried him all the way to that lawn chair.

For one, there was his extreme honesty. Like a child who hadn't yet learned how to lie, Van Damme seemed devoid of guile. "I'm not happy with *Bloodsport*," he admitted on the promotional tour for *Bloodsport*. "It could have been much better casting-wise, directing-wise, music-wise, all for the same money."

Also childlike, and infectious, was his giddiness about whatever was in front of him at the present moment. Van Damme had a philosophy: "Do everything fast. Life is so short." This applied to his dining decisions, with the star ordering the most exotic options available. "The sea urchin is high cholesterol, but it is full of iodine," he explained at a high-end sushi restaurant one night. "After you eat, it is best to go home, make love to your wife." It also applied to his love life, which seemed to be running perpetually on double speed. "If I have a date, if I spend time with a woman, I want to get married," Van Damme admitted, shedding some light on why, in his early thirties, he was already on wife number four, Darcy, a former X-ray technician from Oregon.

As his profile rose higher post-*Bloodsport,* there was plenty of attention available to distract him from whichever marriage was currently going downhill. Van Damme was becoming a heartthrob action star: boyish yet cultured, formidable in combat yet approachable, cheeky yet mysterious.

In 1991, *Playgirl* and *Cosmopolitan* both named him one of the world's ten sexiest men. At a banquet hall in San Diego, as two thousand people gave him a thundering standing ovation, a woman screamed, "Take off your shirt!" And men, too, dug JCVD. "Maybe they like me because gay people love beauty in general," he pondered in 1994. "They have a high level of taste."

But up on the screen it took a while for producers to cotton on to the fact that they had a sex symbol on their hands. After *Bloodsport*, Cannon offered Van Damme three options: *Delta Force 2*, *American Ninja 3*, and an original property called *Cyborg*. He took the last. Written in a single weekend and featuring characters named after makes of guitars and amplifiers, it turned out to be a dystopian bummer of a film. In it, Van Damme's heavily scarred hero, Gibson Rickenbacker, navigates a plague-ridden post-apocalyptic landscape, declining sex from a young woman and enduring a near-fatal crucifixion. It made a fraction of *Bloodsport*'s gross, and saw the star taken to court after striking a fellow actor in the eye with a rubber prop knife during a combat sequence. The actor, Jackson Pinckney, a Fort Bragg–based soldier hired to play a villain, was left partially blinded and awarded $487,000, with Van Damme losing the appeal.

He wouldn't return for either *Cyborg* sequel (though a young Angelina Jolie would appear in the first). Instead, 1989's *Kickboxer* would see him back on safer turf, again entering a Far East tournament, again doing the splits, and having coconuts dropped on his abs in one of many high-intensity training montages. It was another big hit.

And then, the next year, something monumental happened. Van Damme took off his pants.

THE PROJECT'S TITLE had caused much vexation, not least for its director, Sheldon Lettich, who had written *Bloodsport* and *Rambo III* and was now moving behind the camera for the first time. Based on an idea by Van Damme, it was a simple story of a deserter from the French Foreign Legion who arrives in America to avenge the murder of his brother. But nobody could agree on what to call the damn thing, so it ended up with different names for different countries. In France, it was called *Full Contact*. In Germany it was called *Leon*, even though the name of the main character was actually spelled "Lyon." In the United Kingdom it was called *AWOL*, after a producer pointed out that it would then appear at the top of alphabetical lists of video titles. In America it was called *Lionheart*, though some involved disliked the moniker because an Eric Stoltz movie of the same name had been released just one year earlier.

Van Damme had his own suggestion: *Wrong Bet*. "It was called *Wrong Bet* in a number of territories, actually," remembers Lettich. "I think Australia and Belgium called it that. But I thought it was a lousy title. If you're looking at the newspaper going, 'Want to see *Wrong Bet*?,' it'd be like, 'No, we're gonna make the wrong bet if we see that one.'"

A better suggestion from the star came on set one day, relating to the shooting of an intimate sequence. In the scene, Lyon, who has been taken into the home of a lusty femme fatale, is exiting a shower. As he strolled out, wearing only a towel, Van Damme made a suggestion to Lettich.

"What if I drop the towel?" he asked.

The director considered it. Then nodded. A single take was recorded, capturing Van Damme's toned derriere on celluloid for the very first time. It made it into the film. And in movie theaters all over the world, no matter what the film was called, people went berserk when the buttocks were unleashed. "I couldn't describe the reactions, but there were reactions to that," says Lettich with a laugh. "It became the signature for a while. Every movie had to have the bare-ass scene."

As *Lionheart* rolled out globally, there were other reactions that its makers took note of. Namely, sobs. "At the end of the movie, I'd look around and I'd see people actually wiping tears," Lettich says. "We didn't make him a total badass in the movie, except when he

needed to be. He was protective of the niece—he got her a bike—
and we had a number of other scenes that were not your typical
action-guy scenes. And when I talk to women about Van Damme,
I've found over the years that they all love *Lionheart.*"

The actor and director were on to something: sex appeal fused
with sensitivity. And they took it further with their next collaboration, 1991's *Double Impact.* Inspired by a 1941 Douglas Fairbanks
movie called *The Corsican Brothers,* which was in turn based on an
1844 novella by Alexandre Dumas, it cast Van Damme as a pair of
twin brothers, playboy Chad and gangster Alex, who are seeking
revenge for the murder of their parents. Although he was still getting only B-lister money, receiving just $600,000 for the film, he saw
this as a major opportunity to showcase his range. "The Alex character is like the other people I've played," he said. "But my Chad
character looks and acts differently. He's not such an emotionless,
macho hero."

The Van Damme rump was deployed again, this time in a soft-
focus fantasy sequence in which Chad and his love interest roll
around nude, the star's first-ever on-screen sex scene. But also featured were multiple scenes in which Chad cries, something his action rivals (Bruce Willis as John McClane aside) would never do.
"You know, makeup people blow menthol in the eyes of actors
sometimes, to get tears to flow," says Lettich. "I didn't have to do
that with JC. When there were tears, they were genuine."

Some sneered at the results. "Van Damme apparently saw Jeremy Irons as twin brothers in *Dead Ringers* and decided to play
two roles in his latest movie," wrote one critic. "Let's hope he never
sees *Kind Hearts and Coronets,* in which Alec Guinness played
eight roles." But others were delighted by the beaming, romantic
Chad, who is introduced doing the splits in front of an aerobics
class packed with smitten women. "*Double Impact* succeeds because Van Damme provides such a likeable screen presence," went
another review. "It marks his giant step into the big time."

That prediction would turn out to be correct.

VAN DAMME HAD A LONG-STANDING RULE: there was only one fellow action star who could kill him on-screen. "We ended up discussing this," recalls Sheldon Lettich. "He said, 'Bruce Willis? No. Wesley Snipes? Forget about it. Even Arnold Schwarzenegger is not good enough to kill me. But Stallone? I worship Stallone. He can do it.' "

For now, no opportunity to be pulverized by the fists of the *Rocky* star presented itself. But an action script did come along that featured two juicy possible roles: a good guy and a bad guy, both genetically enhanced, reanimated super-soldiers, hell-bent on exterminating the other. Reading the screenplay for *Universal Soldier*, Van Damme liked both characters, the benevolent Private Luc Deveraux and the psychotic Sergeant Andrew Scott. That said, he had no intention of breaking his rule and being impaled on a spike by his co-star, Dolph Lundgren—someone he may have felt a little jealous of, given Lundgren had been recently blessed with a Stallone ass-kicking in *Rocky IV*.

"It wouldn't have worked if Jean-Claude was the bad guy and I was the good guy; the size and everything," Lundgren, who was happy to seize the role of Scott, says with a shrug. "I thought it was good casting. And it was fun, like those old serial pictures where they paired two stars together. We got equal billing and there was a little bit of rivalry."

Van Damme came into the film with more to prove. Afforded a $23 million budget by Carolco, *Universal Soldier* was his first true mainstream project, and director Roland Emmerich hadn't even heard of him when the casting process began. Lundgren, on the other hand, was well known to all as the former Ivan Drago, even if his latest run of films had faltered. So, on the first day of filming, as the two stars prepared for their first scene together—a brutal fistfight at the end of the Vietnam War–set prologue—Van Damme sidled up to Lundgren and told him not to pull his punches. They went at it for real, two action stars thumping it out in front of a startled crew.

"Dolph was a great opponent," remembers Van Damme. "He's a big boy, strong bones, so when he was hitting me on *Soldier* it felt like a mule. I mean, he's a powerful guy. And I'm good at taking blows because I was trained to take real blows in fighting before. It looks good on camera because you don't see so much of the control: you see his meat touching my meat, the impact, the shaking of the body. In slow motion, it has a great effect."

The cameras survived the dust-up. And as the shoot went on, the two stars began to warm to each other, the intensity turning to friendly competition over who could bench the most reps in the trailer that subbed for a gym. Van Damme gave Lundgren shit if he arrived late, ribbing him for movie-star arrogance. Lundgren feigned confusion when he saw Van Damme, asking those in the vicinity, "Who is this?" But they both took their performances as cyber-commandos deadly seriously—Lundgren basing Sergeant Scott partly on Jack Palance in *Shane* and Van Damme patiently standing naked for the obligatory butt shots, while bragging that he could crack a walnut open with his ass cheeks.

What Van Damme termed as a "100% pure beef" experience got even beefier the day Arnold Schwarzenegger flew in on a jet to visit the set. This time, Schwarzenegger recognized Van Damme immediately, offering him a huge cigar. "Too small for me," Van Damme quipped, waving it away. And the Belgian's mischievous sense of humor would extend to the publicity campaign when it launched in Cannes the next summer. There, in the hotel he and Lundgren were staying in for the movie's red-carpet launch, he suggested to his co-star a scheme that would score them newspaper ink.

"He cooked it up before we left the hotel," remembers Lundgren with a laugh. "He said, 'We have to do a fight, you know?' I went, 'What are you talking about?' He was clever, because it had never been done before."

On the steps running up to the town's legendary festival hall, encircled by photographers, Van Damme and Lundgren turned to each other and suddenly began pretending to argue. Van Damme shoved his hand into Lundgren's chest. The giant Swede pushed back. And a buzz of excitement grew in the vicinity as everyone watched two action stars seemingly getting into it for real. It was some of the duo's best-ever acting, though Lundgren admits now that not all of it was fake. "I was with my wife—well, she was my future wife at the time—and one of the security guys jumped in and knocked her back," he says. "Then I got a little pissed. I think that's the big push, when he goes flying back into one of his security guys. So it had a little reality to it."

The fake fracas worked, whipping up chatter around the world. One story leaked out that Van Damme had taken over the movie in the editing bay and that Lundgren was incandescent about some of his performance being cut. But Van Damme couldn't resist admitting the truth on a talk show almost immediately. "Free publicity," he said, grinning. "I'm a businessman."

And his business instincts were paying off. Despite patchy reviews, many decrying *Universal Soldier* as a rehash of *The Terminator* and *RoboCop*, the film made $95 million and would spawn five sequels. It also sparked a lifelong friendship between the two stars. And Van Damme was now officially an A-lister, his asking price $1.5 million and rising, known by a far wider audience.

What would he do next? "I'll do *everything*, I'll do *anything*," he told a journalist over lunch in Cannes. "It's like on this table; I like to try the red wine—that's the action. The white wine is the comedy. This rose, this is the love story. So, I like to try everything. And if I cannot succeed, at least I *tried*."

STEVEN SEAGAL MIGHT have cracked a grim smile in 1991 had he perused Roger Ebert's review of *Double Impact*. In it, the critic went off on a tangent about the greatness of the Great One. "My own favorite is Steven Seagal," Ebert wrote, "because he seems more introspective and thoughtful, a philosopher who has been forced into violence by the nature of our unkind universe."

He wasn't alone in being fascinated by the inscrutable Seagal. As the star shot his fourth movie, *Out for Justice,* in a Brooklyn neighborhood, the production found itself besieged by thousands of fans. "There were so many fans on the streets, we had to get motorcycle cops to drive down the sidewalk to clear them," recalls the film's stunt coordinator, Conrad Palmisano. "I've worked with some of the biggest stars on the face of the earth, but I've never seen fans like that, hanging in trees and off the top of phone poles. Little old ladies saying, 'Thank you, Mr. Seagal, for giving our children somebody to look up to.'" Kelly LeBrock, witnessing her husband's effect on the populace, marveled, "I thought I was with Michael Jackson."

The couple even bought a 176-acre ranch near Michael Jackson's own ranch in California's Santa Ynez Valley, including a fifty-acre vineyard and long lanes of cottonwood trees. It had previously been owned by Tom Selleck, and Seagal made some refinements, adding a martial arts facility and a koi pond by which to meditate. The domestic staff joked that, after watching *Hard to Kill,* they made sure to call him "sir."

Seagal was already acting like a true A-lister, and the Hollywood studio that had put him in this position was still pushing and pushing to make it a reality. When the time came to cast the role of Batman in Tim Burton's superhero film, some within Warner Bros. lobbied for Seagal. After all, he already dressed in black. And who better to kick the Joker's ass than an ass-kicker who never, ever joked? "He had just kind of appeared on the scene, and people thought, 'Holy cow, this guy's badass. He could be Batman,'" recalled the film's screenwriter, Sam Hamm.

Seagal didn't end up getting called in for a script read, let alone dropping Jack Nicholson off a cathedral tower. But the budgets and grosses for his movies were pumping up anyway, with *Out for Justice* costing $14 million and making $40 million. Everything that happened on-screen in his vehicles seemed to be in support of the idea that he was invincible, unstoppable. If you tried to counter him, you'd end up with wrists snapped, crying for mercy. Or, as evidenced in the final scene of *Out for Justice,* knocked down on the sidewalk, Seagal's puppy pissing on your head.

But the more he rose, the more enemies he made, and the more concerning the stories that came out about him began to be.

JULIANNA MARGULIES SAT DOWN on the couch. Then immediately stood back up again. There was, she would recall, a hard object beneath the cushion. She looked across at the man she was in the hotel room with, at eleven o'clock at night. "Sorry," said Steven Seagal. "I must have left my gun there."

The experience was a frightening and surreal one for the actress, who had been summoned to meet with the action star late at night. Officially it was to discuss a role she was after in *Out for Justice,* but Margulies felt weird undercurrents almost immediately. "My stomach was lurching, and I could feel my skin getting clammy," she would say. "He ushered me into the bedroom, which compelled me to talk faster. I was trying to buy time. I had to talk my way out, that much I knew. I had no chance of survival against a giant with a gun." After putting his gun on the bedside table, Seagal informed Margulies that she had weak kidneys and that he could heal them. She fled the room, ultimately getting the part but remaining shaken by the incident for decades to come.

Several action stars would be embroiled in sexual harassment scandals in this period. Van Damme was sued in 1993 by a woman who claimed he forced himself on her in a hotel room; he called it "entirely without merit" and settled out of court. Schwarzenegger would face multiple allegations of misconduct, including grabbing women's breasts and buttocks ("I stepped over the line several times," he would say in 2018). But for Seagal, sordid tales would become a regular feature throughout his career. Margulies called him "a predator" and said, "I was one of the lucky few who got out of there unscathed." Woman after woman would come forward with stories of how this supposed Tibetan Buddhist guru had lured them to some solitary spot, then sexually harassed or assaulted them. Some were unknowns, extras, or production assistants; others were actors themselves, such as Portia de Rossi, Jenny McCarthy, and Katherine Heigl.

Back in the early 1990s, little was known about Seagal's misdeeds. He was still revered by the public and presented by his publicists as a force for virtue. But cracks were starting to show. That picture-book marriage to LeBrock was splintering and finally shattered in 1994 with an ugly divorce. "I had absolutely no self-esteem. I hated myself," LeBrock would say. "I feared everything and didn't want to leave the house."

A few rumors were also starting to leak out about Seagal's work life, at least within the industry. His attitude toward the welfare of stuntmen on his movies was cavalier, bordering on cruel. "He was not very conscientious about how he would hit people and punch people," says director Andrew Davis. "He had these people who were part of his troupe that he would knock down. They would get hurt. He wasn't sweet sometimes, you know?" And on *Out for Justice*, so the legend goes, things came to a head.

The opposing force was a man named Gene LeBell, a former professional wrestler nicknamed "the Godfather of Grappling" and "Judo Gene" who had ended up in Hollywood in the early 1960s. A colorful character, to say the least, LeBell was arrested for the murder of a private investigator in 1976, then fully acquitted. A scene in Quentin Tarantino's 2019 film *Once Upon a Time in Hollywood*, in which a stuntman humiliates Bruce Lee in combat, was based on a story about LeBell doing the same. But the most oft-repeated part of his mythology involves Steven Seagal. On the set of *Out for Justice*, in one version of the tale, the action star was bragging that he was the toughest guy on earth. Then someone on the film's stunt team, who was sore at their treatment at his hands, said, "No, Mr. Seagal. You're the second-toughest guy on earth. The toughest guy is that fat bald guy over there eating tuna sandwiches." Seagal advanced on Gene LeBell, who stood up and casually made an example of him.

That, at least, is the version told by Robert Wall. "Gene put little Steven Seagal down on his knees, choked out," says Wall, who claims LeBell told him the full story on the phone shortly afterward. "He woke up with thirty-two stuntmen and women laughing at him." Seagal, the legend continues, got to his feet and aimed a kick at LeBell's crotch, which resulted in further punishment: a second choke that caused Seagal to lose control of his bladder and bowels. "Gene said, 'I gave him Polish underwear—yellow in the front, brown in the back, so you know which way to put 'em on,'" says Wall. "He was out for a while. And so when he woke up he did the only manly thing he could—he fired Gene."

But as in *Rashomon,* one of Seagal's favorite movies, accounts vary wildly. "It's probably the most exaggerated story I've ever heard in my lifetime in showbiz," says Conrad Palmisano, who was there on the spot. "[Stuntman] Steven Lambert goes to me, 'Hey, Connie, you better come check on Gene. He and Steven are kinda getting into it.' So we go over and they're laughing—it was like, 'Let me show you this move I can do.' I think that Gene got behind him and Steven reached around and slapped him in the crotch. But Steven slapped a lot of guys in the crotch. It's sad for Steven that people love to beat him up over that, saying he wet himself and he pooped his pants. Trust me, if anybody choked out the star of a movie, which would send him to the hospital, it would shut the company down for a day. That's a quarter of a million dollars, right? That guy would go to jail. If it had actually happened, Gene LeBell would never work in the business again."

Palmisano claims he has a letter from LeBell setting the record straight. But in a 2012 interview, Judo Gene poured more gasoline on the conflagration, saying, "If a guy soils himself, you can't criticize him, because if they just had a nice big dinner an hour before, you might have a tendency to do that." And a few weeks later, Seagal himself spoke up.

"If he said that, then he's a pathological scumbag liar," he said on the phone to *The MMA Hour,* still out for justice twenty-one years on. "It makes him look like a demented child."

The LeBell incident occurred in a remote spot, a dirt track on which a foot chase was being filmed. But a few months after *Out for Justice* wrapped, Seagal was to be part of another event that would be whispered about for decades to come. And this time, people all over America witnessed what went down.

STEVEN SEAGAL WASN'T the first action star to host *Saturday Night Live.* Burt Reynolds, David Carradine, and Carl Weathers had all done stints on the legendary comedy skit show. Bruce Willis had made an appearance two years earlier, dancing to the theme music and playing a harmonica. But all those guys had previously displayed at least flashes of humor on-screen. Seagal felt like a different proposition. After the hosting gig was announced as part of the publicity rollout for *Out for Justice,* Arsenio Hall broached the subject with Seagal on his talk show, asking in disbelief, "Are you gonna do that? Have you ever done comedy?"

"Yeah, I used to do stand-up," Seagal responded flatly. After a lengthy silence from the studio audience, he explained, "That was a joke. That's my first attempt at comedy right there and I failed, so maybe I better not do the show."

The room was suddenly ice-cold. "I think you'll be fine," said Hall carefully. "You're just so *intense.*"

"Well, I told them that they're going to have to come up with some real intense shit for me," Seagal explained.

It was not immediately clear if this statement was true or whether it was his second attempt at comedy.

When he arrived at Rockefeller Plaza on Monday, April 15, 1991, things went south almost immediately. As was customary on the show, Seagal met with cast members and writers that day around a long table. There he began to share his vision for Saturday's show. In one sketch he would play a therapist who meets with a patient who has just been raped, then tries to have sex with her. "Some of his sketch ideas were so heinous, but so hilariously awful, it was like we were on *Candid Camera,*" recalled cast member Julia Sweeney. But if reactions to Seagal's suggestions were frosty, he was just as opposed to the ideas going in the other direction. One sketch was proposed in which Dana Carvey and Kevin Nealon, playing Arnold Schwarzenegger fanatics named Hans and Franz, would make fun of Seagal. It got as far as the Thursday rehearsal, where the star, staring into space, said aloud, "I just wish Arnold was here so I could kick his fucking ass."

After a hellish week for all, Seagal finally took to the stage. He sang "Kung Fu Fighting" to a confused studio audience, standing stock still while strumming a guitar; he had nixed the original idea that he would pretend to beat up people while performing.

Then he did the sketch with Carvey and Nealon. In the finished version, after overhearing Hans and Franz rhapsodizing about Schwarzenegger and Stallone, he intones with a poker face, "I don't wanna compare myself to these other stars. They're great and everything. But what I do is unique. You see, I follow Zen." Then he demonstrates his raw strength, defeating them with his little finger alone. "I'm very impressed, Mr. Seagal," gasps Hans. "Maybe we misjudged you." The sketch ends with them replacing their cardboard cut-outs of Schwarzenegger with ones of Seagal.

That night, bewildered *SNL* viewers witnessed a ninety-minute paean to the majesty of Steven Seagal, orchestrated by Steven Seagal himself. The cast would talk of their traumatic experience years later. "You can't explain something to somebody in German if they don't speak German," said Tim Meadows of the star's seeming inability to grasp the concept of humor. *SNL* boss Lorne Michaels banned Seagal from ever appearing on the show again; two years later, when Nicolas Cage faux-fretted in a sketch that he was the biggest jerk to ever host, Michaels replied, "No, that would be Steven Seagal."

One thing was clear as he bid adieu to 30 Rock: while he could make people scream in agony or howl in fear, Seagal could not make them laugh. Or, as David Spade hypothesized long after the nightmare, "Maybe his one-inch ponytail was too tight that night."

CHAPTER 14

...

PLANET ARNOLD

ARNOLD SCHWARZENEGGER had experienced pretty much everything that could be experienced. But on the day he went up to San Jose to see George Foreman, he realized there was something missing. "He had a cougar and he had a black panther," recalls Schwarzenegger of his visit to the boxer. "And they would attack him relentlessly but he would roll around with them. I loved the way he played with his animals, and I always wanted to do that."

That dream of wrestling wild beasts stayed with him. And in the summer of 1989, while shooting a new movie down in Mexico's Churubusco Studios, he finally got a chance to make it a reality. The studio had its own zoo, a collection of animals that could be used in productions. And among them there happened to be a cougar cub and a panther cub. Eyes widening, Schwarzenegger said, "Can you bring these animals every Saturday to my trailer? Instead of having lunch, I will play with them."

As it was decreed, so it went. "Every weekend they brought those animals, and we played and we played and we played," says the star. "Then all of a sudden they weren't three months old—they were six months old, and seven months old, and eight months old. Because the shoot in Mexico took six months."

Schwarzenegger was about to discover what Stallone had learned in his Central Park Zoo days: there was no taming a wild cat. One Saturday lunchtime, as he turned his back on the two large cubs to head to the front of his trailer, one lunged forward and attacked him. "It jumped seven feet through the air, took me down," Schwarzenegger remembers. "I landed on the steering wheel of the truck. And I realized then that the time was over to play with these things. Now it's getting to be serious business. I said, 'Okay, that was the last visit.'"

The attack was a reminder, perhaps a needed one, that even the greatest action star on the planet had his limits. Because there wasn't much evidence of it elsewhere. *Twins* had taken him mainstream. Everywhere he went, people cheered him and chanted his name. He was rolling from one triumph to another.

The only other sign of vulnerability was a recurring nightmare that Schwarzenegger found himself experiencing before he made each new movie. "I sometimes have dreams where you're out there lying totally naked in a forest . . . and you hear somewhere, 'In two minutes we roll,'" he revealed in 1991. "I'm caught totally off guard, like I wasn't prepared."

These images, and the feelings they led to, haunted him. And maybe compelled him to sign up for that film in Mexico. In it, after all, he played a character with a recurring dream of his own.

A FEW YEARS EARLIER, Paul Verhoeven had considered casting Schwarzenegger as the title character in *RoboCop*. But physics had intervened—specifically, the physics of squeezing the onetime Mr. Universe into a costume that was essentially a big tin can. "We discussed Arnold," says Verhoeven. "But then we found out that Arnold in this robotic costume would make RoboCop so over the top, so much bigger than life. Peter Weller is a slim guy of average height and turned out to be the solution for the costume. The costume decided, a little bit, the choice."

The Dutch director and Austrian star never actually met about the project. But after the movie came out in 1987, Schwarzenegger advanced on Verhoeven at a restaurant and stated, "I saw your *RoboCop*. It's fantastic. I would love to work with you someday."

Then, the very next day, he called Verhoeven with the offer of a job: a sci-fi mind-twister to which he owned the rights, titled *Total Recall*.

Back in 1966, the same year that a thousand people gathered in San Francisco to champion LSD, the writer Philip K. Dick had published a short story that was itself a virtual acid trip. In it, office drone Douglas Quail keeps dreaming he is on Mars. After visiting a company called Rekal Incorporated to receive memory implants and thus live out his dream in waking life, he discovers he is actually a spy who has been to the Red Planet. A slippery novella in which reality feels elusive, it had in the 1970s drawn the attention of *Alien* writers Dan O'Bannon and Ronald Shusett, who tapped out an adaptation, renaming it *Total Recall*. But Hollywood just couldn't get a grip on the weird tale. Body-horror auteur David Cronenberg was drawn to it, adding the wrinkle of there being disfigured mutants on Mars. Stars such as Patrick Swayze, Richard Dreyfuss, and William Hurt drifted in and out, while producer Dino De Laurentiis stubbornly held on to the rights, nixing draft after draft.

Through all this, Schwarzenegger, like the Martians in *The War of the Worlds,* regarded the project with envious eyes, and slowly and surely drew his plans. He had heard about *Total Recall* while shooting *Raw Deal* and wanted in; his old foe De Laurentiis, however, had no intention of letting him headline the project. But when De Laurentiis's company collapsed, Schwarzenegger convinced Carolco to buy the rights for $3 million. Then he went about recruiting collaborators for it, starting with Verhoeven.

There was work to be done. A lot of it. Those other stars had been lean, everyman types, but Schwarzenegger's arrival on the scene meant elements of the screenplay—the forty-second draft and counting—would need to be radically retooled so as to orbit around him. "The film had to be adapted to Arnold," Verhoeven explains. "In the original script the guy was a measly accountant, somebody writing numbers in books. We decided we had to change the character completely. We made him a construction guy to explain the muscles. He is not, let's say, an intellectual in any way."

The casting somewhat diminished the edge of the reveal that Quaid (a firmer surname than Quail) is in fact a lethal killing machine; he's Arnold Schwarzenegger, so of course he is. But it did allow Carolco to turn *Total Recall* into a souped-up summer blockbuster with retina-singeing special effects, albeit one with cerebral frills intact.

With *Twins,* Schwarzenegger had propelled himself into uncharted waters. With *Total Recall,* he was doing so again, even though he was back in his action wheelhouse, dispensing such quips as "Consider that a divorce!" (as he shoots his wife, played by Sharon Stone) and "Screw you!" (as he bores into an opponent's innards with a huge industrial drill). Yes, there were gargantuan set pieces, but also many peculiarities. In one scene, Quaid emerges from the body of a middle-aged woman, a futuristic disguise, then battles enemies while wearing a yellow dress. In another, he has a conversation with himself via video screen, a personality cracked in two. Verhoeven, who sported a Jesus watch on his wrist on set, delighted in sneaking as much strange, transgressive stuff as he could into this $60 million film, at the time reported as the priciest ever made.

One scene that would generate a lot of interest featured a triple-breasted female mutant on Mars. "When I was a student at university, I went to some courses about medicine just for fun," Verhoeven explains. "And I saw some pictures of women that have four breasts; the other two are very small. But it was Rob Bottin who said, 'I have a much better idea: it's not four breasts—it's three.' I thought four breasts would have been biologically and anatomically correct, but three is, of course, artistic."

Another sequence was controversial for its violence: the one in which Quaid wields the body of a bullet-riddled passer-by on an escalator, using it as a shield against gunfire. "The original scene was horrible, a bloodbath," recalls Verhoeven, who was commanded by the MPAA to sanitize the scene. "What you see now is a timid version of what that was."

But the real fun of *Total Recall,* for both director and star, was its mind-fucky quality. They had carefully worked out the screenplay so that it is never clarified if Quaid is a hero who saves Mars or if the whole last reel takes place in his subconscious. It was, then, a long way from *Commando*. On set, even the music being piped in to create a mood was highbrow: Shostakovich, operas, symphonies, John Adams's *Nixon in China*—though Schwarzenegger occasionally commandeered the sound system to blast Austrian folk music. Verhoeven, who had studied *The Terminator* obsessively as he geared up for *RoboCop,* taking copious notes about the camerawork and editing, was delighted by the complex performance—or performances—he was getting out of Schwarzenegger. "I could get out of Arnold what others probably would not have tried," Verhoeven says. "And he had no ego at all, which is rare. He is somebody you can really say to, 'That is not good, what you're doing.' And he would say, 'Oh yeah, you're right. Let's do it again.'"

Still, despite his elevated creative ambitions, this was the same old Schwarzenegger. As the six months in Mexico wound on, he bench-pressed and curled as always, before checking the latest box-office report ("What's going on with *The Abyss*?") or indulging in a practical joke (when screenwriter Ronald Shusett made the mistake of falling asleep, he was woken by a stream of ice-cold water to the crotch). His sometimes Neanderthal-like sense of humor found another form one day when he made a loud comment about the alignment of a Mexican stuntwoman's breasts.

Also intact: Schwarzenegger's relentless energy when it came to championing a project. When Carolco balked at the rising budget and pushed for special-effects shots to be cut, the star got on the phone with them and declared, "We will not simplify." Studio chairman Mario Kassar got another call late one night in which Schwarzenegger issued a different one-liner: "Put another million into the promotion." Kassar, who had agreed on a $10 million fee with the star, double what Schwarzenegger had been paid for *Red Heat* two years earlier, said he would. "He got what he wanted and he promoted the hell out of the movie," Kassar says. "That guy, when he starts promoting a movie, forget it. You have to stop him sometimes—he promotes too much!"

The actor even personally intervened in the trailer campaign, annihilating the existing one before it went out and assigning the job to a new promotion firm. "We went from a 40 percent awareness to 92 percent awareness," he later declared with Terminator-esque exactitude. Whether due to that, the quality of the movie, or the wanton carnage, *Total Recall* triumphed at the box office in June 1990, taking the number-one spot in the United States and making $261 million globally. With the success of first *Twins* and now this, plus the arrival of his first child, Katherine, in December 1989—he dubbed the baby "the Schwarzenshriver"—it was looking like things couldn't possibly get any better for him.

Of course, they could.

RIGHT FROM THE END of his *Terminator* experience in 1984, Schwarzenegger had wanted more. No matter that his character had ended up crushed in a steel press, only its CPU chip and one fearsome metal arm left intact. There was a whole future factory full of endoskeletons just waiting to have that famous Austrian face and body grafted onto them—and the star made clear to James Cameron that he was willing to return. An announcement was even made, in December of that year, that a sequel to *The Terminator* was going to happen.

But this time it was legal issues, rather than a waitress from South Pasadena, who shut down Skynet. With Hemdale Film Corporation controlling half of the franchise rights, talks of a follow-up became throttled by red tape. Technology played a part, too. Back in 1980, when Cameron had first dreamed up the whole thing, he had imagined the Terminator as a polymorphic, shape-shifting villain, only reluctantly revising it to a standard metal man when he realized there was no way to put the images in his brain onto the screen. Even years on, visual effects hadn't advanced enough for his liking. Instead, the director considered going in a different direction should the sequel ever happen—a female Terminator, perhaps, or dueling Schwarzeneggers, one good, one bad.

And then *The Abyss* happened. The shoot was a brutal one,

with seventy-hour weeks underwater nearly killing Cameron and star Ed Harris, and reducing actress Mary Elizabeth Mastrantonio to screaming, "We are not animals!" at the end of one take. Neither was it particularly well received critically: of the climax, in which aliens intervene benevolently, the *Washington Post* wrote, "How many times can we be awestruck by Day-Glo Gumbies? And why do these creatures always travel with the Mormon Tabernacle Choir?" But one sequence, featuring an alien using water to appear in human form to the heroes, proved to Cameron that the sophisticated polymorphic effect he had been pining for was finally achievable.

Lighting up with excitement, the director sat down at his keyboard and tapped out a script for *Terminator 2* (the "The": terminated). The writing process this time was aided by Ecstasy tablets. In Cameron's new vision, a juggernaut hero T-800 would face down a smaller and lither but seemingly unkillable liquid-metal foe. "Arnold is like karate and this guy's aikido," he enthused. This "Aikido Terminator," as he referred to it, would be monstrously unstoppable; fighting it would be like battling water. The story he and co-writer William Wisher cooked up did the impossible: it made Arnold Schwarzenegger an underdog.

It sounded extremely cool—to everyone who wasn't Arnold Schwarzenegger. Cameron handed him the freshly printed screenplay on the Carolco jet to Cannes in 1990, and the director remembers, "He read it on the flight over. And then Arnold and I met at one of the hotels for breakfast. I'm just crashed out because I haven't slept in thirty-six hours. And he's got this very worried expression. He says, 'But Jim, I don't *kill* anybody. I'm the Terminator, and I don't *kill* anybody in this. How is this gonna work?' He was horrified. He was petrified. He didn't like it at all."

On the sunny hotel terrace, nibbling oatmeal, the director methodically laid out his case—that creating the unlikeliest hero possible, a robot originally developed for the sole purpose of exterminating life, was a genius move that would blindside fans and finally move them to tears. Unimpressed, Schwarzenegger suggested that he could still rack up a body count before the young

John Connor instructs the new T-800 not to kill. "You got me on a technicality there, Clarence Darrow," Cameron said with a laugh before ruling that out. For a while the star considered walking away from the project, imagining his fans rioting at the prospect of a Terminator who doesn't terminate. But ultimately he trusted Cameron. "He grudgingly went along with it," the director says. "He honestly didn't get it and had huge doubts. But the great thing about Arnold is that he puts his faith in a filmmaker, even if he has to slowly warm to what's being done."

By then, the rights situation had been untangled, in no small part thanks to Schwarzenegger, with Carolco picking them up for $10 million. And on October 8, 1990, the sweeter, warmer sequel to a bleak and brutal sci-fi classic kicked off.

Linda Hamilton was back as Sarah Connor, wirier and far more intense than the 1984 model (her single demand to Cameron had been "I want to be crazy"). First-time actor Edward Furlong, thirteen years old, was ecstatic to be playing John Connor. "I went from going to school every day to working opposite Arnold Schwarzenegger on a huge fucking motorcycle and shit," he recalls. "It was a blast. Arnold kept me laughing throughout the whole movie." And an older but equally green actor, Robert Patrick, who had been trying to claw his way into Hollywood while sleeping in his car, was cast as the liquid-metal terror upon whom the entire endeavor depended. "I mean, if it didn't work, the movie wasn't going to work," Patrick says. "Why that character worked, in my opinion, was because no one had any preconceived notion of me whatsoever as an actor. They didn't know who the fuck I was."

Marshaling the ensemble, shooting like a man possessed, was Cameron. The perceived failure of *The Abyss,* which had barely broken even, had shaken the previously unshakeable Iron Jim, and he would not allow the sequel to his most iconic work to be a disappointment. *Terminator 2* had to deliver the greatest mayhem in motion-picture history. Doing anything less was not an option.

And so, as helicopters were flown beneath freeway overpasses, eighteen-wheel big rigs trashed in San Fernando Valley drainage canals, and nuclear explosions simulated, the six-month shoot became a legend, whispered about in Hollywood like ghost stories around a campfire. So exacting, and vocal about his exactitude, was Cameron that his colorful comments were immortalized on a black T-shirt given to crew members at wrap time. A few choice examples:

"Whose radio was that? Find out and have them shot."
"Just show me something that vaguely resembles a fucking
   frame."
"Having Gavin is like losing two good men."
"Don't give me what I *ask for*. Give me what I *want*."

Even the teenage Furlong was not completely spared from a tongue-lashing. "My very first day of filming, we were shooting a scene in Palmdale, where I'm talking about war being horrible or whatever," he says. "Jim Cameron comes running up to me and he's like, 'That was friggin' amazing—great job.' Then he looks at me closely and goes, 'What the fuck is on your lip?' I'm like, "What are you talking about? I just put on some ChapStick.' And he says, 'Oh my God.' I realized I'd basically destroyed the whole take and had to reshoot it. I was lucky—I was exempted from being yelled at by Jim because I was a kid. But he did call me 'Special Ed' for a while."

INSPIRING ITS OWN WITTY SLOGANS ("*Terminator 2, Crew 0*"; "*T3*, Not with Me"), the production was deeply testing for those on the inside. For those watching from the outside, it looked like insanity. *Total Recall* had been expensive, but *Terminator 2*, at an unprecedented budget of $102 million (fifteen times what the original had cost), was in a different league. Schwarzenegger's salary alone was $15 million, including a Gulfstream III jet. Endless reports in the media shrieked about its unprecedented expenditure. "It was all over the news," says Mario Kassar, "over CNN Business, about how expensive it was, bankrupting the company. They were judging and destroying the movie before seeing a frame. Sometimes, you know, when the media starts on you before the movie's done, they can hurt you. Except *Terminator 2*—they couldn't succeed to hurt us."

Kassar and Andrew Vajna were relaxed partly because they had seen test shots of the T-1000: bleeding-edge moments of spectacle that reassured them they had something special on their hands. "When I saw those—this reel of the black-and-white floor morphing up, the finger, the chrome thing and everything—I went, 'My God, what have we got here?'" Kassar recalls. "For me, that was it. It was done. I didn't care what anybody was saying."

And Schwarzenegger, too, had finally seen the light. He may have only gotten to shoot a bunch of cops in the ankles on-screen, but he recognized the electric charge in his mano-a-manos with Patrick, and embraced the new humor granted to his morally upgraded protagonist. "Chill out, dickwad," the T-800 tells one street punk, employing Angeleno street-slang he's been taught by his young charge. His performance turned out to be complex and impressive: poker-faced and forbidding in the first act, hilarious in the second, and tear-jerking in the third. A metal Hamlet, grappling with metaphysical concepts such as why humans cry and how exactly to execute a proper thumbs-up.

On June 30, 1991, Schwarzenegger climbed into his sand-colored Humvee—he had recently become the first civilian to own one of the vehicles, after seeing one in a military procession while shooting *Kindergarten Cop*—and drove to a hotel near Los Angeles International Airport. After parking the behemoth, which had the word "Terminator" stenciled on its side, he strutted into the building, emerging from a cloud of pink fog onto a stage in a ballroom packed with people. There he stood, scanning the crowd, expressionless. Finally he spoke.

"In the first movie," he declared, "I told you, 'Fuck you, asshole.'"

The crowd went berserk, screaming and stamping their feet.

"But I also told you . . . 'I'll be back.'"

Pandemonium ensued. It was the day before the premiere of *T2*, and the one thousand fans at this *Terminator* convention (which also featured a T-800 look-alike contest) were at peak excitement levels, barging into each other and trying to get closer to their idol. When someone yelled out, "Down in front!," Schwarzenegger repeated again, "Fuck you, *asshole*," triggering more thunderous applause. The star concluded by announcing, "Jim Cameron and I have just decided backstage that we're going to do another *Terminator*. The title will be *The Sperminator*. 'I'll come again.'"

That euphoric room proved an accurate microcosm of what was about to unfold all over America and beyond. *Terminator 2* was huge. Huger than huge. Despite (or perhaps because of) Cameron's fury at the shortcomings of Gavin and the rest, the movie came out a machine-tooled beast of an action picture that steamrolled over its summer rivals, such as *Robin Hood: Prince of Thieves, City Slickers,* and *Backdraft*. Its grand total worldwide: $520.9 million.

For its less experienced cast, its success led to bizarre and mind-boggling experiences. "People who had knife phobias or didn't like scissors would run away from me screaming," says Robert Patrick. "It's funny—from pro athletes to politicians, it seems everyone was traumatized by the T-1000." Edward Furlong would release a pop album, *Hold on Tight,* in Japan. "It's the worst music you'll ever hear in your life," he says. "Let's be honest, I was doing it for the money. It's jerk-off music."

As for Schwarzenegger, *Terminator 2* was his biggest hit to date, and remains so today. Not only was the spectacle transcendent, but his acting had made people weep. "My goal in that movie was to make you cry for the Terminator," says Cameron. "And we succeeded in doing that."

Perhaps this perfect storm of elements, and the self-assurance that comes with having three gargantuan hits in a row, was why Schwarzenegger signed up for something rather surprising. A very public alliance with his two greatest foes.

IT WAS FEBRUARY 14, 1990—Valentine's Day—when the star received an important guest in his trailer on the *Terminator 2* set. Not his wife, Maria, who was en route with the one-year-old Katherine and some heart-shaped balloons, but a film producer named Keith Barish. He and Schwarzenegger had worked together on *The Running Man;* Barish was also behind the likes of *Sophie's Choice* and *The Monster Squad*. But today they weren't together to discuss a movie. Instead, they were talking burgers.

Specifically, Barish was talking, while Schwarzenegger listened. The producer's pitch was simple: he painted a picture of a culinary wonderland, a themed Manhattan restaurant where ordinary people could go to experience a taste of Hollywood glamour. It would be affordable but glitter with stardust, filled with iconic props and occasional cameos from genuine A-listers. Schwarzenegger nodded his way through the presentation. "Count me in," he told Barish.

Next on Barish's hit list was Bruce Willis. The star who had once tended bar thought it sounded like a winner, too. "I needed a place to hang out in New York," he later explained. Though Willis had a condition. Deep into his sideline musical career, having just released his second album, *If It Don't Kill You, It Just Makes You Stronger* (a Nietzsche reference, though it's anyone's guess what Nietzsche would have made of the track "Barnyard Boogie"), he wanted control of the restaurant's tunes as musical director. Barish and his business partner Robert Earl agreed.

Finally, after a flirtation with Warren Beatty—a long phone conversation went nowhere—the last major celebrity endorser materialized, with Sylvester Stallone approaching Barish through a mutual friend. "I begged," explained Stallone in 1993. "They saw me outside on my knees saying, 'Please!'"

It seemed obvious, very quickly, that Café Hollyrock was going to be huge. Especially when it changed its name to Planet Hollywood.

And so began the peculiar chronicle of the chain restaurant with blockbuster production values. The three celebrity shareholders had put aside any differences for the sake of a potentially colossal payday—when asked on a UK talk show why he had gotten involved, Stallone answered with one word: "Greed." With this trio involved, there could be no possibility of failure. The menu may have been humble—a six-ounce burger for $7.50, chicken fingers coated in Cap'n Crunch cereal for $5.95, sweet butter pecan rum cake for $6—but in every other sense this hub of "eatertainment" was designed to be massive, a fulcrum of swirling hype that would fulfill its customers' deepest Tinseltown fantasies.

Oscar-winning production designer Anton Furst, a long-haired Londoner who had recently conjured up Gotham City streets for Tim Burton's *Batman,* was jetted across the Atlantic and given an $8 million budget to make his very first restaurant. Upon completion, the dazed Furst would remark, "We've put it together like a surreal dream."

If anything, that was an understatement. The flagship Planet Hollywood, occupying twenty thousand square feet on New York's West 57th Street, was an overwhelming concoction: visitors would walk in between columns shaped like Marilyn Monroe's legs, to sit at tables with lamps whose bases had been cast from Schwarzenegger's forearm. From the ceiling dangled three motorcycles: one from *Terminator 2,* one used by Steve McQueen in *The Great Escape,* and one previously owned by Elvis. A vast simulacrum of the LA skyline spanned the main room. Items that would amaze movie historians, such as a bell gifted by Vivien Leigh to Laurence Olivier, were positioned alongside ones that probably wouldn't, such as a phone booth from *Commando* and a replica of the beef slab once pummeled by Rocky Balboa. Even wilder plans were reluctantly abandoned, like a huge latex shark that would have splashed out of a pool toward startled diners, or an animatronic Humphrey Bogart.

The grand opening was set for Tuesday, October 22, 1991. And it was as panicky a run-up as the period before any movie premiere. "Last week I wanted to *kill* myself," moaned super-publicist Bobby Zarem that September; the cause of his woe was Bruce Willis, who had agreed to sit atop an elephant for a grandiose magazine photo shoot to promote the occasion, but had turned his Planet Holly-wood baseball cap so that it faced away from the camera. New York zoning codes meant that illuminated signs on 57th Street had to be taken down, though artificial palm trees were allowed to re-main. And flak came flying in from another celebrity restaurant, Robert De Niro's just-opened Tribeca Grill, when De Niro's busi-ness partner, Drew Nieporent, defined the difference between the two restaurants to a reporter: "Like an art movie versus *Total Re-call.*"

But Nieporent had forgotten how much cash *Total Recall* had made. And rather than folding under the pressure—like their Planet Meltdown dessert, a chocolate globe designed to slowly dis-solve beneath hot caramel, revealing the Planet Hollywood logo beneath—his rivals hung tough. "When I tell people the idea," said the bullish Zarem, "people can't fucking-cock-shit-ass imagine why nobody's done it before." The PR maven was starting to see results from his key ploy: sending Planet Hollywood sweatshirts to every famous person he could think of, from Eddie Murphy to President Bush. The *New York Post* ran a photo of Madonna jog-ging in one; talk-show host Regis Philbin held one aloft on TV and announced, "This is *the* shirt of the nineties." Fake Planet Holly-wood baseball caps started being sold on Fifth Avenue before the real ones had even gone on sale.

The restaurant's A-list backers, meanwhile, donned the merch themselves to embark on an out-of-control publicity blitzkrieg that would go on for years. Planet Hollywood would prove to be the thing that finally brought Schwarzenegger and Stallone together, the pair flying around the world together in private jets, chomping on cigars and exchanging war stories. They at last had a common objective: money. On one British talk show, they and Willis domi-nated the episode with such nonstop shilling—it had even been negotiated that they could read from the menu—that an investiga-tion was launched. "The promotion given to the restaurant went beyond acceptable 'plugging' on chat shows and breached the undue prominence requirements of section 10.6 of the Programme

Code," tutted a report by the Independent Television Commission. The horrified host, Michael Aspel, wrapped up the show shortly after, vowing never to front one again.

When opening night in New York arrived, meanwhile, hysteria came with it. Mobs of fans lined the New York street, interested not in the Russian Tea Room a few doors down but in catching a glimpse of Rambo, the Terminator, and John McClane hyping up bowls of Chinese chicken salad. In Cannes a few months earlier, Schwarzenegger had announced, "Seeing the restaurant will be like experiencing a hit movie." It was true, albeit not the kind of movie fans were used to—in this one, the action legends weren't shooting at each other, but clasping hands and grinning like chiseled Cheshire cats. Inside, the trio sat at a special table in the middle of the room, joined by *The Breakfast Club* director John Hughes (it's hard to imagine the small talk). Schwarzenegger pointed out his mother's strudel recipe on the menu. Stallone didn't look too interested in the food; "I'm just not prone to chew a lot," he admitted shortly after. "It doesn't go with my personality." Willis took the first opportunity to hit the stage with his harmonica, entertaining partygoers including Sophia Loren, Jeremy Irons, Kevin Costner, Donald Trump, Elton John, Cher, and Liza Minnelli.

The night was wild, a frenzy of limos and autographs, one of a kind. Except it wasn't one of a kind—because Planet Hollywood spawned sequel after sequel, opening dozens of new restaurants all over the United States and beyond. Maybe it was the chicken fingers, or the memorabilia, or the mind-blowing alliance of three red-hot movie stars. Whatever it was, it worked. Celebrity copycats, like Steven Spielberg's Dive!, a $7 million LA restaurant themed after a submarine, Hulk Hogan's Pastamania, and David Hasselhoff's planned Baywatch Café, filled with bikini-sporting waitresses, floundered and faded away. But, for now at least, Planet Hollywood was the mega-hit it was designed to be. Jean-Claude Van Damme and Steven Seagal would get involved, the latter arriving at the opening of the Vegas branch on the back of an elephant. Besides the lucrative gift store in every restaurant, there was talk of a Planet Hollywood Visa card, a Barbie doll, even an ice cream parlor spin-off.

Robert De Niro had lost the restaurant feud to his muscle-bound competitors far north of TriBeCa. And in a final twist of the knife, De Niro's boxing gloves from *Raging Bull* sat in a glass case at the Manhattan Planet Hollywood, for every tourist to gawk at over their baby back ribs.

CHAPTER 15

...

OLD HABITS

THERE WAS ONE MAN not swept away by *Die Hard* euphoria: its director, John McTiernan. The thirty-seven-year-old watched with curiosity as his film continued to make shock waves in Hollywood, lingering for months in the top ten at the box office, then cleaning up on home video. His eyebrows arched even higher as it became clear that he had made an inadvertent festive classic. "You know, a man who fought in World War II made a Christmas movie called *It's a Wonderful Life*," he says now. "And we decided that our Christmas movie is *Die Hard*. It's got to say something about what's happening with our culture."

McTiernan had made his fun romp about a beleaguered family man in an office block, then moved on to something else: a submarine picture with Sean Connery. But it seemed everyone else in town was still stuck on *Die Hard*. It had captured the spirit of its era perfectly: devoid of the type of geopolitical nonsense that had consumed Rambo and even eventually Rocky, it was a whip-fast yarn that brought the action hero back down to earth. Its humanity, warmth, and wit seemed to infiltrate almost every subsequent major action movie; even *Terminator 2*'s benevolent robot, getting a battering in the third act that makes John McClane's shredded soles look like a mild scratch, owes a debt to the man in the white A-shirt.

Gestating filmmakers studied its camerawork and pacing; a teenage Colin Trevorrow, future director of *Jurassic World,* picked up his Hi-8 camcorder in 1990 and shot a movie he described to his parents as "*Die Hard* with a cat." And studio executives in lots across Los Angeles started dreaming up their own variations on the formula that *Die Hard* had established. A regular-Joe hero, with relatable fears. Villains with big personalities. A specific, contained environment that would function as a battleground.

"*Die Hard* with a cat" would never, alas, become an actual motion picture. But pretty much every other permutation one could imagine was soon on its way.

THE FIRST *DIE HARD* imitation actually had the words "Die Hard" in its title. New 20th Century Fox boss Joe Roth had eyed the studio's 1990 summer slate, realized they needed a biggie, and decided they could hastily turn a script he had just read, titled *58 Minutes,* into a *Die Hard* sequel. The story, based on a recent novel by William Wager, was about a divorced NYPD cop whiling away time at JFK airport when he discovers that villains have commandeered the entire place and are threatening to keep the runway lights off until circling planes run out of fuel and crash. It seemed an easy enough task to switch the name of the hero from Frank Malone to John McClane, and JFK to Dulles. The original's screenwriter, Steven de Souza, was hired to rejigger the story, along with Doug Richardson.

But there could be no sequel without McClane himself. And Bruce Willis wasn't so sure he wanted to come back. "We spent a lot of work on making John McClane a vulnerable, ordinary guy," he had told the *New York Post.* "People know someone like him— he's not some superhero, some Rambo. He's tired and he feels pain and he's afraid." Now, though, he wasn't an ordinary guy, but an extraordinary one whom audiences had seen take down thirteen terrorists. Would they really root for him a second time? Besides, Willis had found his post–*Die Hard* acting gig, as a Vietnam vet in *In Country,* a more rewarding experience. "I needed to know if I could do a movie where I didn't smirk, wasn't wisecracking, and did not get the girl," he explained.

Die Hard 2 seemed to have smirking, wisecracking, and getting the girl as requisites. On the other hand, Fox was offering an even bigger payday than his controversial $5 million one for the first film; this time he would get $7.5 million. Willis signed on.

With McTiernan out of the picture, the studio hired a thirty-year-old Finnish director named Renny Harlin, whose *Nightmare on Elm Street 4: Dream Warriors* had just proven a sizeable hit, to helm the sequel. From the beginning, Harlin felt the crush of expectations weighing down on him. After all, his daunting task was to create a fitting follow-up to the greatest action movie of all time. "You know, Renny, making a sequel is all about replicating the experience for the audience, but not copying the film," producer Joel Silver told him in one of their first meetings. "Because people don't want to see the same film again, but they want to have the same experience."

Harlin's two specific challenges were to provide viewers with more John McClane and more spectacle. And on the first front, he found himself at almost instant loggerheads with his star. "We had a major disagreement about this," he recalls. "Bruce had this notion from the beginning that he now wanted to play John McClane straight and serious. He said, 'One-liners and jokey comments are bullshit: that's not real life. In a real situation, with lives on the line, you can't say that kind of thing.' I said, 'Yeah, not in real life, but this is a movie. This is *Die Hard*.'"

So heated did the argument get that an emergency summit was called, with Harlin, Willis, and Silver sitting down to thrash out the issue. Finally, they agreed that Willis would do as many takes as he wanted of each line, delivering them with deadly gravity; then Harlin would get one single take to do a lighter, humorous version. "He did it reluctantly, and sometimes not so happily," says Harlin, "but he did it. And in the end, every single funny moment that could be caught, even a smile that he might have flashed before he realized the cameras were rolling, every moment of that kind of warmth that was captured on film was cut into the movie."

A seemingly inoffensive scene set at a Dulles rental car counter turned out to be a flash point for the director's and star's differing sensibilities. The script called for McClane to send a fax containing the fingerprints of a dead villain to his cop pal from the first movie, Al Powell. The woman behind the desk is flirtatious, so McClane flashes his wedding ring at her. The *Dragnet*-riffing one-liner written for Willis to deliver, however—"Just the fax, ma'am. Just the fax"—proved a major irritant for the star. "Bruce hated that line," Harlin recalls. "He said, 'It's cheesy. It's stupid. I'm not going to say it.' And it took an hour there at the counter with me begging him and Joel getting involved before he would do it once. We did maybe fifteen takes and that's the one that's in the movie. People love it and laugh at it—plus the moment shows he really cares about his wife. It makes him a relatable and honorable guy."

Character beats, though, were secondary to ensuring that the action provided enough flash-bang-whoosh to rock back audiences' heads. The body count in *Die Hard 2* would be far bigger than in the first—not least due to the crashing of a civilian jet, something the studio fought but ultimately allowed—and so would the stunts. Sequences would see McClane pop out of a cockpit in an ejector seat like a cork out of a Champagne bottle, then blow up a 747 by lighting a trail of jet fuel. But the makers of *Die Hard 2* quickly discovered that shooting in an office building is one thing, and shooting in the great outdoors is quite another. A desperate hunt for snow began, as it first melted in Denver, where the production was based; then in Spokane, Washington, where they had moved; then in two different towns in Michigan. They ended up in the distinctly not subzero Los Angeles, turning three soundstages at Fox into virtual refrigerators and covering the floors with chippings from giant ice blocks.

By then, the $40 million budget they'd been granted was just a memory; *Die Hard 2* had gone off the rails, swelling to nearly $70 million, rocked by one act of God after another. Harlin wasn't bothered by the cold—as a child in Finland, he had frequently played outside in the snow, jousting with other kids using icicles (this happy memory inspired a grisly *Die Hard 2* death, in which

McClane thrusts a spear of frozen water through an antagonist's eye). But the increasing pressure, personified by the increasing number of Fox executives who were standing around on the set, sipping coffee, and staring at him as he worked, was starting to play on his nerves.

One night, as Harlin huddled from an unforeseen blizzard outside a church set in Denver, running behind schedule once again and with costs going up and up and up, Joel Silver took him aside. "He looked deadly serious, and he said, 'This time I just might have too much on my plate,'" Harlin recalls. "And that's when my blood froze. That was the only night where he kind of broke down and was like, 'I don't know if I can handle this. We're just having too much bad luck.' But the storm let up at four in the morning, and we survived the night."

Audiences in early 1990 were treated to a teaser trailer that unspooled austere statistics about Dulles Airport. "It covers 1,000 acres in our nation's capital . . . It handles flights from 84 different countries . . . It takes 10,000 employees to run it." So far, so dull. But then: a flashing red siren, an industrial-looking corridor, a cloud of dry ice, and, dashing through it, John McClane himself. "How can the same thing happen to the same guy twice?" he laments, reloading his handgun. Then he runs off, vanishing back through the steam. The teaser had in fact been specially shot in an LA water treatment plant. And with no snow involved, it came in mercifully on budget.

Most people went to see *Die Hard 2,* aka "Die Harder," because how could you not? In a summer stuffed with sequels—*Back to the Future Part III, Another 48 Hrs., RoboCop 2*—it came in third at the box office, just behind *Ghost* and *Total Recall,* with a haul of $118 million. But while it was slick, bombastic, frequently thrilling, the surprise factor of the original was gone. After all, it was ultimately the same thing, happening to the same guy, twice.

Willis geared up to make an action movie that interested him more, something called *Hudson Hawk,* in which he was planning to truly unleash his comedy stylings. Asked in July 1990 whether John McClane would return, he answered, "Sure, 'Die Hard 3:

He's Dead.' No, I think we've pretty much said everything about
John McClane and terrorists."

THAT WAS, OF COURSE, NOT TRUE: Fox thought there was
plenty left to be said about that particular subject. Steven de Souza
even knew what the milieu for *Die Hard 3* would be. "We had
cooked up the idea that the third one would be set on a cruise
ship," says the writer. "Our thinking was that these were basically
1970s disaster movies, with a layer cake of action laid on. So *Die
Hard* was basically *The Towering Inferno*. The second one was
Airport. So the third one had to be *The Poseidon Adventure*. We
actually worked up a whole storyline involving Bruce and his family going on vacation on a cruise ship."

But that nautical endeavor was torpedoed, brutally and effi-
ciently, by one Steven Seagal.

The star had been looking for a big movie—a really big movie—
for a while. His first four projects had all turned a profit, but they'd
been scrappy, street-level thrillers, nothing pricier than $14 million.
Meanwhile, his bitter rival Jean-Claude Van Damme was busy
shooting a $23 million behemoth, *Universal Soldier,* across town. It
wouldn't do. Seagal informed his patrons at Warner Bros. that he
was looking for something a little more spectacular.

For the studio, *Under Siege* was the obvious answer. Originally
titled *Dreadnought,* it was a spec script by hot young writer J. F.
Lawton, who had started his career with the unpromising *Canni-
bal Women in the Avocado Jungle of Death,* but who had recently
had his screenplay *Three Thousand* turned into the pop culture
phenomenon *Pretty Woman*. His new high-concept idea revolved
around a Navy battleship, the USS *Missouri* (a real vessel that had
been freshly decommissioned in 1992), that is taken over by rogue
sailors. *Die Hard* on the high seas, with nukes to spike up the tension. In lieu of Bruce Willis—or Eddie Murphy, to whom the project was also offered—Warner Bros. dangled it to their homegrown
bruiser. To their surprise, though, Seagal turned it down, multiple
times. One of his objections was the film's female villain, Bambi;

he called her a "bimbo," an element of the film that would make him look bad by extension.

Seagal suggested a fix: Bambi would no longer be the love interest of lead bad guy Strannix, to be played by Tommy Lee Jones, but be rewritten as Playboy Playmate Jordan, who ends up with his own character, ship's cook Casey Ryback. He also insisted on a destined-to-become-infamous introductory scene for Jordan, in which she jumps topless out of a giant cake. "That was Seagal's idea. He gets 100 percent credit for that," Lawton says of the highly gratuitous moment. And Seagal was not shy at reworking other story strands, too. "I completely redid the Tommy Lee Jones character, who was a flat, boring guy in the beginning," the star claims. "And once I redid Tommy, it became interesting to me, and then I was excited to do it. Because, you know, you're nothing without a great nemesis." Lawton, on the other hand, recalls Jones himself being the force behind Strannix's transformation into a leather-clad wild man, who at one point does an impression of the Road Runner ("Mee-meep!"). "Tommy said, 'Why can't I be a rock 'n' roll kinda guy?' It was a little weird, but Tommy made it work."

Director Andrew Davis, who had made Seagal's debut picture, returned to work with the star. He would battle to retain the movie's increasingly comedic tone and even its title: some executives fretted that it was only two words, where Seagal's previous movies had all had three (one suggested to change it to *Sea Under Siege*). Once the title was resolved, there was the question of where to shoot. Davis rejected the studio's suggestion out of hand: "Warner Bros. wanted us to go to Australia and build a battleship there so Steven could surf," he remembers. "I said, 'Are you out of your mind? You can't build this thing!' " Instead, the production headed to Mobile, Alabama, where the Navy allowed them to take exterior shots of an actual dreadnought, the USS *Alabama*. Later, the camera crew would follow the real-life USS *Missouri* to Hawaii to capture footage at the Pearl Harbor Memorial.

But even more tricky than creating the illusion of a 37,970-ton *South Dakota*–class battleship was the prospect of wrangling Steven Seagal. As a sweetener during negotiations with Davis, Warner

Bros. head Terry Semel had pointed out that Seagal would actually have minimal screentime. "Steven's only in the movie for forty-one minutes," Davis says. "Between the Pentagon stuff and all the other cutaways, Tommy is actually in the movie more than Steven." Even so, he proved a handful, for various reasons. "On *Above the Law,* he was easy to work with," the director recalls. "He was happy to be on the set. He wasn't playing prima donna, you know? By the time I went back to work with him on *Under Siege,* it was a different story. Seagal was sort of a pain in the ass."

Casey Ryback would seem to have been designed as a tongue-in-cheek creation: a cook who goes from chopping up onions to chopping up villains when he's left as the last line of defense aboard the *Missouri.* But the kind of quippy banter that came so naturally to Bruce Willis was not an easy mode for Seagal, the action hero with the demeanor of an undertaker. "You know that scene in the kitchen where he's cooking the stew and the guy spits in it?" says Davis. "I couldn't get him to smile. I had to literally do stuff—make jokes and so on—to get a smile."

Neither was Seagal particularly eager for his castmates to have fun in their own scenes. When Gary Busey came across a mention in a book about the USS *Missouri* of an executive officer who had dressed as a woman for a special party on the ship, he decided he wanted to incorporate drag into his villainous performance. "I took the idea to Steven Seagal, who was in a big bus he'd rented from a sheik, with a fifteen-foot fence around it," Busey explains. "He said, 'Whose idea was this?' I said, 'Mine.' He said, 'Okay.' But the next day Warner Bros. called. They said, 'Gary, do not go psychic on us' or psycho, you know what I mean. 'This is not a movie about you as a woman. This is a movie about martial arts with Steven Seagal.' "

Busey being Busey, he ignored them: "I had a 44DD stuffed, I had a Tina Turner wig, and nothing was going to stop me." And he would bump heads with Seagal again later over the star's treatment of Erika Eleniak, the real-life Playboy Playmate who had been cast as the fictional one in the movie. "This guy went overboard with the control master," Busey remembers. "And Erika

Eleniak—the little girl who was in it—I had her under my wing. He was looking to add in a love scene so he could really get down and dirty. She said to me, 'What do I do?' And I said, 'How much time do you have when you're running from us to find a table, lie down, and play plant-the-sausage?' " Neither Davis nor Lawton recall this happening, and Eleniak herself has never corroborated it but does recall Busey and Tommy Lee Jones supporting her when she was struggling with the cake scene. "It was not in the script originally, and I was not super-thrilled about doing that. I was upset and they both sent me yellow roses. Like, the yellow rose of Texas, where Tommy's from, [to say] 'Hang in there, you're going to do great.' "

For Davis, the making of *Under Siege* was a more pleasant experience. The director savored the performance of Jones, who wrote his big villain speech addressing the Pentagon himself. And Davis enjoyed capturing the nautical action, including a miraculous shot of dolphins swimming off the bow of the ship, footage that he says James Cameron considered buying for *Titanic*. But when he remembers the shoot, Davis also recalls a cold pair of eyes, belonging to one of the many shadowy people Seagal enlisted as technical advisers.

"It's really bizarre," the director says. "Steven brought on this guy named Robert Nichols, who was supposedly in the CIA and had these connections. He looked like Clark Gable, with eyes of death. He had the only phone in the world that was a satellite phone, which Steven uses in the movie. And this guy was arguing with Navy SEALS and admirals and all kinds of big shots in the Navy about how to take over a battleship. I'm sitting there between these testosterone flurries from these idiots, talking about what kind of weapons would be needed and how you'd approach the ship."

Davis learned later that Nichols had been under investigation by the FBI. Styling himself as a black-ops CIA agent, who spoke in whispered codes and alluded to a secret global organization called Octopus, he was rumored to be an assassin, a mob associate, even the developer of a high-tech laser gun. It was later alleged that Nichols conned a man out of $10 million using an elaborate plot;

meanwhile, a journalist named Danny Casolaro, who had been investigating one of Nichols's schemes, died in mysterious circumstances in 1991, just a year before *Under Siege* was shot. It wasn't the first time Seagal had brought a shady character onto one of his productions; in *Out for Justice* he'd cast Jerry Ciauri, aka Fat Jerry, a member of the Colombo crime family, as an extra in a bar fight (his character is the one thug Seagal doesn't lay a hand on). But on *Under Siege,* Nichols would be part of the creative process, pitching story beats. "He came up with this whole idea that Seagal should put sides of beef under his jacket," remembers Lawton. "And so when this guy shoots him, the frozen meat stops the bullets. So yeah, there'd be dumb ideas." And the malefactor would even bag a cameo: "Approximately one million people will reach ten thousand degrees Fahrenheit in less than a second," Nichols intoned, as Air Force Colonel Sarnac, in a scene set in the Pentagon.

But not even Seagal's sinister entourage (a promotional party for *Under Siege* aboard the USS *Intrepid* in New York Harbor was hosted by Julius Nasso, Seagal's business partner, who would ultimately spend a year in prison for attempting to extort him) could mar his latest endeavor. *Under Siege* was gigantic. From a $35 million budget, it grossed $156.6 million, more even than *Die Hard* or its sequel had made. A crowd-pleaser that elicited two thumbs-up from Roger Ebert and Gene Siskel, it had something for everyone: blockbuster bombast, a zesty knife fight, Tommy Lee Jones in a bandana.

Even the rarely giddy Harrison Ford, invited to an early screening, was swept away. "The premiere was a Friday, and I got a call Sunday night that Harrison had seen *Under Siege* and wanted me to do *The Fugitive,*" Davis remembers. "Maybe it was the girl jumping out of the cake, I don't know."

Seagal, meanwhile, was happy he hadn't chopped off his signature ponytail for nothing. On the record, he was muted about the film's success: "I don't wallow in joy," he told the *Los Angeles Times* after the opening weekend. But privately he was ecstatic about the reactions to *Under Siege.* He liked to tell the story of the time he attended the funeral for Bruce Lee's son, Brandon, in April 1993, and was approached by a renowned weapons practitioner named Dan Inosanto.

"Man, it's so terrible," Seagal said, regarding the mourners before him.

"Yeah, it's so terrible," replied Inosanto. Then, after a beat: "But that knife fight, man, in *Under Siege*—it's amazing!"

When recounting this story in years to come, Seagal would crack a grin and admit, "It's a pretty good fight."

DIE HARD on a boat had been an obvious enough pitch. The next clone was a little more unexpected.

Renny Harlin, hot after *Die Hard 2*, had been given the keys to another action movie, a Carolco project called *Gale Force*. It was, as the title suggested, about a hurricane—one menacing the Florida Keys, which would be taken advantage of by a band of marauders bent on booty. Only one man could stop them. That man, naturally enough, would be Sylvester Stallone. But *Gale Force* was being rocked by its own headwinds, with an endless parade of writers summoned in to crack the plot. For once, the star was staying out of the process—"All Stallone cared about was on what page did he start getting wet," said an insider—but Harlin was getting increasingly frustrated by the development woes. The final straw came when A-list writer Joe Eszterhas, who had sold *Basic Instinct* to Carolco for $3 million a couple of years earlier, took his own shot at it.

"He was the hottest writer in the world, and we sent him away believing that we would finally have something great," remembers Harlin. "Then we got the script. And it was like *Fatal Attraction* with a hurricane thrown in there. Literally, the hurricane happened in the last eight pages, and other than that it was an erotic drama. We were all just flabbergasted. We didn't even know what we were reading. And that was the final blow to the movie."

Gale Force was dead. But from its ashes rose a new action

movie, from another screenplay that had been getting passed around Carolco. Its name was *Cliffhanger,* and rather than being powered by wind, its unique gimmick was height. Essentially "Climb Hard," it pitted heroic mountain guide Gabe Walker against a group of dastardly robbers in a series of set pieces at fourteen thousand feet. Harlin signed on, despite some reservations about the familiarity of its logline. Stallone, too, clambered on board.

There had been, however, a breakdown in the chain of communication, something that became apparent when the star and the director met in Cortina, Italy, ahead of the start of the shoot. Only hours after Stallone's jet touched down, the two men got together and gazed at the vertiginous peaks of the Alps, jutting into the sky all around them, which in the movie would double for the Colorado Rockies.

"Wow, what a location," marveled Stallone. "So, who's gonna actually go up and shoot there?"

Harlin gulped. "You, Sly," he replied. "We are shooting the whole movie on those mountains."

Stallone's face darkened. "You gotta be kidding," he told the director. "The highest I will ever go is the heels of my cowboy boots."

It turned out that *Cliffhanger*'s A-list star had a lifelong fear of heights. For a project that depended upon its hero credibly dangling off rock faces, this was an issue. So that night Harlin regrouped. And he came up with a scheme.

The following day, he convinced Stallone and his entourage to join a location-scouting trip, in which a helicopter would fly up to view two peaks that had been selected for the shoot. The group disembarked at the larger one and gawped at the astonishing vista, crags emerging from fog far beneath them. While Stallone gazed around, commenting how great it was going to look when the second-unit crew shot up there, Harlin walked backward to the edge—where, unbeknownst to the actor, a wire had been suspended between the two peaks—and was quickly and surreptitiously hooked into a safety line by the stunt team. Then he called out, "Sly, you gotta have a look at this," stepped off the lip of the cliff, and plummeted out of sight.

"Sly pretty much fainted when that happened," says the director with a laugh. "I slid almost to the halfway point between the two mountains, hanging from this thin wire to the main wire, ten thousand feet from the ground. And I said, 'You can do this. We'll shoot it for real, and it's going to be the most amazing thing ever.' I knew, knowing Sly, that he could not say no. All these buff, macho guys were around him, looking at him. And he went, 'I mean, of course. Yeah, I can do that.'"

Stallone didn't do the wire that day. But he did face his fear for the shoot itself, heading up into the clouds on a regular basis and braving not only high altitudes but also conditions so cold that on the second day of filming the cameras iced up and the food for lunch froze solid. He claimed that wind at one point almost swept him off a summit. While shooting a scene where he was trapped under ice, he panicked, blinded by the salt in the water and unable to find his way out. And weeks and weeks of clambering over rocks made his hands so callused that the models he dated would complain about them. "Never again. Never, never, never, never, never again," he said on the press tour.

But the *Cliffhanger* experience proved a good one for the star, in a few ways. Not only had he overcome his own vulnerabilities, with a little nudge from his director, but the film provided a much-needed softening of his screen image—like John McClane, Gabe Walker was a relatable, flawed human, haunted by his failure to save a woman from falling to her death in the movie's prologue. This was Rocky in the Rockies, a throwback to Stallone's start-of-career sensitivity, the bludgeoning brute force and fearlessness of Rambo replaced by a figure who feels emotional pain. Co-opting the *Die Hard* formula proved exactly the right move—after the disastrous run of *Rocky V*, *Oscar*, and *Stop! Or My Mom Will Shoot*, *Cliffhanger* reaped $255 million against its $70 million budget.

A sequel seemed inevitable, and in fact, one was announced in 1994. Called *The Dam*, it would see Gabe defend the Hoover Dam from terrorists. But it never happened. The *Die Hard* effect kept on rippling, though. Wesley Snipes defended a jet plane in *Passenger 57*. Sean Astin safeguarded a school under siege in *Toy Soldiers*. Van Damme, inevitably, got into the action in 1995 with *Sudden Death*, taking the concept to its natural conclusion with a film in which terrorists take over an ice hockey rink, forcing former firefighter Darren McCord to fight back—in one scene while dressed as a penguin.

John McTiernan, who would reenter the fray himself with 1995's *Die Hard with a Vengeance*, continued to observe this seemingly endless wave of *Die Hard* try-hards. "Apparently somebody actually proposed that they make '*Die Hard* in a building,'" he says with a chuckle. "I mean, there's no limit on how silly some people can be."

CHAPTER 16

...

BORN AGAIN

AS THE 1990S KICKED OFF, the man who perfected the round-house kick was considering kicking back. By this point, there was little Chuck Norris hadn't done in the name of righteous mayhem. He had laid waste to armies. He had defeated serial killers, drug syndicates, ninjas, brutes, and shit-kickers. He had won Vietnam. Now, though, he was in his fifties, the oldest of the big-screen action heroes, and despite still having a resting heart rate of forty-eight beats per minute and a more strenuous physical fitness program than ever before, he was considering retiring his fists.

The brutal movies with which he had become synonymous were fading away with the 1980s, and Norris wasn't entirely unhappy to see them go. "Violence is not the answer," he says. "It's love. Love is the strongest emotion in the world. Nothing's stronger than love—it's what life is really all about." On-screen, he was Chuck Norris, the man with the bulletproof beard and flamethrower stare, mowing down Commies and flag-disrespecters without wasting a bead of sweat. In real life, on the other hand, he was Chuck Norris, the shy, soft-spoken Christian who shunned violence at all costs. And people expecting an encounter with the former were often surprised when they met the latter.

One night, while out in the boondocks to shoot an episode of his new hit TV show *Walker: Texas Ranger,* Norris visited a country bar with a few friends. Their preference in alcohol was brandy or whiskey, but this particular joint didn't have any stocked, so instead they ordered beer and sipped halfheartedly. Then, suddenly, a huge man in cowboy garb loomed over them.

"Hey, motherfucker," the guy told Norris. "You're sitting in my booth."

The group fell silent as everyone's eyeballs swiveled to the star, waiting to see how he would react. "I would have said, 'Get the fuck out or I'm going to break your leg,'" says Bob Wall, who was there. "But Chuck reacts totally opposite. Chuck doesn't want you to get in the shit. So he says, 'Oh, I'm sorry, I'm sorry.' Now, this place is empty. But we get up and move. We went to a corner."

The men continued to sip their beers until the doors opened five minutes later and the rest of Norris's party—a dozen black-belt fighters, including two retired cops—strolled in and joined them. For the hulking cowboy in the booth, the penny finally dropped. Taking off his Stetson, he approached the group again, this time with a different demeanor.

"Oh my God, you're Chuck Norris," he mumbled.

"Yes, sir," Norris said.

"I'm so sorry," said the man. "Why didn't you kick my ass over there? I mean, you could kick my ass."

Norris smiled, then replied, "What would that prove?"

Then he invited the cowboy to join them for a beer.

If he was friendly to strangers, he was just as amiable with people in his industry. On the set of *Walker* he offered free self-defense lessons to cast and crew between setups; in a break on one episode, he taught a ten-year-old Mila Kunis how to throw a punch. And Norris's philanthropy extended to acting lessons, too. The man once decried as "a whitebread Bruce Lee, with no screen presence to speak of" was now offering advice to up-and-comers. In 1992, one of his pupils was Jessica Simpson, only twelve at the time and dispatched by her agent to glean craft from the Lone Wolf.

"You have too much expression," Norris said, frowning, as he watched the young Simpson go through a scene. He went on to explain that Denzel Washington was the most powerful actor in the world because he could deliver any line without moving his eyebrows. Then he taped down Simpson's own brows with Scotch tape for the duration of the course.

"Everyone acted like this was very normal," Simpson would recall. "I will say the experience ruined every single Denzel film I've ever seen since. I just watch his eyebrows the whole time, waiting for them to move."

NORRIS'S OWN FINELY honed brow work failed to be commented upon in reviews of his movies. But critics had started to notice a softening, a new warmth, in his performances. Just as the Terminator had learned to become more human, so had Norris. And it began with 1988's *Hero and the Terror,* an otherwise rote cop yarn in which the star's character, Detective O'Brien, does some very un-Norris-like things.

For one, he goes to therapy—therapy!—in an attempt to shake off the haunting memory of being overpowered by an adversary. Then, later, he faints—faints!—at a hospital as his girlfriend prepares to give birth. The latter was in fact an impromptu take that Norris had thrown in as a joke. "I never did it with the intention of it ending up on the screen," he would reveal. "When the director edited it, he called me up and said, 'We're going to leave the fainting scene in the movie.' And I said, 'Oh no, there's no way Chuck Norris is going to faint on-screen. I might do a lot of things, but I'm not going to faint.'"

Norris finally relented, after reflecting on how helpless he had felt when his wife had been in labor with their first child. This most macho of stars was frightened of something after all—allowing himself to look frightened on-screen. "I feel very secure playing a Braddock in *Missing in Action,*" he admitted. "But when you start showing vulnerability on-screen when you're used to playing hard, non-vulnerable characters, it's a risk." Although *Hero and the Terror* got generally lousy reviews, Roger Ebert did salute the actor's change of pace. "A new Chuck Norris is unveiled," the critic wrote. "Maybe he grew tired of kicking people in the face."

It was true: the star was transforming. After releasing a reflective self-help book in the same year as *Hero and the Terror,* titled *The Secret of Inner Strength* (sample secret: "It's just as easy to make a friend as it is to make an enemy"), Norris launched a final flurry of movies before disappearing from the big screen altogether. And only in one of them would he fire a rocket launcher at a demon (*Hellbound,* which would prove to be the final film released by Cannon). The other three, all directed by Chuck's brother Aaron, were designed as movies to inspire kids, studded with family values and delivering as many life lessons as brawls.

They would also see Chuck Norris take on his deadliest enemy: comedy.

Norris was all too aware of the pitfalls that lay in wait for those who dared to lighten up. "Stallone has tried different films and they've been unsuccessful and he's always had to go back to the Rocky and Rambo characters," Norris told one reporter. But he would not be deterred. Hence, 1992's *Sidekicks,* a strange, self-mythologizing project in which he yielded the leading role to a sixteen-year-old named Jonathan Brandis. The story sees asthmatic, bullied teenager Barry (Brandis) get through his miserable days by daydreaming about his hero: movie star Chuck Norris. In Barry's daydreams, he is by Norris's side, kicking foes into submission. Then the real Norris turns up and agrees to help train Barry for a karate tournament. At the end, after the predictable triumph, Norris vanishes into thin air.

If this vanity project, which with a $17 million haul became the star's biggest hit for years, saw him dip his foot into the world of humor, then *Top Dog* seemed set to see him dive right in. Partnering Norris's Jake Wilder with a shaggy police dog called Reno, the 1995 film put out a poster with the briard wearing a hat next to a scowling Norris (the tagline read, "One's tough. One's smart," though it was hard to tell which was meant to be which). The star hyped up the movie as a hilarious family comedy, proclaiming, "Oh man, this is the funniest thing."

But when it arrived, *Top Dog* proved oddly bleak. Norris and his new sidekick were pitted against not bank robbers but neo-

Nazis, who have blown up a building with children inside and also murdered Mexican arms dealers. They are planning another atrocity to occur on Hitler's birthday. Later, the Ku Klux Klan is introduced. As family entertainment went, it was a long way from *Turner & Hooch*.

Top Dog's release was unfortunately timed, coming just eight days after the Oklahoma City bombing, a real-life tragedy that the opening sequence coincidentally echoed. Still, there was no denying that the film was a clunker. "*Top Dog* runs 86 minutes, but so much of it is in slow motion that it would last only about 15 minutes at standard speed," wrote critic Dann Gire. "There are slow-motion shots of people running, slow-motion shots of people shooting, slow-motion shots of people kung-fuing, and even slow-motion shots of Jake Wilder *walking*. Don't look at me . . . I don't know why, either."

If critics found all the hate-group hijinks and half-speed crotch kicks bewildering, they would be left truly confounded by Norris's farewell film. Then again, nobody was ready for *Forest Warrior*.

IT BEGAN IN CHESTER, CALIFORNIA, where Norris had a vacation home. "We were up there for my daughter's basketball game, and I had my niece who was four years old sitting on my lap," Norris remembers. "We're watching the game and suddenly I feel this squeezing on my thumb. And she says, 'I want to see you turn into a bear.'"

Chuck obliged, and in style, he and his brother Aaron teaming up for a kids' film once more despite the travails of *Top Dog*. They cooked up a story in which a mountain man named McKenna, killed in the nineteenth century, returns as a bizarre kind of superhero to defeat a nefarious logging conglomerate. His special power: he can transform into an eagle, a wolf, or, yes, a bear. One might argue that it was overkill; after all, Norris in human form could inflict more damage than most of the animal kingdom put together. But this black-belted environmental fable is responsible for sights never before seen, such as the star of *The Delta Force* stopping a buzzing chainsaw blade with his bare hand. Or swooping down in bird form before kicking a lumberjack mid-transformation.

It was not exactly highbrow cinema. And in fact, *Forest Warrior* never made it to movie theaters, going direct to video in 1996. Norris, though, has no regrets. "It was a great family film," he says, "and like most of my films it has special meaning to me. Truthfully, I'm proud of each one in a certain way."

Chuck Norris would now vanish from the big screen, just as he vanished at the end of *Sidekicks,* not appearing again until 2004's limited-release Christian film *Bells of Innocence,* which also starred his eldest son, Mike. Instead, he'd focus on kicking ass on TV, in *Walker: Texas Ranger.* But weirdly, through this quasi retirement, he would become bigger than ever, his legend continuing to grow and grow and grow. Kids wrote letters to him, telling him how much *Sidekicks* had helped them deal with their own bullies. And "Chuck Norris facts" began to circulate like brushfire on the internet, as well as spawning bestselling books, riffing on his screen persona's seeming omnipotence.

"There is no theory of evolution, just a list of creatures Chuck Norris allows to live."
"Chuck Norris runs until the treadmill gets tired."
"Chuck Norris once killed two stones with one bird."
"Chuck Norris has a diary. It's called the *Guinness Book of World Records.*"
"Chuck Norris makes onions cry."

Says the man himself of the phenomenon: "I consider it a great compliment, for the young people to put me in that category. I don't know why they did it, but I'm completely flattered. What's amazed me is that it has gone all over the world."

In fact, American soldiers in Iraq loved swapping Chuck Norris facts so much that in 2006 a Marine commander contacted the star and invited him to come visit. "So I went to eleven different bases, places no one's ever heard of," he says. "I slept in the hooch with the troops and the latrine would be fifty yards down the road, you know? It was a great opportunity to shake their hand and take pictures with all of them. In fact, one of the tanks had my name on the barrel."

Norris being Norris, he didn't just smile and make it a photo op. He clambered inside the tank, then fired a shell at an insurgent group ten miles away.

JACKIE CHAN WAS BEWILDERED. And the heavy fog of jet lag from his journey to Los Angeles from Hong Kong wasn't helping any. As he wandered from room to room around the vast Beverly Hills mansion, peering closely at every strange artifact he encountered, one word kept arising in his mind: "Why?"

It was May 1993, and the limousine had picked Chan up from LAX after he'd disembarked from the flight. Then it had driven the bleary star north, through Culver City, past Santa Monica, and up into Benedict Canyon, a hushed haven of LA's rich and famous, with stunning views of the Pacific. Finally, Chan was deposited on the driveway leading to an 8,400-square-foot building. This was it— unlike the home gestured at in *Pretty Woman* with the immortal line "That's Sylvester Stallone's house right there," this was the real deal. The residence of the Hollywood A-lister whom Chan had admired from afar but had never actually met or even spoken to.

Chan, initially, was disappointed: there was no Stallone to be seen. Instead, one of the homeowner's assistants granted him access to the facilities: the art gallery, the movie theater, the eight-hole putting green. Chan tried out a few of the gym's twenty-five state-of-the-art fitness machines (though not the one set to a lifting weight of four hundred pounds). Finally he found himself in front of a wall of awards, which in his memory would include—even though Stallone had never actually won one—a golden, gleaming Oscar. Alone, back in this strange land and feeling a jolt of excitement, Chan did what he felt he must.

"I touched it, I kissed it, I smelled it," he later recalled of his reaction to seeing the Academy Award, or whatever it was. "I believe it still has my fingerprints on it."

Chan's strange sojourn at Casa Sly finally came to an end, with the assistant informing him that it was time to finally meet the man of the house. He got back in the car, which wound its way to the set of *Demolition Man*, a new Warner Bros. project. He watched filming of the climactic sequence for a while before Stallone spotted him on the periphery and yelled, "Hey, everyone, it's Jackie Chan!"

For Chan, who had feared there might have been some mix-up involved in his summoning, that the star might have confused him with someone else, it was an overwhelming moment. "Stallone grabbed my hand and walked me around the studio," he remembers. "All the stunt guys started standing up and bowing. I was so totally surprised: 'What's going on? Am I that famous?' I didn't even know. He walked to his trailer and said, 'Jackie, come in.' He pushed a video in, and it was *Police Story*. He said, 'When we run out of ideas, we watch one of your films.'"

Chan was awestruck, so much so that all he could think to say through the provided interpreter was, "Thank you. You are my idol." The next evening, at the premiere of *Cliffhanger*, he was awestruck again as he walked an American red carpet for the first time, trying not to get in the way of the likes of Stallone, Arnold Schwarzenegger, and Dolph Lundgren, plus a cardigan-wearing Jason Alexander.

America had rejected Chan twice before. But as he boarded his return flight to Hong Kong, he took along with him two resolutions: that one day he would hoist an Oscar himself, and that a Hollywood premiere would launch one of his own movies.

He also had a more tangible souvenir: a signed poster of *First Blood Part II*.

A WHILE EARLIER, Chan had actually been sounded out on whether he wanted to play the villain role in *Demolition Man*, the part ultimately taken by Wesley Snipes. But for Chan it just wasn't an option: like Chuck Norris, he did not play bad guys. When he had received an offer to star opposite Michael Douglas in 1988's *Black Rain* as a Japanese killer, he immediately nixed it, too, no matter how much he fancied being part of a $30 million US thriller.

"Being Jackie Chan is not easy," he says. "I have to be very careful what I'm doing, what I'm filming, what I'm talking, what I'm singing. I feel a responsibility. I go jogging in Africa and the children are all following, doing the *Drunken Master* style. All these years later, they still remember this."

As it turned out, he would have a presence in *Demolition Man* anyway. At the end of a scene in the movie where Sandra Bullock's future cop Lenina Huxley defends herself against a gang of thugs, Stallone's John Spartan asks her, "Where the hell did you learn to kick like that?" She replies, "Jackie Chan movies." A line inserted by Stallone as a tribute to his new friend, and an alert to millions of viewers in America that there was somebody special out there worth getting familiar with.

Buzz, as it happened, was building already in the West. The third *Police Story* film, *Supercop,* got a limited US release in 1992, making the jaws of those in the know drop to the floor. "Probably contains the greatest stunts—and that's even including Buster Keaton—ever filmed in any movie ever," Quentin Tarantino would rave. The feats of daring that made him go back to see it again and again were performed by the dream double act of Chan and Michelle Yeoh, the former dangling from a rope ladder attached to a helicopter, the latter jumping a motorcycle onto a speeding train. Off the back of *Supercop,* Yeoh was offered a role in the Bond film *Tomorrow Never Dies.* As for Chan, his reputation as someone who made James Bond look like a slacker was growing fast.

Film festivals devoted to him began to be held in California, New York, and Chicago. In 1994, Hong Kong distributor Media Asia started releasing his Golden Harvest output in the United States. And the star's regular producers, Raymond Chow and Leonard Ho, banking on their feeling that full-blown Chandemonium was inevitable, persuaded him to have one more go at breaking the West. He reunited with *Supercop* director Stanley Chow on a movie set in New York. The title: *Rumble in the Bronx.*

In reality, the rumble went down in Vancouver—despite the many establishing shots of the Statue of Liberty, there was no mistaking the forest-fringed mountains in the background of several scenes. In other ways, too, the Hong Kong crew's re-creation of New York bore little resemblance to the real thing: the cartoonish story saw gun-and-grenade battles breaking out on the streets and a crazed biker gang terrorizing the populace. The dialogue clunked. But Chan determined to make the action so fierce that nobody would be paying attention to the incongruous backdrops or wooden verbiage. And he pulled it off. Unlike in *The Protector,* his last attempt to break into Hollywood, the mayhem in *Rumble in the Bronx* was hugely ambitious, a perfect showcase for his one-man-against-the-world act. As an innocent Chinese guy who gets sucked into a battle against the Big Apple's criminal underworld, Chan utilized such henchmen-smashing props as a refrigerator, a La-Z-Boy, a motorcycle, and, in the climax, a gigantic hovercraft. When he broke his ankle jumping from a pier to the hovercraft, he simply hopped into a wheelchair, covered his cast with a fake rubber sneaker, and rolled back into the fray.

This time he was doing things his way. And that applied not just to the mayhem but also to the film's vibe. No more swearing or tough-guy posturing; here, after reluctantly roughing up a den of goons, Chan's Keung turns to the groaning thugs and says, "I hope next time when we meet, we won't be fighting each other. Instead, we will be drinking tea together."

As Chan recalls, "*Rumble in the Bronx,* I did it with a purpose. Uncle Bill gets married with the Black girl. And I wanted to fill the Bronx with Italian, Spanish, Chinese . . . The first person I punch is a Chinese. I want to show that there are good people and bad people everywhere. In a million years, there will only be one kind of people: Earth people. That's my philosophy."

IN JUNE 1995, two years after Chan touched down in LA for his visit to Stallone's house, he landed again at the same airport. This time his arrival went a little differently.

There wasn't a huge mob to greet him, as there usually was whenever he disembarked a plane in Asia. But by American standards, the welcome party was a surprise: a small throng of twenty-five people, beaming at him and holding aloft signs. A bright pink banner spelled out the words "All Americans love Jackie. Some just don't know it yet."

Chan was there to attend the MTV Movie Awards, where he was handed a Lifetime Achievement award by Quentin Tarantino. "He is one of the best filmmakers the world has ever known," the director pronounced. "He is one of the great physical comedians since sound came into films. Basically, if I could be any actor, I would have the life Jackie Chan has."

The following February, Chan appeared for the first time on David Letterman's talk show. "The number-one box-office star in the world," hyped the host. "We're not talking about here in New York. We're not talking about Phoenix. We're talking about the *world*." An ebullient Chan, in a white turtleneck and black blazer, proceeded to smash a glass on Letterman's desk before clambering onto it and kicking a succession of bottles toward the audience. Then, taking over the host's chair, he barked, "Now—interview!"

He guested on Leno. He mock-battled Conan O'Brien, complete with kung-fu sound effects. He had a breakaway chair smashed over him by Rosie O'Donnell. And even though these TV appearances treated him like something of a joke, the box-office performance of *Rumble in the Bronx* showed that Jackie Chan was to be taken seriously. Released by New Line, after being dubbed into English and slightly reedited from its Asian version, it rocketed to number one in its US opening weekend, beating out *Broken Arrow, Happy Gilmore,* and *Muppet Treasure Island*. The nimble, daredevil, oddly wholesome pugilism of Chan dazzled Americans used to more sluggish one-man armies.

"Any attempts to defend this movie on rational grounds is futile," wrote Roger Ebert. "Don't tell me about the plot and the dialogue. Don't dwell on the acting. The whole point is Jackie Chan—and, like Astaire and Rogers, he does what he does better than anybody."

After fulfilling his dream of getting his own red-carpet premiere for *Rumble*, Chan was invited to leave his handprints in fresh cement outside LA's iconic Chinese Theater in 1997 (he couldn't resist sticking his nose in the sludge, too). Invited to present at the Academy Awards, he was approached there by Tom Hanks, Robin Williams, and John Travolta, who all claimed they were ardent fans. And he received a blizzard of scripts. One, by John Hughes, called *The Bee,* would have seen Chan spending ninety minutes chasing a rogue honey-maker. Another, titled *Confucius Brown,* would have paired him with Wesley Snipes, *Twins*-style, as long-lost brothers. He was offered *Beverly Hills Ninja,* opposite Chris Farley. Bruce Willis sent word that he wanted to collaborate. Steven Spielberg and James Cameron announced themselves as enthusiasts of his brawling techniques. "I want to find out what would happen, my action and their technology," Chan enthused, offering to work with them for free.

None of those projects would happen, however. And although Chan did get the massive American breakthrough he wanted, in the shape of 1998's *Rush Hour,* which paired him with Chris Tucker and made a mighty $244 million, he would come to feel a certain ambivalence about his rebirth, the dream that had come true. Yes, he was now famous everywhere, feted in the West and more bankable than ever. He'd even one day hoisted himself up the iconic Hollywood sign, a daredevil feat to symbolize his US-storming achievement. But part of him quickly came to pine for the creative freedom of Hong Kong, the days where he could wake up, survey his surroundings, then orchestrate bedlam with whatever items were in reach.

"I found out the US market and Chinese market are different," he reflects. "They like talk. Character, story, comedy—*then* action. In Hong Kong, we talk about action first. Fight, fight, fight, fight, fight, fight! In America, they will never let me do *New Police Story*. They will never let me do *Rob-B Hood*. But in Asia, I can do whatever I like to do."

Even so, he would keep pushing, in every project, to distinguish himself from the American action gods with whom he was now in direct competition. Back in that 1996 Letterman interview, he had been asked about those rivals, and tactfully replied, "They're very lucky. . . . The producers, the companies, they won't let them do any stunts. In Asia, life is very cheap, including me."

"So what you're saying," Letterman quipped, "is they're sissies."

Then, Chan had demurred with a laugh. But later that year, during a break on the Hong Kong set of *Thunderbolt*, his follow-up to *Rumble in the Bronx*, Chan flicked through a copy of a local newspaper until he came to an article about the new release *Die Hard with a Vengeance*. In it, a series of photos showed how special effects had combined two shots—one of Bruce Willis lying on the ground, a green background behind him; the other, a car barreling toward the camera—to make it look like the star had been in peril.

Studying the photos, Chan shook his head sadly. If it had been him, he'd have been in front of the car for real. And it probably would have been a truck.

CHAPTER 17

OIL AND WATER

ONE MORNING IN JANUARY 1993, the key players behind the warring-geriatrics comedy *Grumpy Old Men* gathered in a meeting room on the Warner Bros. lot. Stars Walter Matthau and Jack Lemmon were there, plus director Donald Petrie and others, doing one last read-through of the script before they headed to Minnesota to begin the shoot. The mood was light as Lemmon and Matthau sparked off each other, making everyone around the table laugh. Pages flicked by.

Then, two-thirds of the way through the screenplay, a loud thumping began at the door. *Bang! Bang! Bang!*

Petrie got up, puzzled, and opened the door, to reveal a grumpy middle-aged man: Steven Seagal.

"What's going on?" Seagal thundered.

"We're trying to do a read-through with Walter Matthau and Jack Lemmon," Petrie explained.

"Well, I don't care," Seagal said. "I have this room."

As *Twins* writer William Osborne, who was present as an uncredited contributor to the script, remembers, "It was just classic Steven Seagal. He finally stepped out and closed the door. But he was an absolute nutcase. He made those absolutely banging early action films and then he went completely batshit crazy."

Mere months after the release of *Under Siege*, this was Seagal at his absolute zenith. An unstoppable battleship of a movie, it had pounded the global box office into submission, its stunning success definitive affirmation—not that he needed it—of its star's view of himself as one destined for greatness. Seagal's film titles had proclaimed him as *Hard to Kill* and *Above the Law*. It seemed those statements were spot on. Rather than fading away as a fad, he was a monster star, a *kaiju* raging through Hollywood.

Humility, already an alien concept to Seagal, slipped still further away. Now he thumped through the corridors of Warner Bros., the laboratory that had created him, unwilling to accept such slights as, say, an occupied meeting room. The studio had hastily offered him a lucrative four-picture deal, willing to put up with bad behavior in exchange for the promise of more jackpot payoffs. Seagal accepted, and the hunt for his next action movie began. Nothing short of magnificence would do.

Warners decided to try putting him together with the *Die Hard* writer/producer combo of Steven de Souza and Joel Silver. But that idea went south after Seagal was patched into a call with de Souza without realizing the screenwriter was on the line. "Silver's just coasting on Larry Gordon's coattails," Seagal declared before anyone could explain. "And I could write a better script than de Souza with one hand in the dark." The call was brought to a hurried end.

Seagal turned down project after project. Then, finally, something drew his eye. It wasn't so much the quality of the story as the fact that Clint Eastwood—one of his many nemeses, and another house artist at Warner Bros.—wanted it. And the thought of stealing a movie from Dirty Harry made Seagal smile.

"He wanted to fuck over Clint Eastwood," says Ed Horowitz, one of the project's writers. "Clint had just made *The Rookie*, which had bombed. And Seagal had made *Under Siege*. So they gave it to him."

And so was born *On Deadly Ground*, a movie that would unleash Steven Seagal's ego in new, unimaginable ways.

———

IT STARTED, like *The Terminator,* with a fevered vision in the middle of the night. "I had this dream that Arnold Schwarzenegger had been reincarnated as a Native American hero, riding a killer whale on some sort of rescue mission," says *On Deadly Ground*'s other credited writer, Robin Russin. "I woke up and thought, 'Wow, that's intense.'"

He and Horowitz transformed the bizarre reverie into an action screenplay, titled *The Rainbow Warrior,* fusing together a hard-boiled hero, ecological themes (the villains being an oil company trashing the environment in Alaska), and Inuit spirituality. In their heads, the leading man would be someone like Nick Nolte. Instead, to the amazement of the first-time screenwriters, their script made its way to Harrison Ford, Mel Gibson, and Clint Eastwood. "I just started laughing," Horowitz remembers. "I was like, 'This can't be real.'"

Their dream was coming true, in more ways than one. But then came word that the script had reached the offices of Steamroller Productions, Seagal's new shingle, which was positioned directly across from Eastwood's Malpaso HQ in the main Warner building. Steamroller having won this particular gunfight, the two writers were summoned to a meeting with their star.

"Listen, guys," Seagal whispered, leaning against the door frame in a long leather coat and cowboy boots, "I'm going to let you take your pass, then I'm going to come in and make it something really special."

The kicker was this: rather than merely act, Seagal was going to follow Eastwood's lead and direct, too. No matter that he had zero experience, and that this was a complex $50 million production, set to shoot mainly outdoors. If he had any doubts that he could pull it off, there was no evidence of them. In fact, rather than considering budgetary concerns, in script meetings he kept pumping the action up and up, serenely maximizing the carnage.

"Seagal would sit across from me and give me his notes," says Horowitz. "And each one was more insane than the last. My natural response to that kind of absurdity is to make jokes, but I'm fully aware that if I make jokes, he's gonna punch me or roundhouse me or something. One time he said, 'I'm seeing six mercenaries in a Sikorsky [helicopter].' I'm thinking, 'Why would an oil company in Alaska have any mercenaries? I have no fucking idea. This makes no sense.' But I just looked at him and went, 'I'm thinking twelve and two.' And he just breaks into this smile and points at me. While behind me this producer is waving his arms and scowling."

Every edict laid down by the star/auteur was slavishly followed. His character name changed from Ryan Taft to Forrest Taft, to sound more "environmental" ("There's a lot of deep subtext there to be pried out, isn't there?" jokes Russin). The character's partner in the original script was removed; Steven Seagal didn't need help. And a mystical "vision quest" midway through the movie was tweaked, replacing an elderly Inuit lady, an earth mother, with lithe, topless young women. Seagal had decreed: "Sexy it up."

The two writers, new to Hollywood, had a major motion picture on the way, with Michael Caine cast as the villain and a studio throwing its considerable resources behind it. But it had turned into a horror show. "The concept and characters were basically all the same, but there was nothing in that movie left of ours," Horowitz says. Infused with Seagal's ideas, the newly titled On Deadly Ground now made about as much sense as Arnold Schwarzenegger riding a killer whale.

WARNER BROS. had gingerly suggested that the movie be filmed in Montana or Wyoming. Seagal refused. In his mind, it had to be shot in the remote Alaskan town of Valdez, for authenticity. "He wanted that majestic look that Alaska has," said the film's publicist, Tom Gray, at the time. Seagal's demands didn't stop there: he also insisted that a Yup'ik Eskimo tribal chief be cast in a key role, despite having no acting experience, and that Yup'ik be spoken extensively in the film.

Then there was the medicine man. To ensure the success of On Deadly Ground, a blessing ceremony was vital, in Seagal's mind, and so a Tlingit shaman named Cy Peck Jr. was flown by Warner Bros. to Valdez in May 1993. In the production office, accompanied

by another Native American in Athabascan regalia, Peck con-
ducted a forty-five-minute ritual, blessing Seagal and his family.

Bowing to him, Seagal asked, "Do you believe movies can con-
vey spirituality?"

The shaman, who had not seen any of the star's work, replied
that he enjoyed Sherlock Holmes films.

Throughout the shoot, he was to receive regular phone calls
from Seagal, seeking spiritual wisdom. It was the only real evidence
of any insecurity at all. After calling cut on a shot, Seagal would
frequently turn to the crew and ask, "Wasn't that the best thing
you ever saw?" Upon performing a scene in which he ran through
some debris, he strolled over to a huddle of people and said, "Man,
I nailed that, didn't I?"

Watching dailies surely only pumped up his ego further. In
Under Siege, the villains had spent considerable time cataloguing
the attributes of Seagal's hero: "Expert in martial arts, explosives,
weapons and tactics. Silver Star, Navy Cross, Purple Heart with
Cluster . . ." *On Deadly Ground* took this further, with firefighter-
turned-vigilante Forrest's antagonists in awe of his powers. "Delve
down into the deepest bowels of your soul," laments one. "Try to
imagine the ultimate fucking nightmare. And that won't come
close to this son of a bitch when he gets pissed." Another moans,
"He's the kind of guy that would drink a gallon of gasoline so he
could piss in your campfire."

This macho posturing was nothing new. What was novel was
Seagal's new green streak—despite the production leaving Valdez
with the town claiming it was owed $130,000 in unpaid bills, *On
Deadly Ground* was positioned as an urgent message movie, as important as fellow star-turned-director Kevin Costner's *Dances
with Wolves.* "You do whatever you can do to fight the fight," reflects Seagal, decades on. "I don't want to talk about the great suc-
cesses I've had in the environmental world. I've managed to shut
down dirty toxic plants, nuclear power plants that were going to
desecrate holy areas. I've had some luck, you know, but I've also
lost some battles. All I can say is I get out there every day and do all
I can to make the world a better place."

At the LA premiere in February 1994, attended by names such as Sandra Bullock and Arsenio Hall, the anticipation was palpable. "I was sitting in the audience and all around me were people saying, 'This is such an important movie. This is going to change so many minds,'" remembers Robin Russin. "I'm looking around going, 'Man, okay. I mean, your mouth to God's ear, but I don't think so.'" The reels unspooled. Also present, Ed Horowitz turned to his sister midway through and whispered, "Debbie, I wrote this movie and I can't follow it." The film climaxed with perhaps the most unlikely ending for an action movie in history: Steven Seagal, standing in front of a crowd, delivering a seemingly endless speech, complete with slides, on the subject of plankton, toxic waste, and carbon emissions. The on-screen audience is appreciative, with reaction shots of people nodding thoughtfully. Actual viewers seemed generally less enthusiastic.

"All hail the expressionless environmentalist," summed up *Newsday*. Said critic Rene Rodriguez: "Invulnerable heroes aren't much fun, but Seagal has become such an egomaniacal star, he'd probably drop-kick anyone who dared mention this to him. *On Deadly Ground,* which ends with an embarrassingly heavy-handed sermon on protecting the environment, should help deflate his ego."

This was wishful thinking. One person, at least, was delighted with how the movie had come out: the man whose name appeared three times on-screen before its title. "I had many of the greatest directors on earth come to my premiere," Seagal said in an interview shortly after. "And I wasn't really too nervous about it, what they'd think about it, because I was proud of my work." Only one thing soured his mood slightly—a comment by Michael Caine, who had sat next to him and remarked at the end, "I really didn't think it would be anywhere near this good." The suggestion that Caine had once entertained doubts raised Seagal's hackles. "I could have been insulted by what he said," he concluded graciously. "But I didn't, which goes to show how much respect I have for Michael."

Years later, the British actor would speak more freely. "I had broken one of the cardinal rules of bad movies," Caine wrote in his memoirs. "If you're going to do a bad movie, at least do it in a great location."

OVER THE YEARS, *On Deadly Ground* has become a byword for rampant narcissism. It has been mocked by *South Park* and maligned even—or especially—by those involved in its creation. "Whenever I get a green envelope from the Writers Guild with a nice little check," says Robin Russin, "I always say, 'Thank you, Steven. I hate you, Steven.'" At the time, it made a huge loss, garnering only $38.6 million at the box office, a fraction of what *Under Siege* had scored. At least it did well at the Razzies, getting six nominations—Worst Picture, Worst Actor, Worst Actress, Worst Screenplay, Worst Director, Worst Original Song—and winning Worst Director. It was the most public possible humiliation for Seagal, who had swung big and been roundly rejected.

On the film's somber press tour, he went on David Letterman's talk show clad in tassel-shouldered Native American garb and attempted his usual bravado, telling a story about two old women in Japan speculating about the size of his penis. But an impish Letterman seemed to sense blood in the water, repeatedly quipping after Seagal's tales, "That didn't happen," and at one point calling him a "chimp." Around this time, even the genial Jackie Chan fired a shot, saying, "Someone like a Steven Seagal will kill or maim dozens of people in one scene, like he's eating candy. Not even Bruce Lee went through opponents that quickly."

Seagal stashed away the Genghis Khan biopic he dreamed of doing ("I don't know that we have anything in common," he says, "other than that he was the most brilliant military strategist in the history of mankind") and first retreated to what seemed like safe terrain, a sequel to *Under Siege* that swapped the boat for a train. It didn't work—critically lambasted, it made less money than the original while costing more. But his next move would stun the world. It was the last thing anyone expected from this brawling Bodhisattva, who until now had been invincible on-screen.

Yes, Steven Seagal was about to die. Or rather, allow himself to be killed.

It's unknown just how deliberate a career move this was. Was it a reaction to the swelling backlash against him? Or just a way to quickly cash in one of the remaining three chips in his Warners contract? Seagal himself is circumspect. "I kind of wanted to do it to shock people," he says with a shrug. "Warner Bros. wanted me to do it because they knew that Kurt wasn't going to sell that movie alone. They gave me a lot of money—like, a million dollars a day—and so I just said, 'Fuck it, let's try.'"

The movie was *Executive Decision,* and the Kurt was Kurt Russell, one year older than Seagal and the top-billed star of the 1996 picture. As US Army analyst David Grant, Russell would lead a rescue of a hijacked airliner. As the more obviously heroic and manly Lieutenant Colonel Austin Travis, Seagal would be part of the mission until, in a shock twist, he plummets to his death. It was a genius bit of wrong-footing—audiences had been programmed to expect Seagal to make it to the end credits without a bruise. If he could be taken out, anything could happen.

But Seagal was not about to go without a fight. "He was difficult to work with," says Jim Thomas, who wrote the movie with his brother John. "We had several meetings with him, and in one he tried to claim that he had just come back from a CIA mission over the weekend. I mean, seriously telling us this—a couple of writers. Everybody also said that he usually had a gun on him. That's a little unnerving." Given the unusual nature of his role, and his reluctance to sully his screen image, Seagal tussled at length with the writers and studio over how exactly his demise would play out. Eventually an agreement was reached: Travis would heroically sacrifice himself for the good of the team, responding to Grant's wimpish cry of "We're not gonna make it!" with the line "*You* are" and a deliberate plunge to certain death.

Seagal claims he worked just four days on *Executive Decision.* Still, they were memorable ones for those involved. Says Thomas, "Kurt would take the time to sit behind cameras and read lines to him. And then when it was time to switch, Steven would just take off. Later, when we were shooting near Mojave, we kept joking that we ought to have a dummy of him suddenly fall to the ground, right there at the ending of the film. Still in his combat suit. He stayed with us even after he was gone."

For audiences, too, the scene would be the thing about the movie most vividly remembered. A stunning surprise, and perhaps something else, too: a metaphor for the change happening in action cinema, with Seagal's fearless action figure of a character supplanted by Russell's more relatable, anxious regular guy.

Sitting in a movie theater that summer, one person had an even stronger reaction than most: *On Deadly Ground* writer Ed Horowitz. "Seagal died," he says. "It was a shock. And it was a joy. It really was."

FOR THE TWO STARS OF *UNIVERSAL SOLDIER,* the 1990s had very different paths in store. Dolph Lundgren, after his meteoric rise, found opportunities drying up when he moved to Spain in 1994 with new wife Anette Qviberg, a jewelry designer. "It was tough. Some of the toughest times in my life," he says. "My ex-wife hated LA—we never went to LA—so I was out of the loop a little bit. I was going through an inner crisis, I think, as well. I decided to put family first. Inside, I wanted to be back and see what I could do in the business, but the circumstances weren't there."

Lundgren kept acting, and punching, and shooting, but the movies became ones released straight to video, little-seen actioners with titles such as *Silent Trigger, Bridge of Dragons,* and *Jill Rips.* It was a body blow to the ego of the onetime indestructible Ivan Drago. "I felt like I wasn't going anywhere," he admits. "The people I was making the movies with weren't really interested in the quality." But he hung in there, and finally he was pulled out of his doldrums by the same man who had yanked him out of obscurity back in the mid-1980s: Sylvester Stallone. *The Expendables,* a testosterone-soaked harkening back to the glory days of yore, began a whole new lease on life for Lundgren, something that still makes him tear up today. "When I got that call from Sly, I hadn't been on the big screen for fifteen years," he says. "It meant a lot to me."

For Lundgren's onetime screen foe, Jean-Claude Van Damme, on the other hand, the 1990s would prove a nonstop barrage of offers and excess. So much so that early in the decade he coined a new nickname for himself: "Mr. Bulletproof."

Where Seagal presented himself as a man with big things to say, Van Damme did quite the opposite. He was here for a good time, to kick bad guys all day and then party all night. "People, they're trying to make life complicated," he lamented to one reporter. "You go on interviews and they go, 'So what's the message?' Talk to God. I got no message."

Even so, people loved hearing him talk, because unlike most movie stars, Van Damme had zero filter. The Belgian would happily reminiscence, on the record, about his first night with fourth wife Darcy LaPier: "I ate something, but not food. You know what I'm saying." He would muse about his preferred method of death: "What I would love is to have my body dropped where you have those big icebergs and the water is so cold and pure, to be eaten by a polar bear or a seal or an otter." He would cheerfully proclaim *Sudden Death* to be like *Die Hard*, "but better."

And the cheekiness of his real persona began to trickle into his work. Van Damme was done with the somber, glowering vibes of *Bloodsport* and *Kickboxer*. Even 1993's *Hard Target*, the Hollywood debut of Hong Kong action king John Woo, which cast the star as lethal Cajun drifter Chance Boudreaux, was too serious for his tastes, despite featuring a moment in which Van Damme punched a snake. "The action was too much emotion, too much John Woo shit," the star complained, although he liked that the film made him "a samurai with greasy hair." He had seen what lightening up had done for his hero and new pal Arnold Schwarzenegger. And he wanted some of that for himself. To borrow one of his one-liners from the otherwise unmemorable *Nowhere to Run*, also released in 1993, Van Damme was saying, "Au revoir, fucker!" to his old screen image.

So, while part of him was sorry to see the implosion of John

Milius's Alexander the Great biopic, which would have cast Van Damme as the Macedonian conqueror and Sean Connery as his father, he was excited to amplify his inner goofball. Hence his guest appearance on *Friends* as himself, lusted after by Monica and Rachel, a far more successful outing than Seagal's on *Saturday Night Live* (despite claims from the episode's director that Van Damme had inappropriately used his tongue while kissing both Courteney Cox and Jennifer Aniston). And hence the triple bill of big blockbusters with ridiculous loglines upon which he was about to embark.

Sudden Death saw him save a sports stadium, John McClane but better, dispatching one foe using an industrial-strength dishwasher. *Timecop* combined advanced temporal physics with Van Damme doing the splits in tighty-whities, as well as kicking a villain's arm clean off after it's blasted with liquid nitrogen ("Have a nice day," he quips, before chastising himself: "I should have said, 'Freeze!'"). And sandwiched between these two films by director Peter Hyams was Van Damme's first foray into the world of family entertainment.

This was his chance to electrify whole new generations, to truly boost himself onto the A-list. He was also getting an A-list payday. At the junket for *Street Fighter,* he declared that he was taking home $7.2 million for the movie.

IF VAN DAMME SEEMED frenzied in his encounters with the media—and he did—it wasn't entirely down to his naturally exuberant nature. He had always been a man of extremes, aiming kicks at producers' heads, doing interviews at two A.M. because that's when he felt most alert. "Because I come from the street, I like to walk around, sniff around like a dog late at night," he says. "I don't sleep much." But as the 1990s wound on, he turned to chemical assistance. Specifically, cocaine. One of his friends would lay out rails of coke so large that they jokingly called them "freeways."

"Where do you want to go today?" this friend would ask.

"I want LA-Mexico-Tijuana," Van Damme replied. "And I want two lanes."

At his worst, he was snorting his way through ten grams a day. Then he would sit alone, paranoid and dazed, declining to hit the gym and instead working on bits of poetry and reminiscences of his childhood in Belgium. One day he sat in the corner of a Hong Kong hotel room scribbling all of his fears and problems on the back of script pages. He filled eighty sheets, convinced that he was dying. "I did so much damage to myself, the body I created," he would mourn in 1998.

When he arrived in Thailand for the shooting of 1994's *Street Fighter,* Van Damme was in the depths of his addiction. "We had heard rumors about him having substance abuse problems," says Steven de Souza, who had written and was directing the project. "The insurance company said, 'You have to hire a minder.' Unfortunately, the minder turned out to be an enabler. The first night we were in Thailand, there was a dinner party with the whole cast and crew at this big table. The police turn up outside. And it turns out that Van Damme's handler had tried to score marijuana immediately and got busted on the street. Somebody had to bribe somebody to make that go away."

As the weeks rolled on, it became clear that Van Damme wasn't a fan of Mondays. When the weekend was over for everyone else, he remained AWOL, either because he was out partying, conducting what he later termed a "mini-affair" with co-star Kylie Minogue, or else holed up in his hotel room. Assistants dispatched to extract him from his presidential suite would come back relaying increasingly bizarre excuses; one day the message merely read, "I have to pump up my muscles."

For the beleaguered de Souza, for whom everything was going wrong, this was not hugely helpful. *Street Fighter* was a giant gamble, and not just for Van Damme and the first-time director. So large was the project that two major studios—Universal and Columbia—were teaming up to release it. And Capcom, the Japanese video games leviathan, was staking huge amounts of cash and credibility on it. They had even revamped their iconic *Street*

Fighter 2 game—which had been riffed on by Jackie Chan in 1993's *City Hunter*, the star turning himself into various characters from the game—for a limited-edition version boasting Van Damme's face. The Belgian hadn't been their first choice, with Stallone and Schwarzenegger both passing on the script, but now that he was in the picture as military badass Guile they were in full hype mode, trumpeting that fans had unanimously voted in a popular game magazine for him to get the role.

Yet *Street Fighter* was on the ropes. The Thai portion of the ten-week shoot was beset by gangsters, failing equipment, and nonstop rain so loud that sound couldn't be recorded properly. "After two weeks in Thailand, we were seven days behind," laments de Souza. "We had to throw out almost everything we shot there, except for a few of the exterior scenes." Most challengingly, de Souza's game plan—to do dialogue scenes first, so he could train the largely non-martial-arts-adept cast for the fight scenes to come—was shattered when Raul Julia, the actor cast as villain M. Bison, arrived looking haggard. Though it later transpired that he was suffering from stomach cancer, the reason given at the time was that he had picked up an intestinal bug in Brazil from his previous shoot. It meant that the schedule had to be reordered and combat shot on the fly. "I was very aware that the fights we were getting were really, really weak," says the director. "Because there was just no rehearsal time. There's a thing on the outtakes of a weak-ass fight between Chun-Li and Kylie. It was just horrible, so I couldn't put it in the movie."

With Van Damme, at least, there was no prospect of weak-ass moves. And when he was present on set, he was engaged and committed. Too much so, on occasion, as it turned out he had developed a habit of calling "Cut!" himself during scenes.

"There was this one scene where Guile, Chun-Li, and Balrog are under assault against this old temple wall," de Souza remembers. "There's machine gun fire all around, bodies falling and squibs— a very elaborate shot. And he has to say, 'Go free the hostages. I'll see you later.' Well, he does the line and then he yells, 'Cut! Cut! Cut!' I say, 'Jean-Claude, we talked about this before. You don't say cut.' 'Yeah, but I messed up—I was looking at a ladder and so by mistake I said, 'I'll catch up with you *ladder*.' We went to video village, played it back and it turned out he'd said it right. Now we have to wait forty-five minutes for them to check the guns and re-plaster the temple and everything. We do it again and he says, 'Go free the hostages. I'll see you ladder.' "

Aside from the dialogue, there was only one thing Van Damme struggled with. It turned out he was okay with animatronic snakes—like the one he smacked for *Hard Target*—but was terrified of real ones. When Bison's secret underground lair was adorned with a python and a tarantula, production was shut down while the star grappled with his ophidiophobia. "He had no problem with the spider, but he did not enjoy being snake-adjacent," de Souza recalls. "So I put it around my neck while I was typing. My wife, who had been around my son's python, held it. And then once Van Damme's wife, Darcy, put it around her neck, he was forced to work with the snake."

STREET FIGHTER ended up making money. Just under $100 million, in fact, making it his second-biggest vehicle ever, after the same year's *Timecop*. It was, on paper, a double whammy of dreams, solidifying Van Damme as a monster star. But the critical reactions were blisteringly acrid. "The worst movie to date inspired by a video game," wrote Leonard Maltin. "He still delivers dialogue with the puzzled concentration of someone trying to read a ventriloquist's lips," said Desmond Ryan. Van Damme had cashed a giant paycheck, but the extra public exposure, in this case, hadn't done anything for his credibility.

The mid-1990s would prove to be his apex. Like most of his action-star contemporaries, he would transition from huge tentpole pictures watched by everyone back to smaller, more niche action flicks—but he would never stop dreaming big. "An eagle," he replied, when asked which animal he would be if he could. "I can be free and fly anywhere I want, have my own mountains and my females and my eggs."

He would keep winging his way from project to project, directing himself and Roger Moore in 1995's *The Quest*, and teaming up with Hong Kong directors Tsui Hark and Ringo Lam for a string of unpretentious adrenaline shots. He broke the coke habit, returned to the gym, started smiling again. He would never be Arnold Schwarzenegger or Sylvester Stallone. But it turned out he was just fine being Jean-Claude Van Damme.

One summer night in Miami, in 1997, he found himself at Sylvester Stallone's house, partying with the likes of Madonna, Bruce Willis, Shaquille O'Neal, and Don Johnson. He admired Stallone's vintage furniture, smiled at the A-list throng surrounding him, and pondered how far he'd come since those nights sleeping in a car outside Stallone's LA home. Now he was here, one of them, accepted.

Then, like in a scene from one of his own movies, a shadow darkened the door. It was his nemesis. The man who had shit-talked Van Damme incessantly. The Great One himself. Steven Seagal.

The party hushed as Van Damme rushed toward him, shoving him in the chest.

"He was drooling, foaming at the mouth," Seagal claimed later. "I just said back to him, 'When you're sober, if that day ever comes, come and say shit to me. I don't care how small you are or how girlie you are. It won't matter.'"

The host of the party has a different memory. "Van Damme was tired of Seagal saying he could kick his ass," remembers Stallone, who was presumably eying his furniture nervously, "and went right up to him and offered him the chance to step outside so he could wipe the floor with him, or should I say wipe the backyard with him."

"I was pissed a little and said to Steven, 'Come outside!'" Van Damme corroborates. "I waited two hours, but he never came."

A duel that would have made a fortune on pay-per-view TV never came to be—Seagal exited the Miami manse and hightailed it away. "I have to say I believe Van Damme was just too strong and Seagal wanted no part of it," Stallone adjudicated.

Mr. Bulletproof partied on.

CHAPTER 18

THE ICE AGE

SOMETHING WAS CHANGING. They felt it, even as they continued to load fresh clips, chop more solar plexuses, toss further
grenades. As they hoisted their barbells in the gym, sinews straining, a tingle of anxiety ran down their burly backs.

For Stallone, the dark cloud of premonition had drifted into
view at the end of the 1980s. "It was that first Batman movie,"
he would report. "The action movies changed radically when it
became possible to Velcro your muscles on. The special effects became more important than the single person. That was the beginning of the end."

Michael Keaton, a shrimpy Pennsylvanian who had probably
never done an abdominal crunch in his life, was suddenly invading
the territory ruled for so long by the action titans. And his success
was staggering, 1989's *Batman* grossing $412 million worldwide.
Stallone's own offering for that year, *Lock Up,* had made just
$22 million. Harrison Ford and Mel Gibson, as Indiana Jones and
Martin Riggs respectively, had shown already that less muscle-
bound action stars could be box-office dynamite; now a whole new
generation of younger, spryer, not to mention more diverse heroes
were arriving, heralded by Keaton: Keanu Reeves, Will Smith,
Nicolas Cage, Wesley Snipes.

And as Stallone had correctly identified, the ever-brighter dazzle of visual effects was a whole other challenge. Once, Arnold Schwarzenegger's mighty chest had been spectacle enough. Now people wanted more. The sight of a lone cop marching back into battle was starting to no longer cut it, especially as that cop was getting slower and stockier with each picture.

Bruce Willis, the guy who only did *Die Hard* for the money in the first place, seemed to be eying the exit sign. "They're actually starting to lose their appeal for me," he said with a grimace about action movies in 1992. "I'm getting sick of carrying guns in movies. These are the modern generation of cowboy movies, of good guys and bad guys, and I guess that has a certain amount of appeal. I mean, people keep going. I just get a little tired of the guns after a while."

A year later, he would wave a gun, but not fire it, as he reprised the role of John McClane in the spoof comedy *National Lampoon's Loaded Weapon*. And he'd be lured back to McClane again properly, in 1995's *Die Hard with a Vengeance,* reteaming with John McTiernan and bagging a reported $13 million payday. But he was increasingly gravitating to lower-octane projects—*Pulp Fiction, North, Nobody's Fool*—and when he was on an action set, his disdain for the material was becoming ever more evident.

"I did a movie with Bruce called *Striking Distance* where he ad-libbed so much that I had to change the plot in the reshoots," says Steven de Souza. "Literally, because he refused to say things." Willis's additions to the story, a snoozy yarn about a speedboat cop hunting a serial killer, would also cause trouble. "There's a Fourth of July party in the picture where he gets into an argument with someone, and this other cop separates them," de Souza recalls. "Bruce says to another actor, 'Listen, don't push me—throw your beer at me.' Now this actor, he has to listen to the big star, right? But Bruce doesn't tell anybody he has this planned. So the guy throws a real beer bottle full of beer at Bruce, who ducks. It hits an extra, who has to be rushed to the hospital and get nine stitches. That's the kind of stuff going on."

Stallone and Schwarzenegger, sitting next to Willis for their Planet Hollywood–hyping British talk show appearance, grinned as he was grilled by the host about his *Die Hard 3* salary. "We need to get a better agent," quipped Stallone. Unlike Willis, they had no intention of hanging up their firearms—a life of action was the only one they knew. The year 1993 would provide them both with a chance to prove they were still relevant. And that they could still blow shit up better than anyone else in town.

THE FEELING OF BATMAN breathing down his neck only made Stallone hungrier to succeed. He was the same guy who had turned up in New York with chump change and turned himself into a god. That same drive to thrive still pumped through his veins, as well as the same determination to prevail over his foes. He was more forgiving of Schwarzenegger these days, but another old rivalry flared up when he crossed paths with Richard Gere once more. Back on *Lords of Flatbush* they had sparred in a car, Gere daring to besmirch Stallone with mustard; now, in the early 1990s, they squared off in a fancier location, Elton John's house, where they had been brought together for a high-powered dinner party.

The evening started to go off the rails when Gere nestled into the corner of a room with Diana, Princess of Wales, the pair sparking immediately. "As the rest of us chatted, I couldn't help notice a strange atmosphere in the room," John would recall. "Judging by the kind of looks he kept shooting them, Diana and Richard Gere's newly blossoming friendship was not going down well with Sylvester Stallone at all. I think he may have turned up to the party with the express intention of picking Diana up, only to find his plans for the evening ruined."

A short while later, John's partner, David Furnish, was horrified to find Stallone and Gere facing each other down like mad dogs in one of the mansion's corridors, about to take swings. Furnish quickly called them in to dinner. And after an awkward meal with the likes of George Michael, Jeffrey Katzenberg, and Richard Curtis, Stallone stormed out of the house, according to John, with the parting words, "I never would have come if I'd known Prince fuckin' Charming was gonna be here. If I'd wanted her, I would've taken her!"

The guests waited until he'd got into his car before they started to laugh.

Stallone was also getting thwarted, it seemed, when it came to another ambition: to make a science-fiction blockbuster. Unlike Schwarzenegger, whose forays into the genre—*Predator, Total Recall,* the *Terminator* films—had been game-changers, he had never tackled sci-fi, unless you counted *Death Race 2000,* which he didn't. Stallone wanted in on the future. He told his people to bring him something juicy, preferably with laser guns.

Isobar was the first attempt. Its pedigree was immaculate, with the spec script by Jim Uhls grabbing the interest of the *Alien* team of director Ridley Scott and wild-brained Swiss artist H. R. Giger. And though it read a lot like *Alien* reheated—in the exotic future of 2015, a train with a tentacled monster on board flies at twelve hundred miles per hour—it had the whiff of a hit. But then Scott left to do *Thelma & Louise,* a small army of writers descended on *Isobar* to pull the story this way and that, and finally the whole thing derailed entirely.

The second possibility, a few years on, seemed less promising. *Demolition Man* had a twenty-nine-year-old director, Marco Brambilla, who had never made a film, though he had created a series of expensive Diet Pepsi commercials inspired by the movie *Brazil.* And the script, originally by a Quebecer named Peter Lenkoff and recently reworked extensively by *Heathers* writer Daniel Waters, was downright weird. Inspired by an article Lenkoff read about celebrities wanting to be cryogenically frozen, it was about an LA cop, John Spartan, who is put into deep freeze and thawed out thirty-six years later, to continue waging war with old foe Simon Phoenix. Waters had added sci-fi bizarreness and satirical riffs, such as the reveal that toilet paper is replaced by a mysterious process involving three seashells, and future jargon such as "What seems to be your boggle?" In this new city of San Angeles, crime does not exist, nobody smokes or drinks, bad language is verboten, and all guns are confined to a museum.

Not only that, but the hero is mocked relentlessly throughout. John Spartan is regarded as a creaky relic of a defunct era, belittled for his brawn: one character calls him "a musclebound grotesque," another "a Neanderthal." This might explain why Steven Seagal turned down the role when Warner Bros. attempted to shoot it with him in Australia (Jean-Claude Van Damme claims that he was approached to play Phoenix). It might also explain why Stallone passed on the script. "The downside was I, Sylvester Stallone, became synonymous with mindless, monosyllabic violence. I was reduced to this prehistoric, bestial caveman," he explained in 1993. To another reporter, he said, "It seemed like a questionable film that, if not executed properly, could end up being really silly."

But Brambilla and producer Joel Silver, who had been pursuing the star desperately for the project, were determined to identify—and then soothe—Stallone's concerns. So they chased him. "We actually flew to Rome to walk him through the script," remembers Brambilla, "and to make him feel comfortable with the tone, because it was very different for an action movie. Obviously, he had such a persona—his sensitivity was probably that it would parody him. The character is definitely a certain type of dinosaur. But I made it clear that it wasn't really a parody of an action star. The comedy comes from the disconnection between him and the world."

And slowly Sly's concerns thawed. Adjustments were made to the script. And just as he had let himself be hoisted up mountains for *Cliffhanger*, he agreed to be flung into the future for *Demolition Man*.

Things did not start well. The intricate dialogue of Waters's draft was a far cry from the grunting and basic zingers Stallone deployed in his action films, and he struggled to adjust. "The difficult part of this movie has been that in the future, people speak in a very specific manner," he bemoaned on set. "Instead of saying, 'Calm down,' they say, 'Please withdraw your hormones.' I've had to get into these strange kinds of speaking rhythms, so the acting has been really delicate." The physical stuff he was used to, but even that was brutal on this shoot. On Warner Bros. soundstage 26, made up to look like the tale's CryoPenitentiary—the future prison from which Spartan, a veritable Ripped Van Winkle, is released after years of sleep—Stallone had to squeeze his nearly nude bulk into a "freeze pod." A thousand-pound lid was lowered down and sealed shut before glycerine, a viscous liquid, was pumped in, rising higher and higher until only an inch of air remained at the top of this virtual coffin.

"Horrifying" was how the star described it later, claiming that he wouldn't have been able to escape had something gone wrong. "I'm sure he was very apprehensive," says Brambilla. "I designed that set myself, because I wasn't terribly happy with the production designer, who had never designed a science-fiction film. That machine was all on hydraulics. And you had all this weight on top of him in a machine that theoretically could not be opened quickly. You know, it would be something very hard to do."

Human drama, too, again reared its head on a Sylvester Stallone picture. This time, it wasn't a battle with a director or a writer but a failure to sync with a co-star. Lori Petty, who had been cast as future cop Lenina Huxley, with whom Spartan teams up, was ebullient on her third day on set. "We have a really good chemistry together," she said of Stallone, "and we *really* get along well." That same day, she was fired. "That was so sad," Brambilla remembers. "There was just no chemistry between her and Stallone. So we shot the scenes in her apartment, then decided to recast."

Petty now sums up that experience with a single sentence: "It was the most uncool day in Hollywood for me."

BUT EVEN WITH ALL THIS TURBULENCE, and a budget that was flying by its allotted $45 million en route to $77 million, *Demolition Man* was turning out to be something special. For one, the cast were sparking off each other spectacularly. Petty's replacement, a virtual unknown named Sandra Bullock, proved a perfect foil for Stallone, while Wesley Snipes brought endless zest as Simon Phoenix, with bleached-blond hair, different-colored eyes (one blue, one brown; they switch depending on the scene), and a maniacal cackle. "Take away all the guns and the explosions, and this could be considered more of a comedy than an action film," Snipes commented on set.

But it was hard to forget it was an action film with Joel Silver around, and the pandemonium was cranked up to absurd levels, as if all involved realized that the days of big, bombastic action movies—the ones where things were done for real—were drawing to a close. "There are only two digital shots in the film," says Brambilla. "Everything else was done photochemically. Joel was able to find a building in LA that they would let us implode, which I don't think had happened in forty years or something. We had twenty-seven cameras trained on it. And after the explosion it looked like Dresden—you know, it was a completely art-directed, beautiful kind of ruin that was left from the explosion." Another building was detonated by an MTV competition winner. *Demolition Man* was living up to its name.

And then there were the helicopters, a fleet of Chinook choppers that soared above the LA skyline before a stuntman leaped out of one onto the roof of a building. "I was actually in the chase helicopter following the prop helicopter, and the downforce from that helicopter was so strong that we nearly got caught in it and crashed," the director recalls. "We were doing it all for real."

The movie's techniques were, like its main character, prehistoric—soon to be phased out and replaced by much safer and more controllable computer effects. The world Stallone knew was vanishing, and this was an elegy to its old-school charms. But *Demolition Man* would also prove amazingly ahead of its time. The crazy futuristic stylings that the star had worried would come off as silly were actually not only hilarious but oddly prescient. Many of them would, in some form, come to pass.

In December 2020, Elon Musk posted three words on Twitter: "Watch *Demolition Man*." Nine months later, he posted another five: "*Demolition Man* is coming true." He wasn't the only one to notice. Multiple think pieces have been published hailing the movie's uncanny predictions: the video conferencing that predated Zoom; the touch-screen tablets; the wanton political correctness ("John Spartan, you are fined five credits for repeated violations of the verbal morality statute," tuts a machine to the archaic cop, who seems more in danger of cancellation than death); the corporate stranglehold of pop culture (all music in this future world appears to be bite-sized jingles flogging products); the self-driving cars; the extreme proliferation of Taco Bells. As the COVID-19 pandemic began, people even began copying its contact-free greeting, an air high-five that's best concluded with a mutual uttering of "Be well."

"There's a lot in there that deals with human behavior," Brambilla reflects. "And they're the things that hold up now, because they ended up happening. My whole interest in the film was for the social commentary. Then Joel was more interested in the action film. And Stallone was interested in creating the myths of his character. So I was making one film, Joel wanted to make another film, Stallone wanted to make a third, and from that weird spectrum of views came something really quirky."

Whether its star was on board with the quirk or not, the strange alchemy made for blockbuster gold. "I smiled a lot," said Roger Ebert. "Unlike so many other movies in this genre, it really does have a satiric angle to it. It's really trying to be funny, and it's really trying to comment on the nineties from the point of view of the future, and it does so successfully." This was Stallone's *Brave New World*. And a comedy that for once actually made people laugh, not cry, showcasing a new side of him: self-aware, willing to lampoon his own image.

Like John Spartan, rumors of his obsolescence had been greatly exaggerated. By embracing a project that confronted him with the specter of his own irrelevancy, Stallone had managed to burst out of the ice. And the double-whammy success of *Cliffhanger* and *Demolition Man* led to a new surge of profitable, if less memorable, action vehicles: *The Specialist, Judge Dredd, Assassins, Daylight*.

Relaxed, tanned, and smiling once more, Stallone appeared on

David Letterman's talk show in 1994 to reflect on how life was going. "It's tough to get sympathy," he said, mock-wincing, of *The Specialist*'s instantly notorious shower sex scene. "I had to spend twelve hours in the water with Sharon Stone, clad in nothing but cologne, and her, dressed in nail polish. And the guys are sitting there, you know, carrying hundred-pound bags and lights and whatever, and they're going, 'Wait, you're getting paid for this?'"

Then he recalled his response. A Sly zinger for the ages.

"Well, you know, it's tough on the skin after a while."

ON THE GROUNDS of the Long Beach Hyatt Regency hotel in Los Angeles one sweltering day in February 1993, Arnold Schwarzenegger was facing down dinosaurs. But it was the human who looked like he was about to roar. The two giant prehistoric creatures—a *Tyrannosaurus rex* and a brontosaurus—were static models, created to adorn a re-creation of the La Brea Tar Pits on the grounds of the luxury resort. Schwarzenegger, meanwhile, dressed in a tan jacket, blue jeans, and snakeskin boots, was covered head to toe in thick brown sludge and grimacing. Earlier he had been informed that the faux pits' faux tar, a concoction heavy on Oreo cookie dye, was not only edible but delicious. So he'd scooped a dollop of the thick goop into his mouth. And made an appalled noise.

"To me it tastes totally like mud that has fungus in it, and you get diseases," he complained. "And it's 40 degrees, and it's totally uncomfortable."

It was a rare bad day, or so it appeared, on Schwarzenegger's latest bonanza blockbuster. He liked to share a comment that his wife, Maria, had made, that he had never before seemed so relaxed on a shoot. And why wouldn't he be at ease? After all, he had selected the project with the utmost of care. While Stallone had limped into the 1990s, wounded by a string of flops, Schwarzenegger had soared into it. His Rolodex was stuffed with celebrity friends. Every script in town wended its way to his agent at ICM. No other star shone with such diamond brightness.

He turned down one after another. He said no to *Sweet Tooth,* in which he would have played the Tooth Fairy. He declined *The Count of Monte Cristo,* in which he would have escaped from a French prison. He nixed *So I Married an Axe Murderer,* in which he would have married an axe murderer. "People will not accept that I will be lying there worried about my wife when I have destroyed the world five times over in my movies," he explained of the latter, pragmatically. Not a single decision did he ever regret. In one interview he declared, "Everything I turned down ended up looking like shit." But finally something made his steely gaze cease its roving.

In some ways it was an unlikely prospect. The two screenwriters who had originated the project, Zak Penn and Adam Leff, weren't Hollywood insiders but Connecticut university graduates who had been trying to drum up interest for their script about a giant rat in Central Park. With that failing to get a bite, they decided to channel their love of action movies into a story called *Extremely Violent,* in which a teenager gets sucked into one while watching it. "We rented every action movie we could think of and made a checklist," recalls Penn. " 'Does the second-most-evil bad guy die before or after the most-evil bad guy? Does the hero have a Vietnam buddy?' It was fun, although watching Steven Seagal movies one after another can be soul-crushing." *Extremely Violent* would be an extremely violent celebration of the genre, while also deconstructing its many clichés. They named the second lead character, an invincible cop inside the film-within-the-film, Arno Slater— an homage to Arnold Schwarzenegger.

It was a wink, and nothing more, until suddenly a bidding war broke out between the Hollywood studios, and Schwarzenegger himself started taking interest. Remembers Penn: "We never thought we'd actually *get* Arnold. We were just two guys sitting in my apartment, thinking maybe someone would read it and get the reference. When we heard he wanted to do it, Adam and I looked at each other like, 'This is *insane.'* "

Things rapidly got even more so. Columbia Pictures enlisted *Die Hard* director John McTiernan to oversee the project. And *Lethal*

Weapon writer Shane Black was parachuted in to rework the script, which Schwarzenegger had proclaimed "wasn't executed professionally." Penn and Leff were relegated to the sidelines, to watch as the people they had started off lampooning took over their script. And to marvel as the wheeze they had dreamed up while fast-forwarding through the dull bits in *Marked for Death* became not just solid but pumped up to a size that made even old-timers in Hollywood gasp.

Schwarzenegger liked the idea because it reminded him of his childhood, sitting in an Austrian movie theater and wishing he could clamber up through the screen to join John Wayne. As in *Terminator 2,* he would act opposite a kid, a chance to reassert his gentler side, something he sensed his fans wanted. Well, maybe not the teenage fans who came up to him on the street and asked him to say "Fuck you, asshole" (he always declined), but the rest of them. "The country is going in an anti-violence direction," he said. "I think America has seen now enough of what violence has done in the cities." Schwarzenegger himself was feeling more tender these days: he had recently wept while watching both *Field of Dreams* and *Malcolm X*.

But gentleness, he knew, only got you so far. In *Last Action Hero,* the new title of his new movie, he would deliver more thundering spectacle than ever before. He and McTiernan and Black, three kings of carnage, would unite to dazzle the world.

On August 25, 1992, at a "synergy" meeting in LA, seventy Sony executives were shown a sizzle reel of highlights from movies that trio had made. They oohed and aahed over every fireball and overturned car. And then Schwarzenegger took to a podium, lit Romeo y Julieta cigar in hand.

"I want to be involved in every single facet of this film," he told the execs, scanning their faces with Skynet coolness. "From start to finish."

The room erupted into applause.

CONFIDENCE IN THE PROJECT couldn't be higher, it seemed— Columbia chief Mark Canton was already referring to *Last Action*

Hero as a "franchise." But inside the team making it, cracks were already appearing. Shane Black initially had a great time playing around with the meta concept; in one scene of his draft, he had Jack Slater—Arno Slater no more—reach up, grab a scratch on the film, and stab a baddie with it. But he and writing partner David Arnott butted heads with McTiernan, and they, too, found themselves fired. A succession of other writers were paid astonishing amounts of money to fiddle with the story. Oscar-winner William Goldman was given $750,000 for four weeks' work. Carrie Fisher and *The Hunt for Red October*'s Larry Ferguson also had a go. One industry wag cracked that the script had seen "more doctors than Cedars-Sinai."

"Back in those days, that kind of thing was an insurance policy for keeping your job at an executive level," says Black. "A script would be questionable and the trembling executive would give it to a famous writer with a million bucks, so he could say, 'Yeah, it's fortified now. We've given it vitamins. Wait, wait, wait . . . It needs the woman's touch. Give it to Carrie Fisher!' It just made people breathe easier, throwing money at this enormous behemoth."

Fear was rife—how could it not be? "What everyone was desperately afraid of," said one person close to the project at the time, "was making Arnold angry." If he walked, *Last Action Hero* collapsed. But after months of deliberating, the star signed on, even agreeing to a new set piece at a movie premiere where his character would meet the real Schwarzenegger. True to his word, he was getting involved in every detail, even calling in favors from famous friends, from Jean-Claude Van Damme (who would appear as himself at that premiere) to Sharon Stone to *Terminator 2*'s Robert Patrick. "I was doing ADR [additional dialogue recording] for an indie film when I got a call from Arnold," recalls Patrick. "He went, 'Robert, I want you to do the T-1000 cameo you did for *Wayne's World* for my movie.' I think we even talked money, for Christ's sake. It was just, 'You have to do it for me! You *have* to do it for me!'"

Propelled along by the mythic quality of its title, *Last Action Hero* was now not just an action movie. It was the *ultimate* action movie. The budget raced up and up and up; McTiernan grimly speculated that it would hit $125 million. Wild marketing plans cooked up before the shoot had even begun included a $20 million Burger King campaign, an AC/DC music video with a Schwarzenegger cameo, video games, and a $22 Mattel doll of Jack Slater that said, "Big mistake!" when you pressed a button.

Columbia employees were praying they wouldn't be saying the same words in six months' time. "If this movie is a bust, we're fucked," said one, succinctly, to a reporter. Even Canton told the *Los Angeles Times* that summer 1993 was "the season that will make me or break me. This is the big one." Right from the moment the cameras rolled in November 1992, that sense of weight, of sheer significance, bore down on all involved. "During the first week on set we kept screen-testing cars—Arnold and I would drive around in different vehicles, trying to find an iconic car for Slater," says Austin O'Brien, who was cast as child sidekick Danny Madigan. "That was such a strange process. I also remember Slater's boots being a really big deal."

Every detail was micromanaged, but the bigger picture was slipping away from McTiernan, who had captured magic on *Die Hard* but couldn't figure out what his new movie actually was. "The head of the studio couldn't decide whether this was an action movie or a kids' movie," the director recalls. "I was getting pushed in a lot of directions. When I was sent the script, the thing I liked was that it was wildly irreverent. But that was all getting watered down. And we were just trying to get the damn thing finished."

From greenlight to release, they had just nine and a half months to pull *Last Action Hero* together. Often the days on set stretched to eighteen hours. And in postproduction, a desperate McTiernan invited Black to the edit suite to look at what he'd managed to cobble together: scenes involving robots, jokes about Sylvester Stallone, a cartoon cat voiced by Danny DeVito. "It was a mess," remembers the writer. "There was a movie in there, struggling to emerge, which would have pleased me. But what they'd made was a jarring, random collection of scenes. The casting of the little boy

was one of the absolute misfires of Western culture. Also, they rewrote every line of ours, and I don't like the dialogue they wrote."

There was only so much that could be done. At a test screening
on May 1, one audience member commented that *Last Action
Hero* "lay there like a big fried egg." Upon reading the scorecards,
a studio executive suggested that they should be set on fire.

SCHWARZENEGGER WAS NOT one to whimper and despair.
When fellow recruits in the Austrian army had complained about
the early starts, he had bounded with zeal to his waiting tank.
When rival bodybuilders had failed to lift their barbells, he had
grinned and added more iron to his own. And now, as weaklings
around him lamented that *Last Action Hero* was cursed, he stayed
upbeat.

"They're all a bunch of jealous bitches sitting around saying,
'I hope he takes a dive,'" he said of those spreading negative vibes
about the production, including those nicknaming it "Humpty
Dumpty" ("All the reshoots and all the rewrites couldn't put it
back together again"). "What do you think I'm hearing about
Spielberg's picture?" Schwarzenegger confided. "The most *hideous*
things."

"Spielberg's picture" in summer 1993 was *Jurassic Park,* an adaptation of a science-fiction bestseller about dinosaurs resurrected
in the modern world. It was the biggest competition Schwarzenegger faced, but neither he nor Mark Canton seemed to take it seriously, ignoring pleas from inside their camp to move the release date
of their movie. "I rang [Canton] up and said, 'I want to see *Jurassic
Park* more than *Last Action Hero,* and *Last Action Hero* was my
idea!'" says Penn with a laugh. But it would be weakness to retreat,
and weakness could not be tolerated. "Sheer stupidity," concludes
McTiernan, who was plunged back into reshoots after the calamitous test screening. "The studio tried to set us against each other,
which was an idiotic thing to do. Because we weren't the greatest
action movie of all time. We were never supposed to be."

The marketing drive was unprecedented, with a seventy-five-foot balloon of Schwarzenegger holding dynamite inflated in Times Square and $500,000 spent on launching a NASA rocket with the film's name on its side. But again, everything went wrong: the balloon was hurriedly deflated when somebody remembered the recent truck bombing at the World Trade Center, while the rocket launch was ultimately delayed until well after the film's release. And genuine hype stubbornly refused to build. The mood on the studio lot was compared by one employee to that of the Nixon White House in the last days of Watergate. "Columbia's lady with the torch is sweating through her gossamer gown," quipped gossip columnist Liz Smith.

And the *Last Action Hero* premiere, when it finally happened, was even more despondent. Few stars turned up to support Schwarzenegger, and the movie's various writers sat in a gloomy funk. "Everyone ate the food and drank the drink, and nobody said anything to each other about what they'd sat through," says Shane Black. "It was like, 'Don't talk about the movie, but these are some really good fucking canapés.'"

It ended up taking $137 million worldwide, not far off *Demolition Man*'s haul, but for this film it was a big disappointment. "Lizards Eat Arnold's Lunch!" yelled a headline in *Variety; Jurassic Park* had made over $400 million in the United States alone. For Schwarzenegger, tasting the unfamiliar tang of defeat, it was a miserable time. "To be rejected so soundly—it sort of broke his heart," says McTiernan. Even more so than with Stallone and *Demolition Man*, it hadn't just been his face on the poster—it was his image. And this salute to his many years as an action god had fallen flat. Stallone had feared Batman, but it was digital dinosaurs that had toppled Schwarzenegger, harbingers of a new era of cinema that looked to be leaving him behind.

Was he, and his ilk, going extinct?

But this star wasn't built for melancholy, navel-gazing, or remorse. "As always, I had the two voices battling inside my head," he was to explain. "The one was saying, 'Goddammit, oh my God, this is terrible.' And the other was saying, 'Now let's see what you are made of, Arnold. Let's see how ballsy you are. How strong are your nerves? How thick is your skin? Let's see if you can drive around in your convertible with the top down and smile at people, knowing that they know that you just came out with a fucking stinker. Let's see if you can do that.'"

Like the Terminator's lip curling into an approximation of a grin, Schwarzenegger forced a smile each time. His skin was thick. His nerves were strong. His balls were enormous. The man who liked to say "I'll be back" was built for thundering returns. So he lit another Romeo y Julieta cigar and called his friend Jim.

A few months later, on the set of James Cameron's *True Lies*, that smile was back, real, and bigger than ever. Schwarzenegger had implemented a rule with the stunt team: whenever someone made a mistake, that person would have to put a loop of rope around their neck, a big rawhide bone dangling from it, and bark like a dog. The practical joke stuck, and as the production traveled around the United States—the Florida Keys, Downtown LA, Rhode Island—the sound of barking went with it. Then the day arrived to shoot a fight in a public bathroom, as terrorists attempt to machine-gun Schwarzenegger's character, Harry Tasker.

"Arnold had to rip a hand dryer off a wall and clock this guy across the face with it," says Cameron. "With fight choreography, I always try to get in there and do parts of it myself, 'cause I need to feel the body dynamics of it, and I've done a lot of martial arts, so I kind of know a lot of the moves." So the director demonstrated what he wanted: a yank, a whirl, and a thwack.

"Yeah, yeah, I got it," Schwarzenegger said, nodding.

Except he didn't. As he swept the hair dryer around in an arc, his hand hit the side of the bathroom counter and tore open. It swelled up to an unbelievable size, shutting down production for the rest of the day.

"Arnold . . ." Cameron said, with a head shake and a meaningful look.

Schwarzenegger grinned, then began to bark, louder and louder.

As his director friend remembers now, joyfully: "He had to wear the bone."

EPILOGUE

...

THIS TIME THEY CAME BY LAND. And peace, again, became a thing of the past.

It was May 18, 2014, a sleepy Sunday morning in Cannes, with a cerulean blue sky and gentle breeze wafting through the palm trees that line the Croisette. Only the security barriers, newly erected on the beach promenade, and a palpable buzz of excitement gave away that something monumental was about to happen.

Plan A had been a zipline from the roof of the Carlton Hotel down to the shore. A phone call to the insurance company put an end to that. Next, a flotilla of helicopters had been considered. But they were deemed insufficiently dramatic.

And so, at around ten A.M., plan C was activated. With the sound of metal grinding against concrete, two Soviet-era tanks trundled around the corner and into view. The pair of decommissioned BTR-60 eight-wheel armored personnel carriers were traveling east down the Croisette, carrying the kind of personnel one didn't see together every day. Atop one sat Sylvester Stallone, Dolph Lundgren, Wesley Snipes, Jason Statham, Mel Gibson, and Harrison Ford. On the other, Arnold Schwarzenegger, Antonio Banderas, and, rather incongruously, *Frasier* star Kelsey Grammer. Pandemonium ensued: camera phones flashing, onlookers shrieking, Schwarzenegger puffing out cigar smoke, and one frazzled businessman, unable to enter the Carlton for a meeting due to the barricades, screaming, "There are tanks!"

The Carolco party in Cannes from 1990 had finally been eclipsed. This low-speed, high-impact publicity stunt, which had cost a cool $2 million to assemble, was the first time that tanks had been allowed on the streets of France since World War II. And the General Patton who had nodded it into existence was Stallone, director of *The Expendables 3,* the film that all these leathery greats were here to promote. Later, having gingerly dismounted from the BTR-60, Stallone estimated that of the "15 action heroes—real serious ones—in history," at least a third of them had their names on the poster for his movie.

Planet Hollywood had floundered, due to plummeting stock value and declining public appetite for celebrity-endorsed hamburgers. But the endeavor had made its musclemen backers realize they had a taste for peace. At least, peace where there was potential for a mighty payday. And so, after years of brinkmanship, the lone warriors of the 1980s began to form alliances. Schwarzenegger and Stallone would star in four movies together: three *Expendables* and a prison thriller called *Escape Plan.* They also posed for a photo together in 2012, when they found themselves in the same hospital on the same day for simultaneous shoulder surgeries, grinning at each other from their respective beds, a giant syringe plunged into Stallone's neck.

None of those team-ups would rival their earlier individual triumphs. If only their rapprochement could have come in 1987, with them at their pectoral peak. Imagine them taking on the Predator together, or Schwarzenegger facing Stallone in the ring. Then again, without the aggressive posturing that drove all these stars to outdo each other, would we have got the action classics we did? We'll never know.

What we are left with is a collective oeuvre of movies—some great, some lamentable, thankfully only one *Rhinestone*—that changed not only the landscape of the action genre but also, for a while at least, the very concept of masculinity itself. The bulging bodies of these stars, with their ammo belts, gleaming combat knives, and unflinching eyes, became the barometer for what it was to be a real man.

They got old, and so did that paradigm. Today, the definition of an action hero has broadened, becoming more inclusive. In the 1980s, big female-driven action movies were memorable—"I can handle myself," Sigourney Weaver's Ripley told one of the Colonial Marines who surrounded her in *Aliens*—but a rarity. Nowadays that is no longer the case. Following in Weaver's footsteps have come the likes of Geena Davis, Angelina Jolie, Charlize Theron, Milla Jovovich, Halle Berry, Jennifer Lawrence. Not to mention Michelle Yeoh, who in her late fifties kicked ass in 2022's *Everything Everywhere All at Once*, in a role originally created for Jackie Chan. "Your loss, my bro," she told him when he texted her, having heard that the film he'd declined had turned out to be spectacular.

Mainstream action has become richer and more diverse in other ways, too, since those eight dudes ruled the planet. Will Smith, Dwayne Johnson, Simu Liu, Jason Momoa, the late Chadwick Boseman, and many more have headed up blockbuster epics. The likes of *Black Panther* and *The Woman King* have put new kinds of heroes on the screen. Looking back, the action fantasies of the 1980s and '90s now seem somewhat one-note, easily lampoonable by the likes of *Team America: World Police* ("Hey, terrorist! Terrorize this!").

And yet, we keep going back to them. Because for all their limitations, those movies rarely failed to take huge swings, to destroy creatively. They are, in a way, the spiritual successors to the Greek myths of yore, tales of derring-do to stir the spirit and excite the soul. Except Homer never wrote a scene where someone punches a snake.

So we return, year after year, to *Bloodsport*, to *Under Siege*, to *Police Story*. We scour cable and streaming for Rambo, for Conan, for John McClane. Because there's something eternally comforting, in a world increasingly dependent on technology and artificial intelligence, where it's easy to sometimes feel small and insignificant, about cheering on characters who don't need superpowers to make the earth a better place—just bravery, brawn, and a well-placed kick. And in those two hours, we escape from reality to a different world, where it takes much, much more than death to keep a hero down.

JEAN-CLAUDE VAN DAMME finally fulfilled his dream of being killed on-screen by his hero in *The Expendables 2*, with his villain, Jean Vilain, having a knife plunged into his heart by Sylvester Stallone's Barney Ross. Van Damme hopes to return to the franchise as Jean's twin brother, Claude. Though most of his work of late has bypassed movie theaters, he retains cult status, poking fun at his own image in the meta film *JCVD* and the TV series *Jean-Claude Van Johnson*, as well as a string of commercials for Coors beer and one for Volvo in which he does, in his words, "the most epic of splits."

In 1999, he remarried wife number three, former bodybuilder Gladys Portugues, a union that lasts to this day. Together, they attended the unveiling of a statue of the star outside a supermarket in Brussels in 2012. "When people come by here," he said, happily regarding a sea of two thousand fans, "it is not Jean-Claude Van Damme, but a guy from the street who believed in something."

DOLPH LUNDGREN has teamed back up with old friend/foe Van Damme multiple times. Along with two *Universal Soldier* sequels and the submarine thriller *Black Water,* they joined forces in animated form for 2022's *Minions: The Rise of Gru,* Van Damme playing Jean-Clawed (a man with lobster claws) and Lundgren playing Svengeance (an angry Swede).

He has expanded his repertoire of skills, directing six movies to date, including *Command Performance,* a spin on *Die Hard* in which terrorists take over a rock concert (Lundgren plays a lethal drummer). And in front of the camera he has mounted an effective post-*Expendables* comeback, returning to the role of Ivan Drago in *Creed II* and becoming underwater king Nereus for *Aquaman* and its sequel. "I do hardly any action," he says of those parts. "And that's the kind of stuff I wanted to do back then. I had to go through twenty years of whatever—of life—to get to that point."

He claims that his chemical engineering expertise has given him the ability to make an excellent cocktail.

CHUCK NORRIS returned to the big screen in 2004's *Dodgeball: A True Underdog Story,* coming to the rescue of the heroes in a cameo at the climactic tournament, and being cursed in the final scene by Ben Stiller's villain. He professes that he was unaware the movie would end with the phrase "Fuckin' Chuck Norris!" As he remembers, "I said, 'Holy mackerel!' That was a shock. Ben didn't tell me about that!"

He also appeared in *The Expendables 2* as Booker, riffing on the mythos that surrounds him. "I have mellowed," Booker says, explaining why he is no longer called the Lone Wolf. When Stallone's character asks him if it's true he was once bitten by a king cobra, he cheerfully recalls that "after five days of agonizing pain, the cobra died."

With the release of books such as *Chuck Norris Cannot Be Stopped: 400 All-New Facts About the Man Who Knows Neither Fear nor Mercy* and *Chuck Norris: Longer and Harder: The Complete Chronicle of the World's Deadliest, Sexiest and Beardiest Man,* outlandish facts about him continue to proliferate. To date, not one has been proven to be false.

JACKIE CHAN has continued to make kinetic, body-punishing action movies well into his sixties, despite announcing in 2012 that he was retiring from the genre. For 2019's *Vanguard,* he nearly drowned during the shooting of a Jet Ski pursuit; less perilously, he mounted a mad melee inside a Lego store for *New Police Story.* Despite finding huge success in Hollywood with the *Rush Hour* films, the *Kung Fu Panda* animated series, and *Shanghai Noon/Knights,* he's of late headlined mainly Chinese productions, continuing to work with old friends such as Stanley Tong and Sammo Hung. Combined, his movies have grossed over $5 billion at the worldwide box office.

In 2010, Chan paid a visit to Hamleys, the London toy store. While an employee dressed as a pirate distracted shoppers, Chan selected and purchased two stuffed pandas, which he named La and Zy. These pandas would tour the world with him, meeting celebrities from the Clintons to Keanu Reeves. And they would accompany him to the Oscars in 2016, where Chan finally got the gold statuette he'd dreamed of since his visit to Stallone's house. "After fifty-six years in the film industry, making more than two hundred films," he remarked, beaming, while holding his honorary Oscar. "After so many bones, finally."

STEVEN SEAGAL no longer enjoys the backing of a major movie studio—after his final film released by Warner Bros., 2001's *Exit Wounds,* he began his direct-to-video era. But neither shrinking budgets nor an expanding waistline could stop Seagal from pumping out grimy thrillers in which he snaps people's wrists before breakfast. His love of three-word titles has survived the decades, too: since 2010, we've had *Force of Execution, Contract to Kill,* and *Beyond the Law,* in which he is even less law-abiding than he was in *Above the Law*.

A reality TV series, *Steven Seagal: Lawman,* followed the star as he performed his duties as a reserve deputy sheriff in Louisiana and Arizona. "I'm Steven Seagal," he drawled over the opening credits. "That's right: *Steven Seagal,* deputy sheriff." The show ended in controversy in 2011, with Seagal accused of driving a tank into someone's house in a raid that resulted in a hundred dead chickens and a fatally shot puppy. Two years later, the lawsuit brought against him was dismissed by a judge.

Away from the screen, Seagal was granted Russian and Serbian citizenship in 2016, and has spoken of his great admiration for Vladimir Putin, calling him "one of the greatest world leaders." In

February 2023, Putin returned the favor, bestowing on Seagal Russia's Order of Friendship award for his "humanitarian work." Putin hasn't been quite so effusive, with his spokesman reported as saying, "I wouldn't necessarily say he's a huge fan, but he's definitely seen some of his movies."

BRUCE WILLIS did find more to say about John McClane and terrorists, after all. He ended up making multiple further follow-ups to his action game-changer, including a 2020 TV commercial in which he wriggles through another air vent, this time with a Die Hard car battery. Nobody has dared recast the role; when fighting with studio executives during the making of *Die Hard 4.0*, Willis reportedly told them, "Let me ask you a question: who's your second choice to play John McClane?"

Willis has played an array of eclectic characters over the years, from a washed-up boxer in *Pulp Fiction* to a ghost in *The Sixth Sense*. But the gravitational pull of the action genre has always drawn him back, with a recent blizzard of direct-to-the-small-screen thrillers, including *A Day to Die, Out of Death, First Kill,* and *Hard Kill*. He failed to appear entirely in *The Expendables 3*, after reportedly demanding $4 million for four days' work, causing Sylvester Stallone to tweet, "WILLIS OUT . . . HARRISON FORD IN!!!! GREAT NEWS!!!!! Been waiting years for this!!!!," then another post reading, "GREEDY AND LAZY . . . A SURE FORMULA FOR CAREER FAILURE."

In 2022, Willis's family announced that he was retiring from acting due to being diagnosed with aphasia, later identified as frontotemporal dementia. A few months later, he returned to the top of Fox Plaza, the LA skyscraper from which he had once leaped, to quietly celebrate the thirty-fourth anniversary of *Die Hard* with his wife, Emma. Decades on, it remains the film that defines him: in 2006, when a rowdy squirrel took on multiple people in a Florida park, even surviving a pepper spray attack, it was nicknamed "Bruce" in his honor.

ARNOLD SCHWARZENEGGER survived the *Last Action Hero* debacle, hitting big with *True Lies*. He was also to return to comedy with *Junior* (in which he becomes pregnant) and *Jingle All the Way* (in which he pursues a toy with Terminator zeal). On August 6, 2003, however, during an episode of *The Tonight Show with Jay Leno,* he stunned the world by announcing that he was quitting acting to run for governor of California. And despite him having never held public office before, Schwarzenegger, aka "the Governator," aka "the Running Man," won the election by 1.3 million votes.

In 2013, back in Hollywood once again, he unveiled his first leading role in a decade, a sheriff in the action Western *The Last Stand*. While the long-promised *Conan the Barbarian* follow-up has yet to appear, he returned to the Terminator franchise with two more entries (in *Terminator: Dark Fate,* his new T-800 turned out to be a drapery salesman named Carl). He also teamed up with Jackie Chan in 2019 for the bizarre Chinese fantasy *Iron Mask,* and starred in his first TV series, action-comedy spy show *Fubar,* for Netflix in 2023.

Schwarzenegger's lifelong dream of cutting off somebody's arm and then slapping them with it—foiled on *Commando*—was finally fulfilled during the shoot for comedy *Kung Fury 2*. In the same movie, he plays the president of the United States.

SYLVESTER STALLONE, with the release of 2021's *The Suicide Squad,* became the only actor to have a number-one movie at the US box office for six straight decades. This auspicious achievement was made even more remarkable by the fact that in said film Stallone plays a walking, talking, people-munching shark. Sample dialogue: "Nom-nom."

There have been fallow years for the star, with plenty of flops and a short-lived attempt to launch his own brand of bottled glacial water, Sly Water ("It fell from the sky twenty thousand years ago," Stallone explained in a promo interview on *Access Hollywood*). But he has stretched himself, too, in interesting ways. He played a deaf police officer to extraordinary effect in James Mangold's *Cop Land*, and found new, more melancholy hues in the role that made him famous, Rocky Balboa, playing the boxer three further times and earning an Oscar nomination for *Creed II*.

Stallone remains a study in contrasts, the creator of extraordinarily violent tableaux (to date, John Rambo has taken a grand total of 552 lives) who has also made the NRA's "enemy list" for his anti-gun stance. And though he remains best known as a bruiser, off-screen he's never happier than when sitting in a studio, daubing a canvas with wet paint.

"You know, maybe I should have been a painter," he pondered in December 2021 as he unveiled his art collection "Sylvester Stallone: The Magic of Being" in Germany. "It sure would have meant a lot less stress."

ACKNOWLEDGMENTS

...

The past eighteen years have, in a sense, been one extended tooling-up sequence for the writing of this book. In my time at *Empire* magazine, I've been fortunate enough to encounter almost every one of the action titans featured here (Stallone remains sly) and walk away intact.

In Atlanta, I witnessed Arnold Schwarzenegger shoving $10 million down a toilet, on the set of the 2014 thriller *Sabotage*. In Austin, Texas, I sat beside Chuck Norris at a martial arts tournament in a giant stadium shortly before he strode onstage to the sound of Prodigy's "Firestarter." Dolph Lundgren paid a visit to our office, coincidentally syncing with a *Puss in Boots* media drop, resulting in the Swedish colossus posing for photos while cuddling a ginger kitten. I spent a surreal two days in Shanghai shadowing Jackie Chan, which led to us being chased down a city street by Chinese fans before driving away in his BMW, Chan crooning along to a Lionel Richie song. Steven Seagal and Jean-Claude Van Damme I spoke to at length on the phone, each making their views on the other clear ("With the pussies, there is some jealousy," Seagal sniffed; "If Steven Seagal will slap me, I will slap him twice, hard," pledged Van Damme). As for Bruce Willis, I sat opposite him in a Kensington hotel room for the *Red 2* junket, Willis wearing a bathrobe at two P.M. "Can you ask him why he's wearing the robe?" asked a frantic publicist. Alas, I failed to secure the answer.

The book you're reading wouldn't exist without these collective testosterone-soaked experiences, so the hugest of thanks to everybody at *Empire,* past and present. Not least James Dyer, Dan Jolin, Ian Freer, Ally Wybrew, Alex Godfrey, Chris Hewitt, Helen O'Hara, Simon Crook, and Ian Nathan. Plus, of course, my former editors Terri White and Mark Dinning. All of the above are the best of the best at what they do, not to mention enormously inspiring. Though only James has got Seagal-level knife skills.

I'd like to express my deepest gratitude to the many people who helped the book come alive. Thank you to everyone who agreed to an interview, as well as those who lined those interviews up. Much appreciation to Clare Bateman-King, David Baxter, Dan Gagliasso, Jeanette Driver, Jim Hemphill, Victoria Male, Ella Van Cleve, Laifun Chung, Philip Westgren, Stacy Lumbrezer, Jacob Wishnek, Griffin Barchek, Nikhail Asnani, Gail Sistrunk, and Costanza Mauro.

Thanks to my wonderful agent, Felicity Blunt. And to all the fine folks at Crown, Picador, and Curtis Brown, especially my UK editors, Andrea Henry and Paul Martinovic, and Rosie Pierce for answering all my questions, however dull. Most of all to the eagle-eyed and ever-incisive Matt Inman, who once again has guided me expertly and reined me in when my similes got out of control.

The COVID pandemic began one month after I began this book, leaving me stuck at home with tottering towers of Van Damme and Norris DVDs. My sanity might have snapped altogether were it not for a few wonderful, patient companions. To my family, mum Donna and brothers Chris and Phil; faithful reader Neil Alcock; and Winksy, the T-1000 of cats, who may have put me in the hospital over Christmas 2021 but otherwise was most helpful—thank you.

But above all, my gratitude to Maria Costa, for being eternally loving and supportive, and for never tiring of our conversations about JCVD. Sorry there isn't a whole chapter on *Death Warrant* for you.

NOTES

...

PROLOGUE

4   **"The Hollywood of 1990" and following quotes in present tense:** Author interview with James Cameron for *Empire,* April 23, 2020.

4   **"It was an amazing flight":** Author interview with Renny Harlin, October 28, 2020.

4   **"We stopped in Maine to refuel":** Author interview with Steven de Souza, December 27, 2021.

5   **"It's the best party ever done" and following quotes in present tense:** Author interview with Mario Kassar, April 16, 2020.

6   **"Goddammit. You're leading":** Detail from Katya Foreman's article "Arnold Schwarzenegger on Waltzing with Sylvester Stallone," *WWD,* May 20, 2017, wwd.com/eye/parties/arnold -schwarzenegger-on-waltzing-with-sylvester-stallone-10891617.

CHAPTER 1: THE STALLION

12   **"Not too many people":** Lawrence Linderman, "Playboy Interview: Sylvester Stallone," *Playboy,* September 1978.

12   **"It's the only play that Picasso ever wrote":** From Sylvester Stallone interview on *The Tonight Show Starring Jimmy Fallon* (NBC), August 14, 2014.

12   **"It was a giant red appendage":** Ibid.

13   **"Reminiscent of the guttural echoings":** Lewis Grossberger, "The Trouble with Sylvester Stallone," *Rolling Stone,* July 8, 1982.

13   **"I *was* like Mr. Potato Head":** Glenn Plaskin, "Stallone's Long 'Rocky' Road," *Chicago Tribune,* November 4, 1990.

14   **"I was like a poster boy for a nightmare":** Ovid Demaris, "Can He Be More?," *Parade Magazine,* March 31, 1991.

14   **"This boy will never become President":** Linderman, "Playboy Interview: Sylvester Stallone."

15   **"It was like seeing the Messiah":** Demaris, "Can He Be More?"

15   **"The lack of oxygen":** Linderman, "Playboy Interview: Sylvester Stallone."

16   **"I was onstage":** From Sylvester Stallone interview on *City Lights* (Citytv), 1977.

17   **"He would strut around":** Harry Knowles, Sylvester Stallone interview on *Ain't It Cool News,* December 16, 2006, legacy .aintitcool.com/node/30932.

17   **"the inbred cousin":** Ibid.

17   **"He projected for *Death Race*" and following quotes in present tense:** Author interview with Roger Corman, June 2, 2020.

18   **"180 pages of garbage":** Sylvester Stallone, *The Official Rocky Scrapbook* (Grosset & Dunlap, 1977), 14.

18   **"vile, putrid, festering":** Linderman, "Playboy Interview: Sylvester Stallone."

19   **"It was one of those awkward meetings" and following quotes in present tense:** Author interview with Irwin Winkler, May 21, 2020.

20   **"He can hold his head up high forever":** Stallone, *The Official Rocky Scrapbook,* 19.

20   **"We'd watch the sun go up":** Ibid.

21   **"These blasts of gas":** Ibid., 34.

22   **"My first meeting with Stallone" and following quotes in present tense:** Author interview with Garrett Brown, June 9, 2020.

22   **"There's one shot where he walks" and following quotes:** Author interview with Richard Halsey, June 15, 2020.

22   **"When I looked at all the dailies" and following quotes in present tense:** Author interview with Scott Conrad, June 4, 2020.

23   **"I provided them with a presence" and "I was a raving lunatic":** Linderman, "Playboy Interview: Sylvester Stallone."

24   **"a sentimental little slum movie":** Vincent Canby, "Rocky: Pure 30's Make-Believe," *New York Times,* November 22, 1976.

25   **"The movie has made Sylvester Stallone":** Arthur Knight, "Rocky," *Hollywood Reporter,* November 5, 1976.

26   **"He's gloating and gloating":** From Sylvester Stallone interview with *Variety,* youtube.com/watch?v=Ra9Y5QCKw5s&feature= emb_title, 2019.

CHAPTER 2: THE TANK

27   **"You always have to stretch":** George Butler, *Arnold Schwarzenegger: A Portrait* (Simon & Schuster, 1990), 71.

27   **"I didn't get certain things I needed":** Arnold Schwarzenegger, *Arnold: The Education of a Bodybuilder* (Simon & Schuster, 1977), 66.

28   **"My hair was pulled":** Betsy Morris, "Arnold Power," *Fortune,* August 9, 2004.

28   **"He said my weight training was garbage":** Arnold Schwarzenegger, *Total Recall: My Unbelievably True Life Story* (Simon & Schuster, 2012), 615.

30   **"Whatever I thought might hold me back":** Schwarzenegger, *Arnold,* 28.

30   **"I was looking for giant signs":** Schwarzenegger, *Total Recall,* 84.

30   **"A lot of other athletes are afraid of this":** Butler, *Arnold Schwarzenegger,* 31.

31   **"I never saw him read a book":** Ibid., 133.

31   **"The thing that stands out" and following quotes in present tense:** Author interview with Arthur Allan Seidelman, April 23, 2020.

33   **"If you concentrate hard enough" and following rules:** Schwarzenegger, *Arnold,* chapter 4.

34   **"I'm talking to Bob" and following quotes in present tense:** Author interview with Eric Morris, July 19, 2020.

35   **"to be trapped inside a huge":** Vincent Canby, " 'Stay Hungry': Rafelson Film Is About 'New' South," *New York Times,* April 26, 1976.

36   **"Arnold has a gift":** Richard Schickel, "Cinema: A Delicate Beefcake Ballet," *Time,* January 24, 1977.

37   **"Why does a little man":** Dan Geringer, "As They Say in Hollywood . . . Pex Sell Tix," *Sports Illustrated,* December 7, 1987.

37   **"It was not an intellectual process" and following quotes in present tense:** Author interview with Edward Pressman, July 20, 2020.

38   **"We were into Dino-world" and following quotes in present tense:** Author interview with Oliver Stone for *Empire,* June 30, 2020.

39   **"Conan is a barbarian" and following quotes in present tense:** Author interview with John Milius, April 29, 2022.

39   **"I'm interested in pagan mythology":** *Conan: From the Vault,* documentary, 20th Century Fox Home Entertainment, 2011.

39   **"Look, I'm bleeding real blood":** Details from John Milius and Arnold Schwarzenegger audio commentary track on *Conan the Barbarian* Blu-ray.

41   **"a sort of psychopathic *Star Wars*":** Richard Schickel, "Overkill," *Time,* May 24, 1982.

41   **"My goal is to be equal":** *Conan: From the Vault.*

CHAPTER 3: TOOLING UP

42   **"I've been down, and I've been up":** John McCormick, "Without Dubuque There Is No F.I.S.T.," *Telegraph-Herald,* June 26, 1977.

43   **"In true Rocky fashion":** Lawrence Linderman, "Playboy Interview: Sylvester Stallone," *Playboy,* September 1978.

43   **"People like Canby":** John McCormick, "Writers' 'Rocky' Criticism Gnaws at Stallone," *Telegraph-Herald,* June 27, 1977.

44   **"The director never used":** Linderman, "Playboy Interview: Sylvester Stallone."

44   **"nearly two and a half hours":** Richard Schickel, "J.U.N.K.," *Time,* May 1, 1978.

44 **"*Rocky* warmed over"**: Vincent Canby, "Rocky Goes to Limbo in 'Paradise Alley,' " *New York Times,* November 10, 1978.

44 **"Stallone tries to work our emotions"**: Pauline Kael, "Paradise Alley," *New Yorker,* November 20, 1978.

44 **"I received the worst reviews since Hitler"**: Lewis Grossberger, "The Trouble with Sylvester Stallone," *Rolling Stone,* July 8, 1982.

45 **"I was doing a picture"**: Author interview with Scott Conrad, June 4, 2020.

45 **"They say, 'Who is he?' "**: *The Barbara Walters Interview* (ABC), December 5, 1979.

45 **"We felt he was so involved"**: Author interview with Irwin Winkler, May 21, 2020.

46 **"A great movie"**: Roger Ebert, "Watching Rocky II with Muhammad Ali," *Chicago Sun-Times,* July 31, 1979.

46 **"It was a resuscitator"**: Grossberger, "The Trouble with Sylvester Stallone."

46 **"I felt that it was over. I was finished"**: Ibid.

47 **"shrewd and empty"**: Pauline Kael, "Rocky III," *New Yorker,* May 31, 1982.

48 **"I am quite aware that I'm locked into this image"**: Grossberger, "The Trouble with Sylvester Stallone."

48 **"He was a movie star" and following quotes in present tense**: Author interview with Edward Pressman, July 20, 2020.

48 **"Now I'm an 8"**: *Conan: From the Vault,* documentary, 20th Century Fox Home Entertainment, 2011.

48 **"I can absolutely understand"**: *Carnival in Rio* (UNI Distribution Company), 1983.

49 **"I would pay anything"**: Marguerite Michaels, "A Son's Quest to Be the Best," *Parade Magazine,* January 9, 1983.

50 **"We've taken just about all of the blood out"**: Brian Lowry, "Richard Fleischer Directing 'Conan the Destroyer,' " *Starlog,* August 1984.

50 **"I am ambitious"**: Rick Lyman, "Arnold Schwarzenegger," *Panama City News Herald,* July 7, 1984.

50 **"If it doesn't go well"**: Ian Nathan, *The Terminator Vault* (Aurum Entertainment, 2013), 40.

51   *"Man,* that bone structure": Ibid., 42.

51   "Nobody in town" and following quotes in present tense: Author interview with Mike Medavoy, August 27, 2020.

51   "Anybody who tells you" and following quotes in present tense: Author interview with Michael Biehn for *Empire,* April 7, 2020.

51   "You know, I trained in New York": Author interview with Linda Hamilton for *Empire,* July 11, 2022.

52   "I had a toy tank" and following quotes in present tense: Author interview with James Cameron for *Empire,* April 23, 2020.

53   "Erector Set toy-making": *Siskel & Ebert at the Movies* (Buena Vista Television), June 29, 1991.

53   "Protected by the impenetrable thickness": Desmond Ryan, " 'Terminator' Should Be Destroyed," *Philadelphia Inquirer,* November 11, 1984.

53   "Arnold Schwarzenegger was born": Kirk Ellis, "The Terminator," *Hollywood Reporter,* October 26, 1984.

54   "Stallone's career was stalled" and following quotes in present tense: Author interview with Ted Kotcheff, September 12, 2020.

54   "I used to cook pasta" and following quotes in present tense: Author interview with Mario Kassar, April 16, 2020.

54   "I think they were going to lab animals": From Sylvester Stallone interview on *The Howard Stern Show,* March 16, 2005.

56   "I think we both retched": *The Howard Stern Show,* March 16, 2005.

57   "We're beginning to understand": J. Hoberman, *Make My Day: Movie Culture in the Age of Reagan* (New Press, 2019), 163.

57   "I'd sort of conditioned myself": Barbra Paskin, "Sly Flies High," *Film Review,* September 1985.

CHAPTER 4: THE COWBOY AND THE CANNONBALL

58   "I'd never been in a movie" and following quotes in present tense: Author interview with Chuck Norris, "It's Chuck's World—We Just Live in It," *Empire,* May 2007.

60   "Chuck Norris came up harassed" and following quotes in present tense: Author interview with Robert Wall, September 17, 2020.

63 **"He has fluffy blond hair":** Janet Maslin, " 'Eye for an Eye' Is Soft-Core Violence," *New York Times,* August 14, 1981.

63 **"Clearly *The Octagon* is no real threat":** Joseph McLellan, "For the Kill of It," *Washington Post,* August 25, 1980.

65 **"What Norris was really looking for":** Roger Ebert, "Lone Wolf McQuade," *Chicago Sun-Times,* April 18, 1983.

65 **"Mr. Norris is good":** Vincent Canby, "Lone Wolf McQuade," *New York Times,* April 16, 1983.

66 **"decade of darkness":** Jackie Chan, *Never Grow Up* (Simon & Schuster, 2015), 21.

66 **"My master wanted me to do opera" and following quotes in present tense:** Author interview with Jackie Chan for "Jackie Chan Just Wants Some Respect," *Empire,* December 2010.

69 **"America really scares me":** Lou Gale, "The Big Brawl," *Doylestown Intelligencer,* August 29, 1980.

69 **"He spends a good deal":** Al Haas, "Jackie Chan: A Man in Constant Motion," *Santa Ana Orange County Register,* September 5, 1980.

69 **"They don't give me enough time":** Bob Thomas, "Kung-Fu Comeback in 'The Big Brawl,' " *Eureka Times-Standard,* September 6, 1980.

CHAPTER 5: MAXIMALISM

72 **"It's Rambo's tag":** Rick Lyman, "Stallone Experiments with Singing in 'Rhinestone,' " *Brownsville Herald,* June 27, 1984.

73 **"Sly is gorgeous":** Arthur Lubow, "Stallone and Travolta," *People,* March 7, 1983.

73 **"If John keeps it up":** Ibid.

74 **"The only thing we kept":** Glenn Lovell, "Sly Stallone Forsakes Macho Image," *Syracuse Herald-Journal,* June 21, 1984.

74 **"From the several close-ups":** Vincent Canby, " 'Staying Alive' Succumbs to a Host of Missteps," *New York Times,* July 24, 1983.

75 **"No offense to Mr. Robinson":** Lovell, "Sly Stallone Forsakes Macho Image."

75 **"If you take a non-housebroken puppy"**: Michael London, "The Rocky Road to a Hollywood Flop," *Los Angeles Times,* July 20, 1984.

75 **"He got overwhelmed"**: Colin Dangaard, "Dolly Rates Stallone: 'Sly Is a Kisser—The Best,'" *Delaware County Sunday Times,* July 1, 1984.

75 **"It cost more than the three *Rockys*"**: Lovell, "Sly Stallone Forsakes Macho Image."

76 **"Stallone singing"**: Robert Bruce, "Star Billing Can't Save 'Rhinestone,'" *Daily Texan,* June 26, 1984.

76 **"Whether it was a good film"**: London, "The Rocky Road to a Hollywood Flop."

76 **"It's like Edgar Allan Poe"**: Pat H. Broeske, "'Rhinestone' Reflects Glare of Parton, Stallone," *The Register,* June 22, 1984.

76 **"Your deportment in our relationship"**: Aljean Harmetz, "Stallone in Dispute on 'Cotton Club,'" *New York Times,* June 1, 1982.

76 **"Sly is the perfect balance"**: Cliff Jahr, "How I Came Close to Suicide," *Ladies' Home Journal,* June 1986.

77 **"There were days on *Rhinestone*"**: Lovell, "Sly Stallone Forsakes Macho Image."

77 **"took nearly 30–40 pages"**: Harry Knowles, Sylvester Stallone interview on *Ain't It Cool News,* December 16, 2006, legacy .aintitcool.com/node/30932.

78 **"It's one of the few movies"**: *We Get to Win This Time* (Artisan Entertainment), 2002.

78 **"I said, 'Uh-oh'" and following quotes in present tense:** Author interview with Mario Kassar, April 16, 2020.

78 **"I won't allow myself to sweat"**: *We Get to Win This Time,* 2002.

80 **"Just call me Rambolina"**: Deborah Caulfield, "Sigourney Weaver: 'Just Call Me Rambolina,'" *Los Angeles Times*, July 13, 1986.

80 **"After *Rambo,* I'm not that interested"**: Adam Pirani, "James Cameron in Deadly Combat with 'Aliens,'" *Starlog,* September 1986.

80 **"In the script of it that I read"**: Author interview with Ted Kotcheff, September 12, 2020.

80 "People have been waiting": Richard Zoglin, "Rambomania,"
    Time, June 24, 1985.

81 "Immediate attraction": Stu Schreiberg, "Stallone's Smashing
    Foe," *USA Weekend,* November 15–17, 1985.

81 "That was probably before I got kicked" and following quotes in
    present tense: Author interview with Dolph Lundgren,
    "Lost Action Heroes," *Empire,* March 2007.

82 "How do you get any better" and following quotes in present
    tense: Author interview with Irwin Winkler, May 21, 2020.

83 "the greatest fighting machine": Pat Hackett, "New Again:
    Sylvester Stallone," *Interview,* September 1985.

83 "Big, long guys": Author interview with Lundgren, "Going the
    Distance," *Empire,* March 2022.

84 "I just let caution to the wind": Hackett, "New Again: Sylvester
    Stallone."

84 "I'm calling my agent": Knowles, Sylvester Stallone interview on
    Ain't It Cool News.

85 "I could beat Mike Tyson": Rod Lurie, "Dolph Lundgren: Chemical
    Engineer and He-Man," *Greenwich News,* May 21, 1987.

85 "I cannot wait to go into": Schreiberg, "Stallone's Smashing Foe."

85 "Pretty soon my life": Ibid.

85 "It's some of the greatest": Mark Weinberg, *Movie Nights with
    the Reagans: A Memoir* (Simon & Schuster, 2018), 163.

86 "It's always flattering": Jacqueline Trescott and Donnie Radcliffe,
    "White House Starscape," *Washington Post,* October 9, 1985.

86 "Time was limited": Brigitte Nielsen, *You Only Get One Life*
    (John Blake, 2011), 102.

86 "Red Sonja" and details of the relationship: Nielsen, *You Only Get.*

87 "Sylvester made sure": Ibid., 135.

CHAPTER 6: KNOCK KNOCK

88 "He did that to me" and following quotes in present tense: Author
    interview with Jim Thomas, November 17, 2020.

89 "This guy Schwarzenegger": Detail from author interview with
    Steven de Souza, "Bullet Timed," *Empire,* November 2012.

89   "They got together every script" and following quotes in present
      tense: Author interview with de Souza, *Empire*, 2012.

90   "We were sitting next to each other" and following quotes in
      present tense: Author interview with Mark Lester, "Bullet
      Timed," *Empire*, November 2012.

91   "Was Arnold embarrassed" and following quotes in present tense:
      Author interview with Rae Dawn Chong, "Bullet Timed,"
      Empire, November 2012.

91   "Are you scared?": Exchange detailed in author interview with
      Lester, *Empire*, November 2012.

94   "When the director said action": Author interview with Vernon
      Wells, "Bullet Timed," *Empire*, November 2012.

94   "There were sharp metal edges": Author interview with Arnold
      Schwarzenegger, *The Empire Podcast*, Episode 45, January 25,
      2013.

95   "Schwarzenegger has become": Paul Attanasio, "Movies,"
      Washington Post, October 4, 1985.

96   "I could see the potential" and following quotes in present tense:
      Author interview with John McTiernan, November 13, 2020.

102   "*Predator*'s final scenes": Duane Byrge, "Predator," *Hollywood
      Reporter*, June 10, 1987.

103   "I see films as pure entertainment": Frank Sanello, "Arnold Can't
      Dump Guns," *Republic Extra*, June 25, 1986.

103   "He is not my friend": Joan Goodman, "The Playboy Interview:
      Arnold Schwarzenegger," *Playboy*, January 1988.

103   "Seeing him dressed in his white suit": Ibid.

104   "Venusian pimp": Alex Heard, "The Importance of Being
      Arnold," *Washington Post*, January 17, 1988.

CHAPTER 7: THE ALIEN

105   "I like your belt": Details taken from Lawrence Grobel, "Playboy
      Interview: Jean-Claude Van Damme," *Playboy*, January 1995.

106   "It didn't work for nobody" and following quotes in present
      tense: Author interview with Jean-Claude Van Damme,
      "Lost Action Heroes," *Empire*, March 2007.

106 **"The guy in the small village"**: Kris Gilpin, "Cyborg Saviour," *Starlog,* January 1989.

107 **"is like a religion"**: Ibid.

108 **"I suffered many years"**: Author interview with Van Damme, *Empire,* March 2007.

109 **"Big mistake for him" and following quotes in present tense:** Author interview with Robert Wall, September 17, 2020.

111 **"I'm fucked. I'm hungry"**: Details taken from Erik Hedegaard, "Van Damme Kicks Back," *Details,* September 1993.

111 **"I'm a young Chuck Norris"**: Details taken from Grobel, "Playboy Interview: Jean-Claude Van Damme."

112 **"All of which was BS" and following quotes in present tense:** Author interview with Sheldon Lettich, January 21, 2021.

114 **"It looked like a rabbit"**: Nathan Rabin, "Jean-Claude Van Damme," *AV Club,* October 3, 2008, avclub.com/jean-claude-van -damme-1798213466.

114 **"Van Damme, the iron is hot"**: Details taken from Grobel, "Playboy Interview: Jean-Claude Van Damme."

115 **"Buddy, that's it"**: Ibid.

115 **"an incredible, fantastic movie"**: Mark Singer, "Trump Solo," *New Yorker,* May 12, 1997.

115 **"a muscular Brussels sprout"**: Dann Gire, "Bad Guys, Bad Acting in 'Bloodsport,' " *Arlington Heights Daily Herald,* April 23, 1988.

116 **"I like your belt"**: Details taken from Grobel, "The Playboy Interview: Jean-Claude Van Damme."

CHAPTER 8: FOREIGN POLICIES

117 **"Boy, I'm glad I saw *Rambo*"**: Bernard Weinraub, "39 American Hostages Free After 17 Days," *New York Times,* July 1, 1985.

118 **"Well, Jim, *The Sound of Music*"**: Adrian Woolridge, "The Great Delegator," *New York Times,* January 29, 2006.

118 **"reckless *Star Wars* schemes"**: Lou Cannon, "President Seeks Futuristic Defense Against Missiles," *Washington Post,* March 24, 1983.

118   **"The Force is with us":** George de Lama, " 'The Force Is with Us,'
Reagan Says," *Chicago Tribune,* March 30, 1985.

119   **"The film fantasies":** Martin Tolchin, "How Reagan Always Gets
the Best Lines," *New York Times,* September 9, 1985.

119   **"I'm not so much a Republican":** Judy Klemesrud, "His Discovery
Has Norris Excited," *Bedford Gazette,* September 17, 1985.

119   **"If you don't want to win":** Ibid.

120   **"They were getting ready" and following quotes in present tense:**
Author interview with Chuck Norris, "It's Chuck's World—
We Just Live in It," *Empire,* May 2007.

120   **"I actually met him at Chuck's house" and following quotes in
present tense:** Author interview with James Bruner, February 9,
2021.

121   **"The MIA movement was a fetish":** Author interview with Oliver
Stone for *Empire,* June 30, 2020.

122   **"If you want all that realism":** Michael Kinsley, "From 'Rambo'
to 'Platoon,' " *Washington Post,* February 18, 1987.

123   **"I was trying to keep Chuck" and following quotes in present
tense:** Author interview with Andrew Davis, September 15, 2020.

123   **"There's a scene":** Roger Ebert, "Code of Silence," *Chicago Sun-
Times,* May 3, 1985.

123   **"The best compliment I can give you":** Chuck Norris, *The Secret
of Inner Strength: My Story* (Diamond Books, 1989), 165.

124   **"We could say this is mind-bogglingly insulting":** Hal Hinson,
"Missing Everything but Action," *Washington Post,* January 22,
1988.

125   **"I know it's going to happen":** Klemesrud, "His Discovery Has
Norris Excited."

125   **"It's a battle like in *Gone with the Wind*":** Ibid.

126   **"brain-damaged, idiotic thriller":** Roger Ebert, "Invasion USA,"
Chicago Sun-Times, September 27, 1985.

126   **"seemed on the verge of becoming":** Vincent Canby, "Invasion
USA," *New York Times,* September 27, 1985.

127   **"The problem with Rambo as a doll":** Todd S. Purdum, "Coleco
Smitten by 'Rambo,' " *New York Times,* August 1, 1985.

127 "horrible" and "warnography": J. Hoberman, *Make My Day: Movie Culture in the Age of Reagan* (New Press, 2019), 251.

127 **"I fear the United States":** Jay Kesler, "Jesus, Rambo and the Gates of Hell," *Transformation,* January 1, 1987.

127 **"I find it incredible" and following quotes in present tense:** Robert Barr, "Stallone: 'Rambo Goes In to End Conflicts, Not Start Them,'" *Salina Journal,* June 6, 1988.

128 **"Sly took me in" and following quotes in present tense:** Author interview with Peter Macdonald, February 22, 2021.

129 **"There was a huge left-wing demonstration":** Author interview with Sheldon Lettich, January 21, 2021.

131 **"third-rate male models":** Harry Knowles, Sylvester Stallone interview on *Ain't It Cool News,* January 21, 2008, legacy .aintitcool.com/node/35350.

132 **"*Rambo III* has the hardware":** Roger Ebert, "Rambo Lets His Guns Do the Talking in Sequel," *Chicago Sun-Times,* May 15, 1988.

132 **"I'm all for glasnost":** Barr, "Stallone: 'Rambo Goes In to End Conflicts, Not Start Them.'"

133 **"What's he gonna say?":** Robert Barr, "Sticks and Stones Can't Hurt Rambo—but Words Can," *Jacksonville Journal-Courier,* May 22, 1988.

CHAPTER 9: THE GREAT ONE

134 **It was an early afternoon in 1986:** Details taken from multiple sources, including Michael Ovitz, *Who Is Michael Ovitz?* (W. H. Allen, 2018), 225.

135 **"The demonstration was quite miraculous":** Patrick Goldstein, "Steven Seagal Gets a Shot at Stardom," *Los Angeles Times,* February 14, 1988.

135 **"We were all blown away":** Ibid.

135 **"I still can't believe":** John Connolly, "Man of Dishonor," *Spy,* August 1993.

136 **"He just wouldn't leave" and following quotes in present tense:**

Author interview with Steven Seagal, "Lost Action Heroes," *Empire,* March 2007.

136   **"He reminded me of an alien":** Alan Richman, "Black Belt, White Lies," *GQ,* March 1991.

136   **"When I met Steven":** Ibid.

137   **"Many, many different kinds of people":** Ibid.

137   **"When you look at him":** Goldstein, "Steven Seagal Gets a Shot at Stardom."

137   **"Maybe it's this [Eastern] training":** Richman, "Black Belt, White Lies."

137   **"The closest person":** Goldstein, "Steven Seagal Gets a Shot at Stardom."

138   **"Steven was very thin" and following quotes in present tense:** Author interview with Andrew Davis, September 15, 2020.

139   **"The whole motivation":** Goldstein, "Steven Seagal Gets a Shot at Stardom."

139   **"what we're really doing here":** Ibid.

140   **"If we only had a little more money":** Ibid.

140   **"Michael, you really screwed me":** Ovitz, *Who Is Michael Ovitz?,* 225.

140   **"Steven Seagal is a dazzling combination" and subsequent quotes:** Newspaper advertisement for *Above the Law* in *Orange County Register,* April 2, 1988.

141   **"He speaks with a hushed, conspiratorial purr":** Patrick Goldstein, "Mega-Stardom Looms for Tough Guy Seagal," *Winnipeg Free Press,* April 29, 1988.

141   **"exceedingly lacking in story":** Lou Gaul, "Star of 'Above the Law' Is No Cartoon Character," *Montgomery County Record,* April 3, 1988.

141   **"It said in the article" and following quotes in present tense:** Author interview with Robert Wall, September 17, 2020.

142   **"I shouldn't say this":** Gaul, "Star of 'Above the Law' Is No Cartoon Character."

142   **"not a cartoon character":** Ibid.

143   **"Can we change the subject?":** From Steven Seagal interview on *The Arsenio Hall Show* (Paramount Domestic Television), 1991.

143   **"truly amazing"**: Shahesta Shaitly, "Pam Grier Takes Raunch to the Ranch," *The Observer,* December 11, 2011.

145   **"I figured it out"**: David J. Fox, "Fighting Words," *Los Angeles Times,* October 16, 1990.

145   **"I should have my own people in here"**: Goldstein, "Steven Seagal Gets a Shot at Stardom."

145   **"A bunch of Black guys"**: Author interview with Conrad Palmisano, March 13, 2021.

145   **"It was a gut feeling"**: Larry Rohter, "Company News; Small Budget, Small Star, Big Hit," *New York Times,* October 23, 1990.

146   **"Yeah, I could deliver"**: Pat H. Broeske, "Steven Seagal Wants His Oscar," *Los Angeles Times,* October 14, 1990.

146   **"Would you call Tracy a martial-arts guy"**: Richman, "Black Belt, White Lies."

CHAPTER 10: WELCOME TO THE PARTY, PAL

148   **"All we were doing"**: Lawrence Grobel, "Playboy Interview: Bruce Willis," *Playboy,* November 1988.

149   **"The Dalai Lama guy" and following quotes in present tense:** Author interview with Lawrence Gordon, April 27, 2021.

150   **"James Caan told me" and following quotes in present tense:** Author interview with Steven de Souza, December 27, 2021.

150   **"Bruce went and did" and following quotes in present tense:** Author interview with John McTiernan, November 13, 2020.

151   **"They're going to laugh"**: Brian Abrams, *Die Hard: An Oral History* (Kindle, 2016).

152   **"*Nothing Lasts Forever* is truly" and following quote:** Charles Willeford, "Probing Terrorism's Ambiguities," *Miami Herald,* October 7, 1979.

154   **"When I landed"**: Chris Nashawaty, "Bruce Willis: 'If I Hadn't Done *Die Hard,* I'd Rip It Off,'" *Entertainment Weekly,* June 14, 2007, ew.com/article/2007/06/14/bruce-willis-if-i-hadnt-done-die-hard-id-rip-it/.

155   **"I have no idea what's going on"**: Abrams, *Die Hard: An Oral History.*

156 **"I wanted to find the honesty"**: Ryan Murphy, "Bruce Willis: 'Movie Star—That's My Job,'" *Miami Herald,* July 17, 1988.

156 **"It was something I found"**: Ibid.

157 **"I like taking risks"**: Bruce Wills interview on KXAS-TV (NBC5), 1988.

158 **"I did three takes"**: Author interview with Alan Rickman, *The Empire Podcast,* Episode 157, April 17, 2015.

159 **"Manipulative, cold, sexist"**: Steve Copper, "What's Doing?," *Jacksonville Journal Courier,* October 8, 1988.

159 **"a mess"**: Roger Ebert, "Die Hard," *Chicago Sun-Times,* July 15, 1988.

159 **"The filmmakers even"**: Caryn James, "The Police, Terrorists and a Captive Audience," *New York Times,* July 15, 1988.

159 **"Before long you're pummeled"**: Jim Emerson, "High-Rise Adventure Steals the Show," *Orange County Register,* July 20, 1988.

159 **"If she keeps this up"**: Murphy, "Bruce Willis: 'Movie Star— That's My Job.'"

160 **"The '66 was the best Corvette"**: Grobel, "Playboy Interview: Bruce Willis."

160 **"Know why you'll never be"**: Details taken from author interview with Jim Thomas, November 17, 2020.

CHAPTER 11: SUPERCOPS

161 **"*Cannonball Run II* is one"**: Roger Ebert, *Chicago Sun-Times,* January 1, 1984.

162 **"I just didn't want"**: Nadia Bruce Rawlings, Stephen A. Roberts, and Marco Siedelmann, *The Untold In-Depth Outrageously True Story of Shapiro Glickenhaus Entertainment* (Impressum, 2016), 268.

162 **"A cold-blooded killer type"**: Jackie Chan, *Never Grow Up* (Simon & Schuster, 2015), 153.

162 **"Let's just say"**: James D. Solomon, "Worldwide Fame Eludes Jackie Chan," *Eureka Times Standard,* March 13, 1986.

163   "Golden Harvest wants to think big": Ibid.

163   "That film made me angry" and following quotes in present tense: Author interview with Jackie Chan for "Jackie Chan Just Wants Some Respect," *Empire*, December 2010.

164   "Anything less": Jackie Chan, *I Am Jackie Chan* (Pan Books, 1999), 305.

165   "I'd lost my mind": Chan, *Never Grow Up*, 158.

166   "I'm very scared": Jaime Wolf, "Jackie Chan, American Action Hero?," *New York Times*, January 21, 1996.

166   "Until my pictures": Vernon Scott, "Jackie Chan Takes Action," *European Stars and Stripes*, October 12, 1987.

167   "I think I am far better": Cinty Li, "Bruce Lee Heir Does His Own Stunts," *Harrisonburg Daily News Record*, August 18, 1988.

167   "I wondered why": Chan, *Never Grow Up*, 187.

168   "People kind of shooed": Author interview with Lundgren, "Going the Distance," *Empire*, March 2022.

168   "The movie was so powerful": Ibid.

169   "It was Hollywood": Grace Jones, *I'll Never Write My Memoirs* (Simon & Schuster, 2015), 290.

169   The final straw came: Details from ibid., 293.

169   "Suddenly I went": Author interview with Dolph Lundgren, "Lost Action Heroes," *Empire*, March 2007.

169   "I wish. I would have taken it": Author interview with Dolph Lundgren, "Going the Distance."

170   "The cinematographer was really, really mean": Author interview with Quentin Tarantino, "The People vs Quentin Tarantino," *Empire*, July 2019.

170   "There are two sides": Rod Lurie, "Dolph Lundgren: Chemical Engineer and He-Man," *Greenwich News*, May 21, 1987.

171   "I thought it was a joke": Alan Jones, "Masters of the Universe," *Starburst*, December 1987.

171   "What is more important?": Lurie, "Dolph Lundgren: Chemical Engineer and He-Man."

171   "I was walking around": Author interview with Lundgren, "Lost Action Heroes."

171 **"It was all muscles":** Author interview with Lundgren, "Going the Distance."

171 **"I jumped out of a window":** Author interview with Lundgren, "Lost Action Heroes."

172 **"It was a challenging film":** Author interview with Ed Pressman, July 20, 2020.

172 **"Right now, there are only three":** Lurie, "Dolph Lundgren: Chemical Engineer and He-Man."

172 **"His heaving chest":** Stephen Holden, "Dolph Lundgren in 'Red Scorpion,'" *New York Times,* April 21, 1989.

173 **"I was really upset":** Author interview with Lundgren, "Going the Distance."

173 **"could easily be Van Damme–marketable":** *Variety,* December 31, 1990.

173 **"100% pure beef":** *Guns, Genes & Fighting Machines: The Making of* Universal Soldier (Automat Pictures, 2004).

CHAPTER 12: FUNNY OR DIE

175 **"It was just a pile of shootouts" and following quotes in present tense:** Author interview with John McTiernan, November 13, 2020.

176 **"Start with the head":** Ryan Murphy, "Leading Man of Action," *Janesville Gazette,* June 3, 1990.

176 **"He's got muscles":** Jim Murray, "Schwarzenegger Was a Cut Above," *Arlington Heights Daily Herald,* March 25, 1989.

176 **"Arnold is as defined as ever":** Murphy, "Leading Man of Action."

176 **"He was telling me" and following quotes in present tense:** Author interview with Ivan Reitman, August 23, 2021.

177 **"We were like these little terriers" and following quotes in present tense:** Author interview with William Osborne, June 29, 2021.

179 **"He's like a tree":** Jim Emerson, "Schwarzenegger's Twin Shares Some 'Guy Talk,'" *Boston Globe,* December 30, 1988.

179 **"You robbed me blind":** Arnold Schwarzenegger interview on *In Depth with Graham Bensinger,* November 12, 2016.

179   **"Finally, they can see":** Michael Janusonis, "Unlikely Screen
       Pairing Results in 'Twins,' " *Providence Journal,* January 8, 1989.

180   **"I think a lot of times":** Dann Gire, "Move Over, Prince
       Charming," *Arlington Heights Daily Herald,* June 12, 1987.

180   **"I didn't think I would":** Ibid.

180   **"Everybody was kind of tense":** Author interview with Mario
       Kassar, April 16, 2020.

181   **"Animal movies were popular" and following quotes in present
       tense:** Author interview with Rick Gitelson, September 24, 2020.

182   **"Sly's movie didn't open":** Jack Mathews, "Arnold Pumps Up
       Talent with Each New Role," *Los Angeles Times,* September 1,
       1989.

182   **Rumors had swirled around:** Details in this paragraph taken from
       Alan Richman, "Sly Says Bye, Bye, Brigitte, and So a Rocky
       Marriage Ends with a Split Decision," *People,* July 27, 1987.

182   **"It became a prison":** Brigitte Nielsen, *You Only Get One Life*
       (John Blake, 2011), 135.

183   **"It's not the way he should play that":** Details taken from author
       interview with Peter Macdonald, February 22, 2021.

183   **"I wish I could have taken" and following quotes in present tense:**
       Ibid.

183   **"It should be ugly":** Barry Sonnenfeld, *Barry Sonnenfeld, Call
       Your Mother* (Hachette Books, 2020), 230.

184   **Details of Jeffrey Katzenberg call and following quotes in present
       tense:** Author interview with John Landis, July 8, 2020.

187   **"There isn't a laugh":** Roger Ebert, *"Stop! Or My Mom Will
       Shoot,"* *Chicago Sun-Times,* February 21, 1992.

187   **"*Stop! Or My Mom Will Shoot* plays":** Vincent Canby, "Take His
       Mother, Please," *New York Times,* February 21, 1992.

187   **"The worst film I've ever made":** Harry Knowles, Sylvester
       Stallone interview on *Ain't It Cool News,* December 4, 2006,
       legacy.aintitcool.com/node/30869.

187   **"He totally went for it":** Ben Pearson, "Arnold Schwarzenegger
       Confirms One of Hollywood's All-Time Great Troll Moves,"
       Slash Film, October 9, 2017, slashfilm.com/553774/arnold
       -schwarzenegger-beyond-fest.

CHAPTER 13: DOUBLE IMPACT

188　"I can come up with script": Erik Hedegaard, "Van Damme Kicks Back," *Details*, September 1993.

189　"I'm so flexible, smooth": Diane Goldner, "You Have to Do What You Have to Do," *USA Weekend*, July 10, 1992.

189　"I'm not happy with *Bloodsport*": Rod Lurie, "An Interview with Jean-Claude Van Damme," *Greenwich News*, May 26, 1988.

189　"Do everything fast" and following quotes in present tense: Author interview with Jean-Claude Van Damme, "Lost Action Heroes," *Empire*, March 2007.

189　"After you eat": Alan Richman, "Four Weddings and a Front Kick," *GQ*, August 1995.

189　"If I have a date": Ibid.

190　"Maybe they like me": Stephen Rebello, "The 8 Million Dollar Man," *Movieline*, August 1994.

191　"It was called *Wrong Bet*" and following quotes in present tense: Author interview with Sheldon Lettich, January 21, 2021.

192　"The Alex character": Thomas D. Elias, "Van Damme Wants to Follow in Arnold's Steps," Scripps Howard News Service, August 20, 1991.

192　"Van Damme apparently": Chris Hicks, *Deseret News*, August 16, 1991.

192　"*Double Impact* succeeds": Lou Gaul, "Van Damme Fans Can Double Their Enjoyment," *The Intelligencer*, August 9, 1991.

193　"It wouldn't have worked": Author interview with Dolph Lundgren, "Lost Action Heroes."

194　"Too small for me": Hedegaard, "Van Damme Kicks Back."

194　"He cooked it up" and following quotes: Author interview with Dolph Lundgren, "Going the Distance," *Empire*, March 2022.

195　"Free publicity": Jean-Claude Van Damme interview on *The Arsenio Hall Show* (Fox), Season 4, Episode 173, July 7, 1992.

195　"I'll do *everything*": Philip Thomas, "Jean-Claude Schwarzenegger," *Empire*, September 1992.

195　"My own favorite": Roger Ebert, "Double Impact," *Chicago Sun-Times*, August 9, 1991.

195 **"There were so many fans" and following quotes in present tense:** Author interview with Conrad Palmisano, March 13, 2021.

196 **"I thought I was with Michael Jackson":** Alan Richman, "Black Belt, White Lies," *GQ,* March 1991.

196 **"He had just kind of appeared":** Jordan Zakarin, "How Tim Burton's Batman Set the Stage for Comic Books' Hollywood Takeover," *Syfy Wire,* June 20, 2019, syfy.com/syfy-wire/steven -seagal-was-considered-for-bruce-wayne-and-other-burton -batman-facts.

197 **"My stomach was lurching":** Julianna Margulies, *Sunshine Girl* (Ballantine Books, 2021), 145.

197 **"I stepped over the line":** Lou Schuler, "How Arnold Became Arnold," *Men's Health,* October 10, 2018.

198 **"I had absolutely no self-esteem":** Jeff Maysh, "Kelly LeBrock Emerges from Hiding," *Mail Online,* August 27, 2013, dailymail .co.uk/tvshowbiz/article-2402408/Kelly-LeBrock-comes-hiding -photoshoot-reveals-toll-drugs-divorce-took-her.html.

198 **"He was not very conscientious":** Author interview with Andrew Davis, September 15, 2020.

198 **"Gene put little Steven Seagal down" and following quotes in present tense:** Author interview with Robert Wall, September 17, 2020.

199 **"If a guy soils himself":** Gene LeBell interview on *The MMA Hour with Ariel Helwani* (Vox Media), 2012, youtube.com/watch ?v=S2hCGD62Ru0.

199 **"If he said that":** Steven Seagal interview on *The MMA Hour with Ariel Helwani* (Vox Media), 2012, youtube.com/watch?v= G9y1VSpH04c.

200 **"Are you gonna do that?":** Steven Seagal interview on *The Arsenio Hall Show* (Fox), Season 3, Episode 18, October 3, 1990.

200 **"Some of his sketch ideas":** Tom Shales and James Andrew Miller, *Live from New York: The Complete, Uncensored History of* Saturday Night Live (Little, Brown, 2002), 423.

200 **"I just wish Arnold was here":** From Dana Carey interview on *The Howard Stern Show,* May 22, 2019.

201　"You can't explain": Shales and Miller, *Live from New York,* 423.

201　"Maybe his one-inch ponytail": David Spade interview on the *Literally! with Rob Lowe* podcast, August 6, 2020.

CHAPTER 14: PLANET ARNOLD

202　"He had a cougar" and following quotes in present tense: Author interview with Arnold Schwarzenegger, *The Empire Podcast,* Episode 45, January 25, 2013.

203　"I sometimes have dreams": Bill Zehme, "Arnold Schwarzenegger: Mr. Big Shot," *Rolling Stone,* August 22, 1991.

203　"We discussed Arnold" and following quotes in present tense: Author interview with Paul Verhoeven, October 6, 2020.

206　"What's going on with *The Abyss*?": Jack Mathews, "Arnold Pumps Up Talent with Each New Role," *Los Angeles Times,* September 1, 1989.

206　a loud comment about the alignment: Ibid.

206　"He got what he wanted" and following quotes in present tense: Author interview with Mario Kassar, April 16, 2020.

207　"We went from a 40 percent awareness": Arnold Schwarzenegger, *Total Recall: My Unbelievably True Life Story* (Simon & Schuster, 2012), 352.

208　"How many times": Rita Kempley, "The Abyss," *Washington Post,* August 9, 1989.

208　"Arnold is like karate": Jim Emerson, "Director Cameron Stretches Outer Limits of Sci-Fi," *Orange County Register,* June 30, 1991.

208　"He read it on the flight over" and following quotes in present tense: Author interview with James Cameron for *Empire,* April 23, 2020.

209　"I went from going to school" and following quotes in present tense: Author interview with Edward Furlong, "20 Years Since *Terminator 2!*," *FHM,* October 2011.

209　"I mean, if it didn't work" and following quotes in present tense: Author interview with Robert Patrick, "20 Years Since *Terminator 2!*"

211 **"In the first movie":** Details taken from Zehme, "Arnold
Schwarzenegger: Mr. Big Shot."

212 **"It's the worst music":** Author interview with Furlong, "20 Years
Since *Terminator 2!*"

213 **"I needed a place":** David Handelman, "Soon to Be a Major
Gimme-Cap-and-Sweatshirt-Dispensing Restaurant," *Spy,*
September 1991.

213 **"I begged":** Sylvester Stallone on *Larry King Live* (CNN),
October 9, 1993.

214 **"Greed":** Sylvester Stallone interview on *Aspel and Company*
(ITV), May 16, 1993.

214 **"We've put it together":** Greg B. Smith, "Star Vehicle Goes into
Orbit," *San Francisco Examiner,* October 22, 1991.

214 **"Last week I wanted":** Handelman, "Soon to Be a Major Gimme-
Cap-and-Sweatshirt-Dispensing Restaurant."

215 **"Like an art movie":** Ibid.

215 **"When I tell people":** Ibid.

215 **"This is *the* shirt":** Smith, "Star Vehicle Goes into Orbit."

215 **"The promotion given":** Independent Television Commission
report, July 1993.

216 **"Seeing the restaurant":** Anne Thompson, "Cannes: 1991,"
Entertainment Weekly, May 24, 1991.

216 **"I'm just not prone to chew":** *Aspel and Company,* May 16, 1993.

CHAPTER 15: OLD HABITS

218 **"You know, a man" and following quotes in present tense:** Author
interview with John McTiernan, November 13, 2020.

219 **"We spent a lot of work":** Jason Bailey, "How *Die Hard* Changed
the Action Game," *Vulture,* July 10, 2018.

219 **"I needed to know":** Hal Lipper, "It's a 'Hard' Life," *Tampa Bay
Times,* July 3, 1990.

220 **"You know, Renny":** Details from author interview with Renny
Harlin, October 28, 2020.

220 **"We had a major disagreement" and following quotes in present
tense:** Ibid.

222 **"Sure, 'Die Hard 3' ":** Joan V. Vadeboncoeur, "Willis: Critics Jaded," *Syracuse Herald American,* July 1, 1990.

223 **"We had cooked up":** Author interview with Steven de Souza, October 21, 2018.

224 **a "bimbo":** David J. Fox, " '*Under Siege*' Blasts Off," *Los Angeles Times,* October 20, 1992.

224 **"That was Seagal's idea" and following quotes in present tense:** Author interview with J. F. Lawton, January 27, 2023.

224 **"I completely redid" and following quotes in present tense:** Author interview with Steven Seagal, "Lost Action Heroes," *Empire,* March 2007.

224 **"Warner Bros. wanted us" and following quotes in present tense:** Author interview with Andrew Davis, September 15, 2020.

225 **"I took the idea" and following quotes in present tense:** Author interview with Gary Busey, "Shut Up, World. Gary Busey Is Talking," *Empire,* January 2012.

226 **"It was not in the script originally":** Erika Eleniak interview on the *Reliving My Youth* podcast, November 7, 2018.

226 **one of the many shadowy people:** Details on Robert Booth Nichols from various sources, including Guy Lawson, "The US Government Is a Sham," *New York,* June 29, 2012; Guy Lawson, "Get Rich or (Pretend to) Die Trying," *The Independent,* September 3, 2012; and Jennifer Reingold, "How a Con Artist Got Conned," *Fortune,* July 20, 2012.

227 **"I don't wallow in joy":** Fox, " '*Under Siege*' Blasts Off."

228 **"All Stallone cared about":** Anne Thompson, "Sylvester Stallone's *Gale Force,*" *Entertainment Weekly,* October 4, 1991.

230 **"Never again":** Bob Strauss, "The Hazards Were Real in *Cliffhanger,*" *Chicago Tribune,* June 17, 1993.

CHAPTER 16: BORN AGAIN

232 **"Violence is not the answer" and following quotes in present tense:** Author interview with Chuck Norris, "It's Chuck's World—We Just Live in It," *Empire,* May 2007.

233 **"I would have said" and following quotes in present tense:** Author interview with Robert Wall, September 17, 2020.

233 **"a whitebread Bruce Lee":** John Corry, "Chuck Norris In *Silent Rage,*" *New York Times,* April 2, 1982.

234 **"Everyone acted like":** Jessica Simpson, *Open Book* (Dey St., 2020), 62.

234 **"I never did it":** Brad Webber, "Chuck Norris May Be Tough, but He's No Bad Guy," *Arlington Heights Daily Herald,* November 25, 1988.

234 **"I feel very secure":** Ibid.

234 **"A new Chuck Norris is unveiled":** Roger Ebert, "Hero and the Terror," *Chicago Sun-Times,* August 26, 1988.

235 **"Stallone has tried":** Webber, "Chuck Norris May Be Tough, but He's No Bad Guy."

235 **"Oh man":** Marilyn Beck, "Funny Script Attracted Chuck Norris to 'Top Dog,'" *Orange County Register,* December 9, 1994.

236 **"*Top Dog* runs 86 minutes":** Dann Gire, "Stupid Plot Makes Norris' 'Top Dog' a Mutt," *Arlington Heights Daily Herald,* April 29, 1995.

238 **"I touched it":** From Jackie Chan's acceptance speech for honorary Oscar, November 13, 2016.

239 **"Stallone grabbed my hand" and following quotes in present tense:** Author interview with Jackie Chan for "Jackie Chan Just Wants Some Respect," *Empire,* December 2010.

240 **"Probably contains the greatest stunts":** Quentin Tarantino interview on Sky Movies, 2009, youtube.com/watch?v =Zv0WlHbBhdc.

242 **"The number-one box-office star":** Jackie Chan interview on *Late Show with David Letterman* (CBS), February 13, 1996.

242 **"Any attempts to defend this movie":** Roger Ebert, "Rumble in the Bronx," *Chicago Sun-Times,* February 23, 1996.

243 **"I want to find out":** Jaime Wolf, "Jackie Chan, American Action Hero?," *New York Times,* January 21, 1996.

244 **"They're very lucky":** *Late Show with David Letterman,* February 13, 1996.

CHAPTER 17: OIL AND WATER

245　**"It was just classic Steven Seagal":** Author interview with William Osborne, June 29, 2021.

246　**"Silver's just coasting":** Detail taken from author interview with Steven de Souza, December 27, 2021.

246　**"He wanted to fuck over" and following quotes in present tense:** Author interview with Ed Horowitz, December 13, 2021.

247　**"I had this dream" and following quotes in present tense:** Author interview with Robin Russin, December 10, 2021.

248　**"He wanted that majestic look":** Yereth Rosen, "Alaska a Hot Spot for Films Needing Northern Exposure," *Arlington Heights Daily Herald,* August 6, 1993.

249　**"Do you believe":** Details of exchange taken from "Tlingit Adds Blessing to Making of Seagal Movie," *Daily Sitka Sentinel,* May 19, 1993.

249　**"You do whatever you can do" and following quotes in present tense:** Author interview with Steven Seagal, "Lost Action Heroes," *Empire,* March 2007.

250　**"All hail":** Terry Kelleher, "Steven Seagal's Ego Gushes Crude in *Deadly Ground,*" *Newsday,* February 22, 1994.

250　**"Invulnerable heroes":** Rene Rodriguez, "No Action, Adventure in *Deadly,*" *Burlington Times,* February 27, 1994.

250　**"I had many of the greatest":** Steven Seagal interview on *The Beat* (ITV), March 15, 1994.

250　**"I had broken":** Michael Caine, *The Elephant to Hollywood* (Hodder & Stoughton, 2010), 257.

251　**"Someone like a Steven Seagal":** Jackie Chan, *I Am Jackie Chan* (Pan Books, 1999), 302.

252　**"He was difficult":** Author interview with Jim Thomas, November 17, 2020.

253　**"It was tough" and following quotes in present tense:** Author interview with Dolph Lundgren, "Going the Distance," *Empire,* March 2022.

254　**"People, they're trying":** Tom Russo, "Damme Nation," *Premiere,* January 1995.

254 **"I ate something"**: Stephen Rebello, "The 8 Million Dollar Man," *Movieline*, August 1994.

254 **"What I would love"**: Lawrence Grobel, "Playboy Interview: Jean-Claude Van Damme," *Playboy*, January 1995.

254 **"but better"**: Russo, "Damme Nation."

254 **"The action was too much"**: Ibid.

254 **"a samurai with greasy hair"**: Grobel, "Playboy Interview: Jean-Claude Van Damme."

255 **Van Damme had inappropriately:** Details of Van Damme's actions on the set of *Friends* taken from " 'The One We Wouldn't Normally Do': The Uncensored Story of the 'Friends' Super Bowl Episode," Mara Reinstein, *Hollywood Reporter*, January 28, 2021.

255 **"Because I come"**: Author interview with Jean-Claude Van Damme, "Lost Action Heroes," *Empire*, March 2007.

255 **"Where do you want to go today?" and details of Van Damme's drug habit:** Peter Wilkinson, "Van Dammaged," *Us*, October 1988.

256 **"I did so much damage"**: Ibid.

256 **"We had heard rumors" and following quotes in present tense:** Author interview with Steven de Souza, December 27, 2021.

256 **"mini-affair"**: Author interview with Van Damme, "Lost Action Heroes."

256 **"I have to pump up"**: Keith Stuart, " 'I Punched Him So Hard He Cried': Inside the Street Fighter Movie," *The Guardian*, July 16, 2018, theguardian.com/games/2018/jul/16/inside-street-fighter -movie-jean-claude-van-damme-kylie-minogue.

258 **"The worst movie to date"**: Leonard Maltin, *Leonard Maltin's 2007 Movie Guide* (Plume, 2006), 1277.

258 **"He still delivers dialogue"**: Desmond Ryan, " 'Street Fighter' a Worthless Brawl," *Syracuse Herald Journal*, December 28, 1994.

258 **"An eagle"**: Jim McClellan, "Damme Buster," *The Face*, March 1992.

259 **"He was drooling"**: Keith Valcourt, "Steven Seagal: A Dangerous Man," *Hustler*, October 2009.

259 **"Van Damme was tired"**: Harry Knowles, Sylvester Stallone interview on *Ain't It Cool News*, December 16, 2006, legacy .aintitcool.com/node/31032.

259   "I was pissed a little": Jean-Claude Van Damme interview on French TV, 2010, youtube.com/watch?v=THsEWTClnjc.

259   "I have to say": Stallone interview on *Ain't It Cool News,* 2006.

CHAPTER 18: THE ICE AGE

260   "It was that first Batman movie": Geoff Boucher, "Sylvester Stallone Springs Back into Action," *Los Angeles Times,* July 18, 2010.

261   "They're actually starting": Bruce Willis interview on *Aspel and Company* (ITV), May 16, 1993.

261   "I did a movie with Bruce": Author interview with Steven de Souza, December 27, 2021.

262   "As the rest of us chatted": Elton John, *Me* (Macmillan, 2019), 274.

264   "The downside": Bernard Weinraub, "After Rocky Start, Sly Finds His Role," *New York Times,* June 10, 1993.

264   "It seemed like a questionable film": Marc Shapiro, "Demolition Man," *Starlog,* October 1993.

264   "We actually flew to Rome": Author interview with Marco Brambilla, April 7, 2021.

264   "The difficult part": Shapiro, "Demolition Man."

265   "Horrifying": Ibid.

265   "We have a really good chemistry": Shapiro, "Demolition Man."

265   "It was the most uncool day": Marlow Stern, "Lori Petty on the Halycon '90s," *Daily Beast,* July 12, 2017, thedailybeast.com/lori-petty-on-orange-is-the-new-black-the-halcyon-90s-and-discovering-jennifer-lawrence.

266   "Take away all the guns": Shapiro, "Demolition Man."

266   "Watch *Demolition Man*": Elon Musk post on Twitter, December 3, 2020.

266   "*Demolition Man* is coming true": Elon Musk post on Twitter, August 14, 2021.

267   "I smiled a lot": *Siskel & Ebert,* Season 8, Episode 8, 1993.

268   "It's tough to get sympathy": Sylvester Stallone interview on *Late Show with David Letterman* (CBS), September 23, 1994.

268   "To me it tastes": Nancy Griffin, "Fire & Reign," *Premiere,* June 1993.

269   **"People will not accept"**: Steve Pond, "Some Kind of Hero," *Us,* July 1993.

269   **"Everything I turned down"**: Ibid.

269   **"We rented every action movie" and following quotes in present tense**: Author interview with Zak Penn, "Too Big to Fail," *Empire,* November 2011.

270   **"wasn't executed professionally"**: Aljean Harmetz, "Five Writers + One Star = A Hit?," *New York Times,* May 30, 1993.

270   **"The country is going"**: Griffin, "Fire & Reign."

271   **"more doctors than Cedars-Sinai"**: Pond, "Some Kind of Hero."

271   **"Back in those days" and following quotes in present tense**: Author interview with Shane Black, "Too Big to Fail."

271   **"What everyone was"**: Harmetz, "Five Writers + One Star = A Hit?"

271   **"I was doing ADR"**: Author interview with Robert Patrick, "20 Years Since *Terminator 2!*," *FHM,* October 2011.

272   **"If this movie is a bust"**: Pond, "Some Kind of Hero."

272   **"During the first week"**: Author interview with Austin O'Brien, "Too Big to Fail."

272   **"The head of the studio" and following quotes in present tense**: Author interview with John McTiernan, "Too Big to Fail."

273   **"They're all a bunch"**: Pond, "Some Kind of Hero."

274   **"Columbia's lady with the torch"**: Liz Smith column, *New York Post,* June 1, 1993.

274   **"Lizards Eat Arnold's Lunch!"**: Leonard Klady, *Variety,* June 21, 1993.

274   **"As always"**: Arnold Schwarzenegger, *Total Recall: My Unbelievably True Life Story* (Simon & Schuster, 2012), 411.

275   **"Arnold had to rip" and following quote in present tense**: Author interview with James Cameron, "The People vs James Cameron," *Empire,* January 2019.

EPILOGUE

278   **"15 action heroes"**: Catherine Shoard, "Sylvester Stallone in Cannes," *The Guardian,* May 18, 2014.

279   **"Your loss, my bro"**: Steve Ross, "How *Everything Everywhere* gave Michelle Yeoh the Role of a Lifetime," *The Guardian,* May 13, 2022.

280   **"When people come by here"**: Jean-Claude Van Damme interview, *On Demand Entertainment,* October 2012, youtube.com/watch?v =OOO1mffekkw.

281   **"I do hardly any action"**: Author interview with Dolph Lundgren, "Going the Distance," *Empire,* March 2022.

281   **"I said, 'Holy mackerel!' "**: Author interview with Chuck Norris, "It's Chuck's World—We Just Live in It," *Empire,* May 2007.

282   **"one of the greatest"**: Ben Child, "Steven Seagal: Vladimir Putin Is One of the 'Great World Leaders,' " *The Guardian,* March 28, 2014.

283   **"I wouldn't necessarily say"**: Andrew Pulver, "Putin Proposed Steven Seagal as Russian Envoy to US," *The Guardian,* April 22, 2015.

283   **"WILLIS OUT"**: Sylvester Stallone post on Twitter, August 6, 2013.

284   **"It fell from the sky"**: Stallone interview on *Access Hollywood,* April 2006, youtube.com/watch?v=EZwo0xlnFhM.

285   **"You know, maybe"**: Pat Maio, "Sylvester Stallone Unveils Over 50 of His Impressionist Paintings," *Mail Online,* December 3, 2021, dailymail.co.uk/tvshowbiz/article-10272941/Sylvester -Stallone-unveils-50-artworks-Germanys-Osthaus-Museum.html.

INDEX

...

NICK DE SEMLYEN is the editor of *Empire*, the world's biggest movie magazine, and the author of *Wild and Crazy Guys*. As a film journalist, he has also written for *Rolling Stone, Stuff*, and *Time Out*. He lives in London.

Also available from

NICK DE SEMLYEN

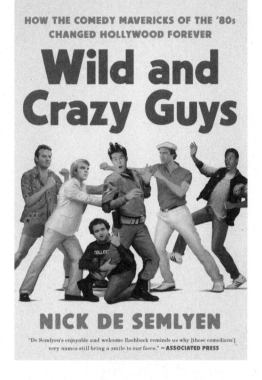

"The definitive account of the golden age of
American comedy—if it were any more addictive to read,
these wild and crazy guys would probably have tried
to snort it in the '70s. Riveting."

**—DAVID EHRLICH,
senior film critic, *IndieWire***

CROWN
NEW YORK

Available wherever books are sold